THE GERMAN TRADITION
OF SELF-CULTIVATION

THE GERMAN TRADITION
OF SELF-CULTIVATION

'BILDUNG' FROM HUMBOLDT TO
THOMAS MANN

W. H. BRUFORD

Schröder Professor of German, Emeritus, in the
University of Cambridge and Former Fellow of
St John's College

CAMBRIDGE UNIVERSITY PRESS

Published by the Syndics of the Cambridge University Press
Bentley House, 200 Euston Road, London NW1 2DB
American Branch: 32 East 57th Street, New York, N.Y.10022

Library of Congress Catalogue Card Number: 74-79143

ISBN: 0 521 20482 8

First published 1975

Printed in Great Britain
at the University Printing House, Cambridge
(Euan Phillips, University Printer)

CONTENTS

ACKNOWLEDGEMENTS

Chapters 1, 2 and 7 are completely rewritten versions of papers which originally appeared as follows: Chapter 1 – 'The idea of *Bildung* in Wilhelm von Humboldt's Letters', *The Era of Goethe: Essays Presented to James Boyd* (Oxford, 1959); Chapter 2 – 'Goethe's *Wilhelm Meister* as a picture and a criticism of society', *Publications of the English Goethe Society*, N.S. ix (Cambridge, 1933); Chapter 7 – 'The idea of *Bildung* in Friedrich Theodor Vischer's *Auch Einer*', *Essays in German Language, Culture and Society*, ed. S. S. Prawet, R. Hinton Thomas and L. Forster (London, 1969).

INTRODUCTION

In a lecture which Thomas Mann gave to a group of republican students in Munich in 1923, he spoke about what he saw as the deeper causes of the lukewarmness about politics at that time of the educated middle class in Germany, and of their consequent failure to support the new Weimar Republic. He made his main point in the following paragraph:

The finest characteristic of the typical German, the best-known and also the most flattering to his self-esteem, is his inwardness. It is no accident that it was the Germans who gave to the world the intellectually stimulating and very humane literary form which we call the novel of personal cultivation and development. Western Europe has its novel of social criticism, to which the Germans regard this other type as their own special counterpart; it is at the same time an autobiography, a confession. The inwardness, the culture ['Bildung'] of a German implies introspectiveness; an individualistic cultural conscience; consideration for the careful tending, the shaping, deepening and perfecting of one's own personality or, in religious terms, for the salvation and justification of one's own life; subjectivism in the things of the mind, therefore, a type of culture that might be called pietistic, given to autobiographical confession and deeply personal, one in which the world of the *objective*, the political world, is felt to be profane and is thrust aside with indifference, 'because', as Luther says, 'this external order is of no consequence'. What I mean by all this is that the idea of a republic meets with resistance in Germany chiefly because the ordinary middle-class man here, if he ever thought about culture, never considered politics to be part of it, and still does not do so today. To ask him to transfer his allegiance from inwardness to the objective, to politics, to what the peoples of Europe call *freedom*, would seem to him to amount to a demand that he should do violence to his own nature, and in fact give up his sense of national identity.

The free development and enjoyment of all the resources of the mind came to be regarded in Germany in Goethe's time, as Mann says, as a kind of 'salvation', a goal to be valued far more highly than all the ordinary things men live for, such as money, power and pleasure. It is well known that a great change came over the general

vii

temper of German thought in the course of the nineteenth century. As W. H. Dawson wrote in 1908: 'A century ago, idealism was supreme; half a century ago it had still not been dethroned; today its place has been taken by materialism.' It is obvious that this change was closely connected with the industrialization of Germany, and the transformation of the country in two or three generations from a loose confederation of mostly unambitious small states into a highly organized and dynamic world power.

The literature, philosophy and scholarship of Germany in the late eighteenth and early nineteenth centuries meanwhile gradually became known in Europe and America, from soon after the end of the Napoleonic Wars, and came to constitute in several countries, for a generation or two, a dominant intellectual influence. The Victorian 'sages', Carlyle, Coleridge, J. S. Mill and Matthew Arnold, for example, were greatly attracted by German ideas about personal culture and used them as a counterblast to the materialism which had become rampant in this country from the 1820s, owing to the remarkable results of the industrial revolution. It was through these writers that the notion of the 'good' Germany of Goethe's age gained acceptance, while in Germany itself things were taking the turn described above in Dawson's words. Carlyle in 1870 was still so sure of the moral superiority of Germany to France that in a letter to *The Times* he welcomed the prospect of such a 'noble, patient, deep, pious and solid' country being 'at length welded into a nation, and becoming Queen of the continent'.

The real difficulty for admirers of the older Germany, then and later, was simply to imagine how anyone imbued with the spirit of Goethe could ever bring himself to tolerate declarations and actions by his own countrymen, which to public opinion outside Germany seemed to be utterly inhumane. There were occasions of this kind at the beginning of the First World War and repeatedly throughout the years of National Socialism. Whole libraries of factual information, on the political, economic and social history of Germany and the story of her relations with the rest of the world, have not entirely removed, for many of us, our sense of shock on becoming aware of what seemed so abrupt a change in national character. It seems clear that there were always people true to the old tradition, but forced to look on impotently at what they abhorred. There was a considerable resistance movement towards the end which deserves all credit. But there are well-attested examples throughout of highly cultivated men who in whole groups, so it seems to us, spoke and acted completely out of character as products of the old Weimar tradition, groups of writers and other intellectuals under Hitler, for example, and particularly university faculties, whose spirit had been illiberal as far back as the 1890s at least. Even much further back, in the days of Kant and Goethe, we miss in Germany any widespread indignation of ordinary citizens at the so-frequent interference with the freedom of the person, and Goethe himself, talking to Eckermann (12 March 1828) draws a contrast between the sense of freedom in England and the atmosphere he finds in German families and schools, and in the streets of Weimar.

Was there then perhaps some inherent defect from the beginning in what Mill calls 'the culture of the inward man' in Germany, and if so, how did it reveal itself before it was put to the supreme test in the Second and Third Reichs? That is the question to which I am attempting to find an answer, by examining particular examples of German writings, throughout the nineteenth century and down to Thomas Mann, writings conceived in the spirit of the tradition of personal culture, 'Bildung', but necessarily reflecting the mind and character of the author and the political, social and intellectual climate in which he lived. I have selected for study, after Wilhelm von Humboldt and Goethe, the two most important sources of this way of thinking, seven distinguished writers of various kinds, a theologian, two philosophers, three novelists and a professor of aesthetics turned novelist at the age of seventy, in all of whom the gospel of 'Bildung' is a central feature in at least one major work. For each author I have tried to find one work suitable for special examination, so that the reader may be brought, through quotations, as closely as possible into touch with the mind it reveals. The extracts are translated, in the hope that the matter under discussion may prove to be of some general interest as a partial answer to the intriguing historical question of 'the two Germanys'. I have included some general comments by other writers which I have found illuminating, and the book ends with a chapter on Thomas Mann's writings and speeches on current affairs from about 1914 to 1948, tracing his steady development from a position of Romantic disdain for politics to a public-spirited concern for the enlightenment of the German people about politics, as an essential part of a humane life. This chapter draws together the main lines of the book in connection with Mann's fight against Hitlerism, and it points forward to some such development as we now see in the Bundesrepublik, as it plays its part in the life of the European Community.

WILHELM VON HUMBOLDT

IN HIS LETTERS

The name of Wilhelm von Humboldt is inseparably connected with the growth of German ideas about 'Bildung', or self-cultivation. The importance of his personal influence on university and school education in Prussia and in Germany as a whole is beyond all question. A great deal has naturally been written about these activities and about the theory of 'Bildung' that occupied so much of his attention, long before he was entrusted with the reform of the Prussian educational system after the battle of Jena.[1] This chapter is not directly concerned either with Humboldt's reforms or with his theory. It attempts rather to outline the development of his notion of 'Bildung', as it was evoked by his own experience of life and is reflected in his letters and diaries, documents from which it is a pleasure to quote, because they are so much better written than Humboldt's early essays, about which he himself said, in 1816, that it was the inner plague of his life to have been always full of ideas for a book, but never able to complete it.

Wilhelm and Alexander von Humboldt came of a Pomeranian noble family with a previously undistinguished intellectual record and were educated in the usual way by private tutors, on their father's estate at Tegel, a few miles to the north-west of Berlin. Their father died when Wilhelm, the older of the two brothers, born in 1767, was twelve years old, and it was about this time, he tells us, that he first took a liking to ancient history and began to read about it, with great interest, for himself. It was in his twelfth year too, according to the fragment of an autobiography that Wilhelm wrote down in 1816,[2] that he began, 'entirely of his own accord', to exercise self-control, apparently just to prove to himself that he was capable of it, and not because he thought it was virtuous or likely to prove useful in later life. He says expressly that this idea was awakened in him by the Ancients and continued to attract him to them. 'I started from the pure essence of Stoicism, to will for the sake of willing.' But the notion of stoical self-respect, of inner freedom, the 'No man need say "I must"' of Lessing, was of course one of the central ideas of the German Enlightenment, the philosophy of all Humboldt's teachers. It was generally combined here, however, with humanitarian feeling, a brotherly respect for other men, what Unger calls 'a secularized echo of Christian ethics'. This element was never to be important, as Spranger admits in his great study, *Wilhelm von Humboldt und die Humanitätsidee*, in Humboldt's form of humanitarian philosophy. For him, as for Goethe and Schiller in their maturity, there was something distastefully utilitarian in the Enlightenment's version of Christian charity.[3] He was generous, as a gentleman should be, but good works did not arouse his enthusiasm and we never find him crying, like the young Schiller in the 'Hymn to Joy', 'This kiss to the whole world!' His aristocratic reserve would have held him back even if he had felt himself in that mood, but in fact, according to the autobiographical fragment, his deepest impulse was to keep the world at a distance, 'in an attitude of critical scrutiny', and it was only through the strictest self-control that he could make himself as independent of it as he wished to be. Throughout the *Briefe an eine Freundin* he urges his unhappy friend to cultivate a similar detachment. In his attempts to know and to master himself, he says, he has always aimed at two things,

to be ready to welcome any joys that life may offer and yet...to remain independent, not to have need of anyone, nor of any favours from fate, but to stand on my own feet, and to build my happiness in and through myself.[4]

Stoicism is an oddly unyouthful attitude to find even in a rudimentary form in a boy of twelve, and several of Humboldt's biographers have felt that he only really became himself in old age. In Rudolf Haym's words: 'There was always more of a Nestor than of an Achilles in him. Only now, when he has made his way safely from the stream of life to the bank, does he appear wholly as himself.'[5] When nearly twenty-two, Humboldt himself wrote to Karoline von Dacheröden, his future wife: 'To be older was always something that I fervently longed for.' She would pity him and bless the God who had brought him through all the trials of his boyhood and youth, he says, if she only knew what they had been. 'My childhood faded away joyless and desolate.'[6] He had lost his father early, it is true, and his mother does not seem to have won the affection of either of the sons

2

of this, her second marriage, but no childhood could have been more sheltered and outwardly fortunate than theirs, and it is hard to imagine more conscientious and devoted teachers than those their mother chose for them, yet somehow Humboldt felt that he was completely misunderstood by them and wrongly handled, because they never left him alone, and allowed his character no free expression. He therefore began to conceal his real feelings and interests, while complying externally with what was required of him. J. H. Campe, one of the best-known children's writers of that time, was tutor to the Humboldt boys' step-brother and gave them their first lessons before joining Basedow at his Philanthropinum, the leading experimental school of the German Enlightenment. Then, when Wilhelm was seven, a young tutor fresh from the university, Herr Kunth, was engaged, who stayed on with the family as confidential agent long after the boys were grown up, and later had a successful career in the Prussian civil service, as one of Freiherr vom Stein's chief assistants. He must have been able and trustworthy, and he did his best for the boys in his stiff and pedantic way, helped by temporary teachers for special subjects. In the last year or two before going to the University of Frankfurt an der Oder Wilhelm heard regular lectures, of which his notes are to be found in the *Gesammelte Schriften* (Band I), on economics and statistics, by Geheimrat von Dohm of the Foreign Office, on natural law by Kammerrat Klein, an eminent jurist, and on philosophy, 'almost always merely on matters of logic, entirely in the tradition of Wolff', by J. J. Engel, who was soon to perform the same office for the Prussian Crown Prince.

It was through Kunth and these distinguished Berlin friends and teachers that the Humboldts were introduced to the Jewish intellectuals, mainly women, who first made the inner life an exciting and absorbing pursuit for Wilhelm. The brothers were taken along to the Tuesday Reading Society of which their four teachers were regular members, together with Markus Herz, the leading Berlin doctor, who gave well-attended lectures in his home on natural philosophy. Among the other members were his beautiful young wife Henriette and her friend Dorothea, Moses Mendelssohn's daughter, married to the banker Veit. The boys were soon close friends of Henriette and her circle, and for a year or so Wilhelm, like Schleiermacher and many others later, was quite fascinated by Henriette, who delighted in

3

intellectual flirtations, but was equally expert in kindling and in damping down such flames. It is well known that in the quarter of a century between the end of Frederick the Great's reign and the Wars of Liberation the intellectual and social life of Berlin was strongly influenced by a small group of Jewish hostesses. Together with the French colony they helped to leaven its native heaviness, to support new ventures in music and the theatre and to encourage a more adventurous taste in literature. The Weimar writers and Goethe in particular found their most receptive readers, from the 1790s, in these circles, and they prepared the ground for the Romantic movement in Berlin. Moses Mendelssohn and a few of his Jewish contemporaries had started the process of emancipation, favoured by the tolerant atmosphere of Frederick's reign, and the continued exclusion of Jews from the craft guilds and from trade in many staple commodities made them all the more prominent in the callings that were permitted to them, banking, medicine, and the 'free arts' in particular. As Schleiermacher wrote to his sister in 1798:

That young scholars and men of fashion frequent the big Jewish houses in Berlin is very natural, for they are much the wealthiest middle-class families here, almost the only ones which keep open house and in which, because of their extensive connections in all countries, one meets foreigners of every rank. So anyone who wants to see something of good society in a very unceremonious way obtains an introduction to such houses, where any man of talent, even if it is only social talent, is welcome and will certainly find plenty to amuse him, because Jewish women – their husbands are rushed too early into trade – are highly cultivated, can talk about everything and are usually very accomplished in one or other of the arts.

Here then, through Henriette Herz, before he went to the university and before Herder, Goethe or Schiller could have had any real influence on him (he had read hardly anything of Goethe's before he went to his second university, Göttingen, and it was only here, in 1789, that he encountered even *Werther*) Humboldt learned to distinguish general culture from useful knowledge. 'It is only what we love that ever helps to cultivate us', he wrote, in the first of his letters to Henriette that we have.[7] Ultra-sentimental as these letters certainly are, by a perhaps natural reaction in a reserved young man, brought up in a family where the expression of feeling was not encouraged – Frau von Humboldt was descended from French

4

Huguenots and Scottish merchants – they exhibit the same interest of the writer in the analysis of his own psychological states and the same urge to reveal them to a sympathetic woman that we find in the remarkable series of letters to his wife and in the *Briefe an eine Freundin* of his later years:

The pleasures of the heart, Henriette, [he writes] are, I swear, the only ones which bring real happiness, real bliss. Compared with them, what is all the pleasure that comes from satisfied vanity, ambition, the desire for fame, even from learning and the cultivation of the intellect?[8]

It is not altogether surprising, in an age of declining faith, when secret societies with a highly edifying purpose, like the Freemasons and others, had many adherents, to find Wilhelm, the devotee of self-control, founding along with Henriette a small society which they called a 'Tugendbund', an association for mutual self-improvement. This happened late in 1787, during Wilhelm's first semester at Frankfurt an der Oder, and the first fellow-members the two admitted were Dorothea Veit and Karl von Laroche, the son of the famous Sophie, Wieland's first muse. A few lines from a revised draft of the rules prepared for the 'lodge' by Wilhelm and sent to Henriette in a letter from Göttingen a year later are enough to show the pre-Kantian beginnings of Wilhelm's ideas on 'Bildung':

Since the aim of our lodge is happiness through love, and the degree of happiness in true love is always exactly proportionate to the degree of moral perfection in the lovers, it follows that moral cultivation is what every associate most ardently seeks. The associates have abolished amongst themselves all barriers of merely conventional propriety. They enjoy every pleasure which is not purchased through the loss of higher pleasures.[9]

Though the associates despise the conventions, it is a Platonic love, evoked by the moral qualities of the beloved, which binds them. In the autobiographical fragment of 1816 Humboldt insists that his cult of self-control, though inspired by the example of the Stoics, has never included as part of its aim the avoidance of experience, with its joys and pains. It is not in that sense ascetic, but 'gives free rein to desire and sees in enjoyment, even in forms which many would call intemperate, a great and beneficent power'. Some deliberate excesses would be approved, then, but he does not like to lose his temper or be carried away by emotion, though he recognizes the compelling

5

energy of a passion that appears in a man as a force of nature. In the much earlier expression of his views in 1787 we see a naïve combination of eudaemonism with a vague idealism that is still very much of the Enlightenment, in its later sentimental phase. A small self-conscious group has to underline its unconventionality if each member is to be kept aware of his ideal self. If challenged, they would no doubt have maintained that theirs was a 'natural' ethic, neither Christian nor Greek nor Jewish, but simply human, like the natural religion that was found by Lessing at the core of all historical creeds. The group consists here of some half-dozen members of both sexes, but we read in that age of many essentially similar associations that are confined to two, sometimes both men (e.g. Schiller and Körner), sometimes a man and a woman (e.g. Fürstin Gallitzin and first Hemsterhuis, then Fürstenberg, or Frau von Stein and Goethe). Reading some of the letters exchanged in the Tugendbund, one is struck by the frequent references to affectionate embraces, and cannot avoid the suspicion that for all the talk about virtue, a diffused eroticism played a considerable part in holding the members together, always at the risk that it might become powerful enough to lead to secessions from the group.

It was in fact such a secession that led to Humboldt's marriage and to the correspondence with which we shall be principally concerned in this essay. The 'Bund' was started late in 1787. In January 1788 Karl von Laroche took up a post near Magdeburg and in the spring Wilhelm went on from Frankfurt an der Oder to Göttingen university. In August he paid his first visit to Karoline von Dacheröden, a candidate for membership of the Bund, proposed by Laroche, who had known her for some time and was thought by the other members to be half engaged to her. In Göttingen meanwhile Wilhelm had met and been much attracted by Therese Forster, the highly intelligent daughter of the great Greek scholar Heyne, with all the characteristics of the emancipated woman. Heyne, Therese and her famous husband were all important in Humboldt's development in their different ways, as was also Georg Forster's friend F. L. Jacobi. Hearing of Humboldt through Laroche, Karoline, an only child who lived with her father, Kammerpräsident von Dacheröden, now retired, in the winter in Erfurt and in the summer on their estate, Burgörner, invited Wilhelm in July 1788 to come and stay with them,

6

suggesting as a pretext a visit to the first steam engine in Germany, installed near their home. The letter with which this young lady of twenty-two opened a correspondence destined ultimately to fill seven large volumes shows her as fully ready to enter into the spirit of the Bund. 'I cannot deny my heart the pleasure of writing a few lines to you ['Dir'], dear Wilhelm', she begins. Members of the Bund, despising convention, were on Christian name terms with each other from the beginning, and addressed one another with the familiar 'Du' and even as 'brother' or 'sister'. A candidate on probation like Karoline was expected to do the same, even to a correspondent she had never met. She continues:

Karl von Laroche will bring them to you, and will join with me in asking you to visit me. Do not let me ask you in vain, dear brother. Remember that I live in a wilderness, where my heart lives on memories and hopes. Karl will tell you that I am kind and have a warm, loving heart in my breast, that I wish to join with yours by sacred bonds, and that it strains forward to meet you with pure sisterly love.[10]

In his bread-and-butter letter of 1 September Wilhelm responds nobly:

O Lina, it is a week today since I saw you! Why could I not prolong them to a lifetime, those moments when I lay in joyful rapture in your arms! You were happy too. I could read it in your eyes.[11]

Towards the end of the letter we have the first of an unending series of references in the correspondence to the ennobling influence of women:

You women are so fortunate in this, you can exert so strong an influence on not wholly unworthy young men, can make them happier and thereby better.

Wilhelm refers to this remark a few days later when he writes to his Berlin friends:

O! Jette, o Brenna! How much K[arl] and I will still learn from you, how much better we shall become through you! Only recently I said this in a letter to Kar[oline]. If I am good, it is through Jette.[12]

From his next letter we learn that Karl had suggested he should spend a couple of months in Erfurt to be near Karoline and to get to know the Governor who represented the Elector of Mainz there, Karl Theo-

7

dor von Dalberg, later a close friend, but he is still undecided. He defends Karoline warmly however against the criticisms of Jette and Brenna, who have called her 'gushing', because she has not learnt as well as they have to bear the burden of life. He finds her a very sensible girl. Was she not reading Gibbon's *Decline and Fall* when he visited her? He even agrees with her views about personal survival after death, as Jette should know, or has she forgotten those divine hours, unforgettable to him, when on his last visit to Berlin they had sat hand in hand on her sofa, debating this very question, 'and searching for any grounds we could find to recommend to our reason what was so dear to our hearts'.[13]

The emotional currents revealed in the correspondence between these young people, a year before the French Revolution, are a fascinating psychological study, and the climate of feeling behind these letters is perhaps just as important as any intellectual factors for a sympathetic understanding of the German passion for 'Bildung' in that age. We are aware of a certain jealousy on the part of the Berlin ladies, and of a surprising desire in Karl, still unofficially engaged to Karoline, to throw her into Wilhelm's company. Wilhelm says he is studying her character and trying to correct any faults he sees in her, as they have all undertaken to do to each other. It is in this letter that he suggests the new formulation of their rules, already quoted. At Karl's suggestion he is going to try to find time to go to Erfurt or Rudolstadt to admit Karoline to their society, and he asks Karl for more of his impressions of Karoline from his talks with her, 'exact description, not just admiration'. He enquires also about admitting Karoline von Beulwitz, the elder of the two Lengefeld sisters and a friend of Karl and of Karoline von Dacheröden. It was through her that he was soon to be introduced into the Schiller circle. Therese Forster was the sixth and last member to join the Bund.

Karoline von Dacheröden and Therese Forster, who were capable of genuine and deep feeling, soon objected to that sharing of all their secrets with their fellow-members on which the shallower Berlin ladies pedantically insisted. Humboldt too was now restive, Therese Forster having for the moment put Jette and Brenna completely in the shade. He wrote in his diary in Göttingen on 9 December 1788, only a month after the last letter mentioned, that some lines he had received from Jette made him laugh, and only at the third reading moved him a little, so that his answer, he admits, was written with assumed feeling. Probing into his own mind as usual, he finds two causes for his disillusionment, first of all a desire for change: 'The principle that one must have been in many situations of every kind is now so well established with me that any new situation is agreeable just because of its newness.'[14] We shall find that he often returns to and reasserts this principle in various forms. The second cause he finds in the emptiness of Jette's letters, which are 'like cake without spice', and he now feels the same about all their group, meaning, no doubt, the original members. Therese's letters give him ample food for thought, but she is unattainable, and soon we find him sending all her letters on to Karoline von Dacheröden, who was drawing away from Karl, for her unvarnished comment, for he is sure Therese and she would mean much to each other. Karoline cannot agree: 'I think I should admire her more than I should love her, but certainly love her more than she could me', she writes back. One passage in a letter from Therese had moved her in particular, and she quotes it: 'No union with any human being can do me any good. You can give me nothing' – a cry of despair, she feels, because for her the whole happiness of life lies in the give-and-take between hearts,[15] or what we now call personal relationships.

The end of the Tugendbund was evidently in sight, yet even in August 1789, when Humboldt, at the end of his third semester at Göttingen, had accepted an invitation from his old teacher Campe, who had great hopes for mankind on hearing of the radical resolutions passed by the French National Assembly, to accompany him to Paris, the letter he wrote to his associates shows him apparently still full of the old ideas. It is quite evident however from this letter that his feeling was no longer, as he still pretends, a diffused one for the whole group, but that it had crystallized round Karoline. After a further month or two of travel, in the course of which he saw the Forsters again, at Mainz, met Schiller's teacher Abel at Stuttgart and heard him lecture, and visited Lavater at Zürich, he went to Erfurt again and became engaged to Karoline in December 1789. They were married on 29 June 1791. The self-improvement group had been reduced to two members, and for the next few years at least it often sounds, from the correspondence, like a mutual admiration society. A year after their engagement he writes:

9

I used to pray to unknown, longed for, imagined beings, but now, now my longing, my admiration, my worship are clearly defined and no longer range uncertainly, now I worship the pattern of all beauty, to which the sight of you raises my thoughts.[16]

It would be easy to compile an anthology 'In praise of women' from these letters. Here are two quotations, widely separated in time:

That I am one with myself, that I am what I had the native endowment to become, that I see truth, that I feel harmonious beauty, that is your work, yours alone; and it is my work, mine alone, that you too are what you were meant to be, that you too see truth, and experience beauty and harmony.[17]

And again, twenty-two years later, after innumerable cloying instances of similar, to our ears rather self-satisfied protestations, we read: 'The advice of women is like a star which guides us through the wilderness of life.'[18] Once at least it is too much for Karoline, and she exclaims: 'We are surely not going to begin exchanging compliments with each other.'[19] But usually she is as generous with her praise of Wilhelm as he could wish, though it is as an individual that she extols him, not as one of a morally superior sex.

Humboldt's marriage would seem then, on the evidence of his correspondence, to have been a singularly happy one. Expressing his gratitude to Karoline in superb letters, he tries repeatedly to find the secret of their success, in view of the many failures among their friends. 'In most people, men and women, the best and tenderest feelings are blunted when they marry', but they themselves have retained the freshness of their feeling, perhaps because they have been at one in seeking always 'the simplest and highest in life...the purely human', not looking for any other goal in life but life itself.[20] Yet it was clear even to Haym a century ago, and later biographers have emphasized the point, that Humboldt's character was not nearly as harmonious by nature as it might seem from his writings, and that his married happiness too was something achieved by conscious effort.

If Humboldt's friends had been asked beforehand whether he would make a good husband, some of the more intimate of them would certainly have said that he was too cold and sceptical. This was the impression he made in the Berlin salons and places of pleasure which he and his highly gifted but dissolute friend Gentz frequented in his bachelor days. This is how he appears in Karl Hillebrand's

10

striking picture of those circles.[21] He had great charm and a brilliant wit, it was thought, but no one ever knew what he really felt. He continued to have this reputation throughout his active career, and it fits in well with his self-confessed determination to keep his emotions under strict control, to remain an uncommitted spectator of life. The remark already quoted from his autobiographical fragment about the beneficent power he saw in enjoyment makes his friendship with Gentz, who could appreciate his intelligence better than most, at least understandable, and it even prepares us for an otherwise astonishing entry to be found in Gentz's diary, on 1 July 1815, when he was Secretary to the Congress of Vienna and had again seen a great deal of Humboldt, one of the leaders of the Prussian delegation: 'Passé une heure avec Suzette, très belle personne que Humboldt m'a léguée.' Humboldt was after all, we must remember, a child of the eighteenth century, a gentleman from the Mark Brandenburg, who characteristically wore a pigtail down to 1809, when such a sight was rare. For all his freedom of mind, he could not quite escape from the ideas of his class and age, and at this same Congress of Vienna fought a duel with the Prussian Minister of War, Boyen, when both were involved in most important negotiations. His letter to his wife about it is a masterpiece of irony. Here is one delightful touch. When Boyen objected to sharing a carriage with him on the way to their encounter, he quoted to him, he says, a precedent from Ariosto, who makes two knights in a similar predicament even ride the same horse together.[22] All these things do not shake our conviction, after reading Humboldt's intimate letters, not only to his wife but to close friends like Goethe and Schiller, that there was a real Humboldt capable of deep and lasting feeling, but, as Goethe would well understand, he was 'a man with his contradictions'.

A more serious potential danger to Humboldt's marriage was what Leitzmann calls, with considerable exaggeration, I think, 'the sadistic colouring of sexual feeling in Humboldt', in his comment on a passage in Humboldt's diary of his first journey to France, where he describes what he felt as he watched a girl working the Duisburg–Krefeld ferry. 'When thoughts about women first began to occupy my mind', he writes, 'I always imagined them as slaves, burdened with all kinds of work, tortured in a thousand ways, treated with the greatest contempt. Such ideas are still not strange to me.'[23] He goes on to say

11

how important feelings of this kind have been for his whole development. How they occupied his imagination much later in life is clear from poems like *Die Griechensklavin*, but they come out too in the otherwise very puzzling story of his love for Johanna Motherby, when he was in Königsberg in 1809, busy with the reform of the Prussian educational system, and his wife was still in Rome. Frau Motherby, a doctor's wife, was something of a siren, who later fascinated even the sturdy Ernst Moritz Arndt. Her hospitable home was for Humboldt the only good thing in a wretched town, and he continued to write to her for some years, until she found Arndt more interesting. From Vienna in 1813 he wrote that through her he had hopes of 'a deeper and much more individual kind of love. This love consists in the woman's being absorbed by the man, so that she has no separate existence apart from his will, no thought but what he demands, no feeling that does not submit itself to him.'

It is strange to find in Humboldt at the age of forty-six this almost Kleistian desire to be completely the dominant partner in love, for there is no hint of it in his letters to Karoline, either because she was too strong a personality in her own right, or because with her he was capable of genuine self-surrender and the imaginative sharing of another's life. But that this desire to have complete control of a woman's will, obscurely connected, one feels, with the still older impulse to be master of his own, remained strong in him to the end, is evident to anyone who reads the *Briefe an eine Freundin*. These are actual letters, published of course long after Humboldt's death, which were almost compulsory reading a century ago for self-respecting young ladies, the only writings of Humboldt's to reach a wide public. (I have a copy apparently abandoned in 1914 by the Association of German Governesses in England!) In the midst of his labours in Vienna, about a year after Frau Motherby had disappointed him, he received and answered an appeal for sympathy and advice made, on the strength of a passing acquaintanceship at a spa in 1788, by Charlotte Diede who, after an unhappy married life, was now living separated from her husband. It was a pathetic story, and Humboldt gave help in full measure. After a sporadic beginning the correspondence went on uninterruptedly, and without the knowledge of Karoline, until Humboldt's death. This stream of letters from a distinguished statesman and scholar in retirement to an always ailing, lonely woman whom he hardly ever saw, a mine of profound reflections on the conquest of life's difficulties through the proper use of the mind and will, a manual of the inward life, was prompted certainly by generous sympathy, but one cannot but be struck by Humboldt's insistence on absolute compliance with the instructions he gives, down to the exact date when Charlotte is to write. Here he had at last the completely obedient woman he had always dreamed of.[24] Of his wife he always wrote in these letters with devoted affection, Charlotte in no sense supplanted her, but he felt the need to keep part of himself secret even from his wife. 'Friendship and love call for trust, as deep and genuine as possible,' he explained, 'but in superior souls no surrender of privacy.'[25] There were times too, as his biographers remind us, when Karoline herself was apparently less interested in her highminded husband than in nonentities like Wilhelm von Burgsdorff and J. F. Koreff.

Allowing full weight to the disturbing irrational elements in Humboldt's character, it is still very difficult to go all the way with scholars like Siegfried Kaehler and Werner Schultz in their opposition to the 'legend' of Humboldt's serenity, especially when one remembers how many similar legends were destroyed between the wars of this century. Haym had said of Humboldt: 'We do not call him a great man, we call him a happy, wise and good man.' Schultz would reverse this judgment, calling him great rather than happy, great in a Faustian way, as one struggling bravely with the tensions within him. A generation later, many of us will see in this opinion the stamp of the period when disillusionment concerning traditional values had reached a new peak in Germany, after a lost war and the uncertainties of the inflation. The idea of salvation through culture had never had less appeal, and the way was open to a Kierkegaard revival and the beginnings of Existentialism. Humboldt himself, at any rate, would have seen in these newer critics' discoveries, we feel, an overstressing of what he called the contingent or fortuitous in his character, as opposed to his 'individuality'. As he wrote to Schiller, when he thought that Körner was trying to 'correct' his friend's natural self:

Everyone must seek out his own individuality and purify it, ridding it of the fortuitous features. It will still be individuality, for a portion of the fortuitous is inseparable from the make-up of every individual, and cannot and should not be removed. It is really only in that way that character is possible, and through character greatness.[26]

Like Goethe's Wilhelm Meister and like Goethe himself he did not want his character to be a product of chance, though he knew well that he could never be, and did not wish to be, other than himself. 'Bildung' meant for him the weeding of his mental and emotional garden, the Ciceronian 'cultura animi' in its original sense, that of the Greek 'paideia' as it was understood in the Hellenistic age. M. Marrou, in his *Histoire de l'education dans l'antiquité*, reminds us of a phrase used by Plotinus, 'modeler sa propre statue', which he paraphrases as follows:

Se faire soi-même; dégager de l'enfant qu'on a d'abord été, de l'être mal dégrossi qu'on risque de demeurer, l'homme pleinement homme dont on entrevoit la figure idéale, telle est l'oeuvre de toute la vie, l'oeuvre unique à laquelle cette vie puisse être noblement consacrée.

These words admirably describe Humboldt's ideal of life at the time of his marriage, and as we have seen, he himself said later that it was the Greeks who had first suggested to him the idea of self-mastery. For a little more than a year (January 1790 to May 1791) he had served in the Berlin Kammergericht or Court of Appeal, but Karoline and he had agreed during his first summer leave that when they married he should retire from Prussian service and live for the free development of his faculties. His means allowed of it, and after some hesitation he had convinced himself that it would not be selfish to follow his deepest instincts in this matter. A long letter to Karoline explains how he had first wondered whether, not having creative genius, he ought not to devote himself to useful work. Jacobi and Forster however, among others, had turned him against a career in public office, and he had come to think 'that only that is truly valuable that a man is in himself', and finally 'that a man always does good to the extent that he becomes good in himself'.[27] When Forster, a man of a restless, reforming nature, whose sense of political commitment was soon to declare itself during the French occupation of Mainz, had urged upon Humboldt the necessity of activity for the general good, Humboldt had summed up his own views in the words: 'The first rule of a true ethical code is "Improve yourself", and "Influence others through what you are" comes only second.' This 'Yogi' attitude to life, to borrow a term from Mr Koestler, no longer came easily to either the nineteenth or the twentieth century, though it left its traces, as we shall see. We find even Haym pointing to the epicureanism prevailing in the Berlin of those days, as well as to the inefficiency and low moral tone encountered by Humboldt during his brief experience as a civil servant, as contributory causes of his decision to resign his post, while Schultz, less convincingly, finds here an example of Faustian restlessness. It seems on the whole far more likely that it was a genuinely ethical decision, from motives the roots of which we have found in Humboldt's earlier history, and which were soon to be reinforced by his friendship with Goethe, Schiller and Körner.

After his marriage, Humboldt may be said to have lived, for all but eleven years, as a free intellectual with scarcely any commitments, except to his family and to the estates which made his independence possible. For the first three years he led the life of a studious country gentleman, mostly at Burgörner, his wife's estate, reading and translating Greek, with the advice and help of the great scholar F. A. Wolf. Before the birth of their second child they moved to Jena and spent the better part of three years there, in the incomparable intellectual atmosphere of the years when Schiller was bringing out the *Horen* and the *Musenalmanach*, and had won Goethe as a collaborator and friend. Humboldt was treated by both poets as a friend and equal, greeted each new product of their genius with enthusiasm and constructive criticism and continued the essays towards a theory of 'Bildung' which had occupied him since before his marriage. On a prolonged visit to Berlin, where his mother was very ill, he wrote to Schiller in 1796:

If we imagine a man whose sole aim in life is to cultivate himself, his intellectual activity must finally be concentrated on discovering (a) *a priori*, the ideal of humanity, and (b) *a posteriori*, a clear picture of mankind in reality. When both are as precise and complete as possible in his mind, he should, by comparing them, derive from them rules and maxims for action.[28]

The best known of the fragmentary writings which resulted from this aim is *Ideen zu einem Versuch, die Grenzen der Wirksamkeit des Staats zu bestimmen* (The Limits of State Action), two sections of which appeared in Schiller's *Neue Thalia* and three more in the

15

Berliner Monatsschrift. There were difficulties with the censorship, publishers hesitated and Humboldt himself had doubts about some of the essay's political content on reading Burke on the French Revolution, so that the complete text did not appear till 1851, long after the author's death. The leading idea of the essay comes at the beginning of the extract made by Schiller, in a passage quoted by J. S. Mill in his *On Liberty*:

The true end of man, not that which his transient wishes suggest to him, but that which eternal immutable reason prescribes, is the highest possible development of his powers into a well-proportioned whole. For culture of this kind freedom is the first and indispensable condition.

Humboldt's view of the state and its functions follows from his conception of the good life, for if people are to be as fully developed as possible as individuals, there must be a minimum of interference from without and a maximum of variety in their opportunities for experience. Humboldt's *bête noire* is the mechanical efficiency of benevolent despotism, with its ideal of running its subjects' lives for them according to a pre-conceived system for what it alleges to be the general good. His 'grand, leading principle', as Mill rightly saw, so that he used this sentence from Humboldt as the epigraph of his *On Liberty*, 'is the absolute and essential importance of human development [i.e. 'Aus-bildung'] in its richest diversity'. In Humboldt's ideal social world there is 'a contest of personalities for moral and intellectual influence in which it is as blessed to receive as to give...By being oneself one enriches the world as it presents itself to others, who, in turn, perform the same service for oneself.'[29] In much the same way Goethe frequently said (e.g. to Eckermann, 20 October 1830) that he had done more for the world by developing and expressing his own personality than he would have done by deliberately working for the good of the whole. This is of course far from being the whole truth about social relationships. The conception of freedom involved is negative freedom, freedom from interference, and as Sir Isaiah Berlin has pointed out, 'liberty in this sense is not incompatible with some kinds of autocracy, or at any rate with the absence of self-government'. It is arguable, he says, that in the Prussia of Frederick the Great men of creative genius felt themselves freer than in many an earlier or later democracy.[30] Humboldt however, disillusioned by his own experiences, sees all the efforts of the state through its elaborate bureaucracy for the positive welfare of the people as harmful because they stifle individual initiative. He illustrates the evil results in military matters, education, religion and morality and discusses the kind of laws that are in his view necessary, a very small number, mainly for defence and the maintenance of order. This conception of a 'nightwatchman-state', as Lassalle was to call it, is a typical product of the idealistic, unpolitical Germany before the Napoleonic wars.

It is the creative mind which most obviously needs a maximum of freedom, and it often seems as if it were the creative life that Humboldt really had in view as his ideal, as when he says:

Thus peasants and craftsmen of all kinds could perhaps be developed into artists, that is, into men who loved their particular work for its own sake, improved it through their own initiative and inventiveness and so cultivated their intellectual powers, ennobled their character and refined their pleasures.[31]

Here he comes close to the idea later put forward by Goethe at the end of the *Lehrjahre*, that it is not the form of a man's activity that matters, but the spirit in which it is exercised. At another point in the essay Humboldt in fact says this in so many words.[32] But it is the purely mental side of the activity which interests him most, considered apart from its results, for his ideal is as usual to be as independent as possible of everything external. He puts this thought in its most extreme form perhaps in a fragment, probably of 1793, on the theory of 'Bildung', in which he asks himself why we set out to study this and that, and answers that we are not really concerned about what we learn or how we improve the world outside, 'but only about the improvement of our inner selves, or at least about satisfying the inner restlessness which consumes us'.[33] Another might have said that it was to escape the boredom which always threatens an over-leisured class, not compelled by any external necessity to exert itself, but Humboldt makes a free man's religion out of his pride in his spiritual self-sufficiency, as we see from the following passage in *The Limits of State Action* (Section 7). Religion he explains as the outcome of psychological needs, and after a fine page on the integrating effect of belief in a personal Deity on the whole life of the soul, he goes on:

17

Although the influence of religious ideas is certainly a powerful element in the pursuit of inner perfection, it is not an indispensable one. The idea of spiritual perfection in itself is great and satisfying and inspiring enough not to be in any need of a veil or personal form. And yet every religion is based on a personification, on an appeal to the senses, on a higher or lower degree of anthropomorphism. That idea of perfection will still hover perpetually in front of a man, even if he is not accustomed to thinking of the sum of all moral good as combined in one absolute ideal, and of himself as standing in a personal relationship with this Being. The idea will rather be a spur to activity, the substance of all his happiness. Firmly convinced by experience that his mind can grow continually in moral strength, he will strive with eager courage towards the goal which he has set himself. The thought of his possible extinction will no longer fill him with fear when once his imagination has conquered the illusion that non-being will be conscious of its own non-being. His dependence on external fate does not depress him; relatively indifferent to external enjoyment and deprivation, he has eyes only for the purely intellectual and moral, and no freak of destiny can disturb the inner depths of his soul. His spirit feels itself to be independent through its self-sufficiency, raised above the flux of things through the abundance of its ideas and the consciousness of its inner strength. When he reflects upon his past, retracing step by step how he has made use of circumstances, now in this way, now in that, how he has gradually become what he now is, when he sees cause and effect, ends and means, all united in himself and then, full of the noblest pride of which finite beings are capable, cries:

> Hast du nicht alles selbst vollendet,
> Heilig, glühend Herz?*

how then all those ideas of loneliness, of helplessness, of lack of protection and comfort and help vanish, which are generally believed to assert themselves when a personal, guiding, rational cause of the chain of finite being is lacking.[34]

Compared with later passages we shall quote in praise of the inward life, e.g. from Schleiermacher and Schopenhauer, this is woolly and self-satisfied, but it reminds us how much in Humboldt's praise of individuality goes back to the *Sturm-und-Drang*, preromantic genius cult of twenty years earlier, the inspiration of Goethe's marvellous ode, 'Prometheus', from which he quotes. Before he left Jena, Humboldt seems to have come to feel that as an end in itself, the pursuit of harmonious and fully developed faculties was not as satisfying as he had hitherto thought. Living in close touch with Goethe and Schiller at the height of their powers he realized, as he put

---

* Have you not accomplished everything yourself, holy, ardent heart?

it later, that he had never been capable of their at times almost fanatical concentration. 'A man must give himself up to *one* limited, definite objective and lose himself, at least for a time, in its pursuit.'[35] He could help Schiller to think out his ideas by his intelligent, sensitive response to them in conversation, he could help Goethe (perhaps not so successfully) with the hexameters of *Hermann und Dorothea*, once they were in existence, but he was no poet, and his attempts at aesthetic theory are not generally considered to go much beyond reformulating rather confusingly the classical aesthetics of Goethe and Schiller. Schiller praised his essay on *Hermann und Dorothea*, but Goethe had to confess that he could not follow its complicated argument. Recent work has suggested however that Humboldt anticipated some modern ideas about the status of the work of art, its existence in its own right, as something that not merely humanizes nature, but takes its place.[36] Certainly Humboldt was not content to stand for ever in the shadow of his great friends and in 1797, as there was some prospect of peace in Europe, he decided to go abroad, naturally to one of the centres of culture, Paris or Rome.

Both Karoline and he would have preferred Italy, Karoline because of her delicate health and Wilhelm because of his passion for the ancient world, but as fighting soon broke out again in northern Italy, they had to be content with Paris and spent the next four years there, with a long and adventurous family holiday in Spain in the autumn and winter of 1799–1800. It was now that Humboldt first became interested in linguistics, particularly in the problem of the Basque language, and after reading all round the subject in Paris he returned to the Basque country a year later for three months. This was the first step towards the distinguished scholarly work that Humboldt was to do in the linguistic field in his retirement. At the very beginning of his stay in Paris he had written to Gentz that his views had changed considerably since his first visit in 1789. Then he had firmly believed that a man only counts through what he is, not through what he does. Now however, he felt that it was high time for him to produce something, to have something to show for his time on earth. But it was many years before he discovered his real vein, and in Paris he was still feeling his way, occupying himself in a dilettante way with the literature, art and institutions of France and above all studying human nature, for he enjoyed the social life of a great capital, with his

19

wealth and rank he had the *entrée* everywhere, and he soon became a sort of cultural ambassador of the new Germany, one of the chief informants above all of Mme de Staël. Humboldt himself became more and more clearly aware, during this long period of residence abroad, of his essentially German nature, he began to understand the meaning of political, as opposed to cultural nationalism, and the way in which national differences are reflected in the concrete realities of everyday life and social institutions, thus preparing himself unconsciously for the work of administrative and educational reform in which he was soon to take so large a share. Current political events are still scarcely mentioned in his letters, but he was acquiring a clear understanding of lasting social forces and losing his doctrinaire prejudices. Even in questions of art his letters to friends like Goethe and Körner are far richer in concrete personal perceptions than, for instance, his essay on *Hermann und Dorothea*, written during his first months in Paris. The most important of these letters, the one to Goethe on the performances of French tragedy which had so much impressed him in Paris, strongly reinforced the anti-naturalistic trend of the Weimar Theatre with specific suggestions from French practice.

In August 1801 the Humboldts returned to Berlin for a year, in the course of which Wilhelm applied for and obtained a minor diplomatic post in Rome. His motives, as he explained to Schiller in a letter from Rome, were still personal. He had been in search of some practical activity, even of a routine kind, if it seemed to lead somewhere. In return for performing the light duties of Prussian Envoy to the Holy See he had a substantial supplement to his income, very welcome to the prudent father of five children, and good prospects of a continued diplomatic career. Above all, to the open envy of Goethe, he had an opportunity of living for years in the capital of the ancient world, still, in spite of Napoleon, the favourite resort of the aristocracy and cognoscenti of Europe, where he could muse over ruins in the warm sun of the south.

Humboldt was much more of a sentimental traveller than Goethe, as is plain from letters to his German friends, full of the romantic sense of the past: He writes to Körner (8 June 1805):

It is only here, in fruitful loneliness, that the shapes of this world unfold themselves clearly in peace; thought and feeling melt into each other in

clarity; melancholy and cheerfulness in serenity. On the boundary between life and death one plays one's part more easily in the one and
prepares oneself more gently for the other.

The finest of these much-pondered letters is the long one of 23 August
1804 to Goethe, in which he tries to determine how much of the effect
Rome has on him is 'objective'. It is for the traces it shows of a better
world, pagan antiquity, that Rome fills him 'with reverence for the
Gods and a longing for home', like a line from Homer, for it stands out
among cities as he does among poets. It is not Christian or even
Renaissance Rome that stirs his feeling, but the ruins of ancient
Rome, with its memorials of a nobler race of men, for Greece and
Rome seem to be fused for him into one vision of perfection, and like
Winckelmann and Goethe, he has no wish to move on from Italy to
Greece. Quite in the spirit of Schiller's 'Die Götter Griechenlands',
he declares that with the coming of Christianity, 'natural tranquil-
lity, undisturbed inner peace' were for ever lost to mankind. 'The
nature of man came to be divided, the life of the senses to be set up
against a pure spirituality, and men's minds were filled with ideas of
poverty, humility and sin which never lost their hold.' A full
awareness of this gulf between ancient and modern is essential for
Humboldt's twilight mood in Rome. 'It is only from a distance, only
in isolation from common things, only as past that antiquity must be
seen by us.' To excavate the ruins is sacrilege, a gain for learning at the
cost of the imagination, and equally disastrous would be any attempt
to cultivate the Campagna or to turn Rome into a well policed city.
From his comfortable house above the Spanish Steps, after one of
Karoline's parties for Roman painters, he must be able to stroll out, he
seems to imply, through picturesque squalor to dream among the
ruins. 'If it were not for this heavenly anarchy in Rome, and round
about Rome this priceless wasteland, there would be no room left for
the shades, each one of which outweighs in value the whole race of
today.'[37]

In Rome Humboldt still expressed regret from time to time at
producing so little, but he was becoming reconciled to his limitations
and more and more sure of his 'individuality'. As early as 2
February 1796, in the letter to Schiller from which we have quoted,
he had distinguished two equally satisfying ways of life from a third,
the one characteristic of their own age, and for him utterly

repugnant. The first was the creative life, the attempt to discover, to create or to be something which would inspire others and add to man's inheritance. The second was the carefree enjoyment of life, 'when a man is content to exist in happy innocence'. He probably came nearer to this idyllic state in Rome than ever before, though he also experienced there, for the first time, profound sorrow. In Rome, he wrote to F. A. Wolf, enjoyment became a fruitful occupation and made one look upon work with a kind of contempt. What he all through despised as illiberal was the third way of life, that of the ordinary 'philistine', a wretched man, he thought, who was not even happy *most* of the time, but lived for work, work for the satisfaction of merely material needs.[38] In his laudable preference, following the Greeks, for things and states of mind valuable in themselves, ends rather than means, Humboldt seems to have been strangely blind to the necessary material basis of the higher life, and this again is typical of the aristocrat in him. Nine-tenths of his fellow-countrymen, after all, could not do otherwise than work for a mere subsistence, many of them supporting absentee landlords like himself. Goethe, equally aristocratic in his outlook, was at least more realistic. As a young member of the Weimar court he fully understood how much they all depended on the exploitation of the peasantry, greenflies swollen with sap, as he put it in one of his letters, that were sucked dry in their turn by ants; and in old age he made the lumbermen in the Masque in *Faust II* remind the fine ladies and gentlemen;

> Denn wirkten Grobe
> Nicht auch im Lande,
> Wie kämen Feine
> Für sich zu Stande,
> So sehr sie witzten?
> Des seid belehret!
> Denn ihr erfröret,
> Wenn wir nicht schwitzten.*

Humboldt was in fact, as we have seen, an individualist of the type so common in the age of German Idealism, self-centred from what seemed to him the highest motives. 'This code of ethics', Spranger says in his admirable analysis, 'puts all culture inside the individual', not

---

* If there were no crude ones like us in the country, how could refined ones be there at all, no matter how clever? Remember this: we have to sweat, to keep you from freezing. (Translated by Barker Fairley.)

in a system of universal objectives or social aims, not in the establishment of some form of community life or even in a high standard of living. It is exactly the mood which led Schiller to put the question: 'Can a man be meant, in the pursuit of any object, to neglect his own inner self?'[39]

This way of thinking was not in Humboldt, as in so many, the result of a boyhood steeped in the atmosphere of Pietism. He inherited the effects of a Pietism that had already been given an aesthetic twist, as in the theories of art of Kant and Schiller. To quote Spranger again:

Just as a work of art serves no purpose outside itself, but is experienced as a whole existing for and in itself, so the purpose of man lies in himself alone. It is, by implication, the enjoyment of the self that is proclaimed here as an ethical system (even if the deduction is not drawn, as by Schopenhauer and Nietzsche later, that the world is only justified as an aesthetic phenomenon).[40]

In his letters to his wife, both in the Italian period and in the following eleven years of intensive official activity, Humboldt repeatedly speaks of the need he feels of cultivating detachment, 'of looking at the world as a spectacle, rather than as a serious concern in which one must actively intervene', 'of learning to see one's actions as a negligible factor in the world process and only important for one's private view of things and private evaluation of them'.[41] A successful man of action, he knows well, must always be ready to assert himself vigorously, but he contrasts himself with such a man much as Schiller opposed the Idealist to the Realist: 'One who is right down in it, only seldom and abstractedly looks beyond the present, and one who needs a broad view of things, rarely involves himself deeply.' Even in the midst of momentous negotiations in 1813, during the armistice following the battle of Bautzen, Humboldt writes: 'One must have a world of one's own within, over which the waves of life roll on, while it quietly grows unseen.'[42]

Humboldt was not of course completely detached, or he would not have become one of Prussia's leading statesmen. In Paris and Rome he became conscious of the ties that bound him to Germany, and especially after the battle of Jena, to Prussia. Nor was he perhaps quite so free from the love of power as he imagined. He was pleased, at any rate, to be offered so important and congenial a task as the reorganization of the Prussian educational system. His wide culture, complete integrity, strong sense of justice and outstanding intellectual

23

ability made him extremely successful, in spite of great difficulties, both as head of the Department of Education and later in the highest posts in the Prussian foreign service. If he had had a spark more of ambition in him he might have taken Hardenberg's place as Prussian premier in 1817. But he could not intrigue for power, and though admired for his energy and skill, he was constantly reproached for his apparent lack of 'Gemüt' or temperament. His comment was:

To that I can only reply that I thank my Creator that I have not got what these gentlemen call their 'Gemüt'. I should indeed have a poor opinion of mine, if it just lay on top like a plant in the sand, to be conveniently skimmed off by them.[43]

There is the pride and traditional reserve of the gentleman in these words, but also the attachment to the inward life which makes him add: 'It is terrible to see how all the people who talk like this are buried in reality and all its trash.'

Although Humboldt had so little good to say of worldly success, it was not pure introspection or day-dreaming that delighted him, not mental activity with no external object, but on the contrary a ceaseless turning over in his mind of the results of his experience in his quest for understanding, a distillation of the widest possible experience of life into wisdom. It is in this sense that he aimed at universality. While at his busiest with plans for educational reform he writes:

My life must continue to be, as before, one of contemplation and reflection. In general, perhaps the best thing a man can do with his life is to take away with him a living picture of the world, properly unified. For me in particular no task is more suited, more imposed upon me by my nature.[44]

He had said the same in the early days in Rome:

He who can say to himself when he dies: 'I have grasped and made into a part of my humanity as much of the world as I could', that man has reached fulfilment...In the higher sense of the word, he has really lived.[45]

The same thought occurs earlier still in the poem 'An den erwarteten Sohn', written in Spain, and it is the burden of the *Briefe an eine Freundin*.

To feel and to understand life in its fullness, there is indeed something Faustian in this aim, and within his limits Humboldt steadily pursued it. When he and his wife, after twelve years of great happiness together, experienced their first great sorrow, at the sudden death of their nine-year-old son, Humboldt was at first inconsolable, but he applied his whole mind and will to the conversion of this suffering into a positive gain, as he did with all forms of experience. In his frequent references in the correspondence with his wife to the family bereavements which they felt so deeply, we see clearly how much more of the Protestant than of the Stoic tradition entered into his attitude to life in maturity, in spite of his calling himself 'a poor heathen, who cannot bear the churches'.[46] He does not wish to shelter himself from suffering, or to cultivate indifference to it, for life resides for him in feeling. He never speaks of nature, like Goethe, as a kindly mother. He was not much interested in nature unless it had been humanized, as he found it in the landscape of France and Italy, and natural science he left to his brother Alexander. He did not habitually think of the world and man as under the protection of a watchful deity. He saw every man open to pain and calamity without warning, with no protection but the resources of his own mind. After the death of a second child he writes:

It is as if fate purposely went such hidden and mysterious ways, in order to test the heart in sorrow and in joy, to make of life a labyrinth, in which every moment one loses the objects around, to find home only in oneself.

External events are governed by laws indifferent to man. 'Feeling winds its way through them and developes and strengthens itself in the process, and it remains victorious in the end, because it is always able to remain independent.'[47] Or again four years later:

There is only one summit in life, to have taken the measure in feeling of everything human, to have emptied to the lees what fate offers, and to remain quiet and gentle, allowing new life freely to take shape as it will within the heart.[48]

The way in which Humboldt achieved his kind of spirituality was still by 'Bildung', by training his imagination to hold every event in life at a distance, abstracting its essence from its practical import for him. In a letter to Princess Luise from Vienna he said that when anything unpleasant happened to him, his first reaction was to try to laugh at himself. In English we should say that such a man had a sense of humour, and we do hear from many who knew him that he saw the funny side of everything and kept his family at table in fits of laughter, a thing one would never guess from his published work or even from his letters. All reality, he explained, affected him through the imagination. The pleasure he felt in the well defined character of men and things, their essence, one might say, outweighed for him their immediate effect and that of the personal relation in which he stood to them. Haym, who quotes this passage, says of Humboldt's religion: 'Humboldt's religious feeling...sprang from exactly the same source as had been the origin of the *Reden über die Religion*',[49] the Discourses on Religion of Schleiermacher, which H. A. Korff too sees as a kind of gospel of 'Bildung'. Like the intellectuals to whom Schleiermacher primarily addressed his words, Humboldt had early been estranged from Christianity by 'Enlightened' criticism of its incompatibility with modern thought, its unacceptable mythology, its claim to the exclusive possession of the truth and so on, but when he re-read the Bible late in life, he was surprised to find how strongly it appealed to him. He was strongly attracted too, however, by the Indian *Bhagavadgita*, which he read in 1825 and expounded to the Berlin Academy of Sciences. He thought he found here his own doctrine of detachment and his own belief in the immateriality of the soul. Like Goethe, he found it inconceivable that the miracle of personality achieved by man could perish with him. This thought had occupied him, as we have seen, since he had discussed it on that sofa in Berlin with Jette Herz. After assuming many forms, the idea seems to come very close to Goethe's of a selective immortality, as it is expressed at the end of the Helena act in *Faust II*.[50] More often however he speaks of it as a hope, and one on which we should not allow ourselves to lean too much, lest it should make us unfaithful to the earth.[51]

To judge from the *Briefe an eine Freundin*, Humboldt came in his later years to think more and more in terms of Christian symbolism, interpreted however for the most part in humanistic ways. He can still write: 'The true aim of earthly existence, in my view, is not just happiness, but the development of all the germs that lie in the individual endowment of a human life.'[52] But this universalism gives way more and more, in the second half of the letters, written after his

26

wife's death in 1829, to praise of a life led in and for thought, for ideas, as something desirable in itself, and at the same time the best preparation for death and the life to come. Self-cultivation comes to be thought of as pursuit of 'the salvation of the soul'. Humboldt is constantly using expressions like 'passing over', 'taking over', implying a transition from one form of life to another after death, in which some quintessential of humanity, like 'Faust's immortal elements', survives the change. More and more, life comes for him to be directed towards the distillation of these elements out of human experience. Life is a task to be carried through to the end, and death is its last stage, or 'Earth is a place of testing and development, a stage towards something higher and better; we must gain the power here to comprehend what is beyond the earthly. For heavenly bliss too cannot be a mere gift, but must always in a certain way be earned.'[53] Salvation of the soul then is the final aim of self-cultivation:

I use this expression intentionally in order not to exclude any means that a man may choose for his spiritual improvement. For he can raise himself to a higher stage of spirituality by a continually fuller and purer development of his ideas, by more and more vigorous efforts to improve his character, or he can reach the same goal by the shorter path of simple piety.[54]

It is inevitably only an incomplete impression of Humboldt as man and writer that can be conveyed by any selection from his letters. Too little has been said about his scholarly work, especially in linguistics, where his range is amazing; nothing about the achievements in diplomacy of one whom Talleyrand counted among the three or four outstanding statesmen he had known in Europe; and hardly anything about his personality as it appeared to others. The brilliant appreciation written in 1837 by Varnhagen von Ense gives us on this last point the views of a younger contemporary, not blinded by any excess of sympathy, yet unable to withhold the highest praise. In his picture of Humboldt we see a man of unlimited intellectual capacity who, in conversation with slower-witted companions, used to frisk playfully all round them in humorous sallies which, though never unkind, sometimes reached a Mephistophelian pitch of audacity. Behind his mask of reserve, however, Varnhagen insists, he hid a sensitive nature and great depth of feeling, only expressed without embarrassment in his old age. The feature Varnhagen puts first in his characterization and stresses throughout is Humboldt's independence of age and circumstance:

Of Humboldt, if of anyone, it can be said that he made his own circumstances, that his mind held unfettered sway over them, using everything fate offered him in his own way, rejecting some things, dismayed by none, rising superior to most, and in this respect too always able to summon up greater powers when he wished.[55]

In making this the central feature in his analysis, Varnhagen confirms what Humboldt frequently asserted about his own efforts since boyhood, to make of himself what in the depth of his heart he wished to be, the efforts we have followed through many phases. Further confirmation comes from the most kindred to him in spirit among all his distinguished friends, the one he held to be the greatest man he had ever known, Schiller, who, in his last letter to him in April 1805 said that the distance between them now in space had never prevented their full understanding of each other as of old, for they were both idealists, and would be ashamed to have it said of them 'that it was things that shaped us and not we who shaped things'.[56] If we include among the raw material to be shaped by the spirit, as Schiller certainly would, the cruder elements in a man's own nature, we may take this idea of the primacy of the will as an indication from two devotees of 'Bildung' of what they held to be its very essence.

2

GOETHE: WILHELM MEISTERS
LEHRJAHRE (1795–6)

In a famous 'Fragment' published in 1798 in the periodical of the
early German Romantics, the *Athenäum*, Friedrich Schlegel described the French Revolution, Fichte's *Wissenschaftslehre* (1794) and
Goethe's *Wilhelm Meister* as the three greatest 'tendencies' of the age,
and from his following remarks it is clear that he was challenging
normal opinion by putting the appearance of a philosophical and a
literary work on the same level of cultural importance as a political
event already generally regarded as a turning point in history. This
assessment and his long review of the *Lehrjahre*, the series of letters
written by Schiller between 1794 and 1796, as Goethe sent him
successive books of it before publication, and admiring comments by
innumerable German writers and critics down to Hofmannsthal,
Hermann Hesse and Thomas Mann, above all perhaps the fact that
the novel has been imitated in a whole series of 'Bildungsromane' and
made this *the* German species of the novel, all this indicates that it is
felt to be peculiarly German and representative. The rather luke-
warm appreciation of the work by English critics apart from Carlyle
tends to reinforce this view. When T. S. Eliot wrote in 1929 that
Goethe, unlike Dante, 'always rouses a strong sentiment of disbelief
in what he says', he was not going any further than D. G. Rossetti and
several others down to D. H. Lawrence. They find Goethe thought-
provoking but difficult, and if their ignorance of German cuts them off
from his poetry, they have not the patience to explore what is so
obviously an alien tradition. Though the early books of the *Lehrjahre*
are a good story by any standards, the novel as a whole is evidently,
like so many German novels, intended to interest the reader at least as
much by its ideas as by its presentations of character and events. Our
purpose is to study it primarily as an interpretation of life, an
expression of Goethe's mature thought but also, through him, of his
age and its inherited traditions.

In a typical 'Bildungsroman' we are shown the development of an intelligent and open-minded young man in a complex, modern society without generally accepted values; he gradually comes to decide, through the influence of friends, teachers and chance acquaintances as well as the ripening of his own intellectual and perhaps artistic capacities and interests as his experience in these fields grows, what is best in life for him and how he intends to pursue it. We see him learning to deal with the common problems of personal and social relationships, acquiring a point of view in practical matters and above all a 'Weltanschauung', a lay religion or general philosophy of life, or perhaps one after another. Adventurous episodes may be introduced by the author to maintain interest, but in general there is enough variety if the hero meets well contrasted friends in different social milieux, and of course falls in love with more than one kind of girl, some appealing to his senses and some to his mind. The novel usually ends when he has attained to some degree of maturity, and what he does with his life later is not revealed to us. There is often a large autobiographical element in such novels, so the favourite hero is a writer or artist, not a man of action. There had been 'artist-novels' in Germany from Wieland's time, and there was a fresh outcrop with the Romantics, but in these the hero is more fully conscious of his own unique personality and more eager to take the lead than Wilhelm Meister and the normal dreamy 'Bildungsroman' hero.

It is true that in the first version of *Wilhelm Meister*, not published by Goethe but known from a manuscript copy made by a friend in Zürich, only discovered in 1910, the centre of interest is Wilhelm's own career as a dramatist, actor and theatre-manager in the making, who lives for the ambitious dream of reforming the German theatre and making it into a means of educating the public through art, exactly the kind of dream which inspired Schiller's address about the possible effects of a good standing theatre to the 'German Society' at Mannheim in June, 1784, while he was engaged as theatre poet by the Mannheim National Theatre. When Goethe sent him, ten years later, the proofs of the first book of *Wilhelm Meister*, Schiller wrote back that he could remember only too well his own experience of life and love in a theatrical troupe such as Goethe had so well described. In his lecture, partly to please his bourgeois audience, he had adopted the tone of the Enlightenment and said things like this:

The stage is the channel, open to all, into which the light of wisdom pours down from the superior, thinking part of the people, to spread from there in milder beams through the whole state. More correct ideas, sounder principles, purer feelings flow from here through all the veins of the people. The mists of barbarism, of dark superstition vanish, night gives way to victorious light.

The thinking is as mixed up as the metaphors, but many shared these opinions. Iffland had been sent to the theatre by his father at the age of eight to see Lessing's *Miss Sara Sampson* because it 'taught a good lesson' and decided on the stage, instead of the church, as a career, thinking of it as he did as 'a school of wisdom, of beautiful feelings', and from the same Hanover school K. P. Moritz had run away with similar intentions but eventually taken to writing and become the author of *Anton Reiser*, an autobiographical novel of which one is often reminded in reading *Wilhelm Meisters Theatralische Sendung*. When Goethe wrote his novel of the theatre, between 1777 and 1785, he was busy, amongst many other things, with the amateur theatre at the court of Weimar, doubling the role of *maître des plaisirs* of the Duke with that of minister and member of the small governing council of state. Like Wilhelm, he traced his interest in the theatre back to his grandmother's gift of a puppet-theatre when he was a small boy, and he had been writing plays and reading and seeing French classical drama since boyhood. Herder had made him an enthusiastic admirer of Shakespeare at twenty-one, and Goethe's 'Shakespearian' historical play, *Götz von Berlichingen*, had made a name for him in Germany a year or more before his European success with the novel *Werther*. The atmosphere of the time and his own close acquaintance with the German theatre as dramatist and writer of operettas performed in many places, and further as a leading spirit in the amateur theatre in Weimar for several years, made it quite natural that he should conceive the idea of a theatre novel reflecting the striking developments which had taken place in Germany in forty or fifty years round the middle of the eighteenth century, and especially the establishment of National Theatres and the gradual transformation of the repertoire by the inclusion of Shakespeare and plays in the English tradition. It is interesting to note that there was nothing national in the normal sense of the word about the National Theatres, except that they presented their plays in German, unlike the French players and Italian opera troupes hitherto occasionally invited to entertain German courts. They put on original German plays by preference, but there were not nearly enough to go round, and much use had to be made of translations, at the first National Theatre in Hamburg, 1767–9, where Lessing was engaged as 'Dramaturg', and at all its successors in Vienna, Gotha, Mannheim, Berlin, Weimar etc. They were essentially subsidized repertory theatres, mostly, unlike the first one, in one of the capitals of Germany's many small states and so often described also as court theatres. They tried to raise the status of actors by taking them off the road and paying them better, but their economic situation was usually precarious, even in Vienna and Berlin. There were far too many of them for a poor country to support, but this was of course the beginning, fostered by inter-state rivalry, of the later German system of state and municipal theatres, through which a good theatre, for drama and opera, has come to be considered just as essential to the cultural life of any centre of population as libraries and art galleries.[1]

When Goethe resumed work on the novel in 1794, after a break of eight or nine years, he found it necessary to revise drastically what he had written to bring it into line with his new conception of the central theme. In spite of these changes the point of transition from the old material to the new, at the end of what is now the fifth book, was unmistakable even before the discovery of the Zürich manuscript. Up to this point the style is realistic. Except for two obviously poetic or symbolic figures, Mignon and the Harpist, the characters and action produce the illusion of being described from life in all its complexity and unexpectedness, not constructed and arranged following a plan. This freshness is more marked in the *Theatralische Sendung* itself. Goethe's skilful use of Susanne von Klettenberg's papers in the sixth book of the *Lehrjahre* gives it too something of the same depth and unpredictability, but the last three books lack this irrational charm, being too obviously didactic and utopian. They were written much more quickly than the earlier books, and in writing them Goethe has evidently always followed closely a systematic plan like the one he drew up for *Faust* when he tried to complete in the 1790s a drama of which the beginnings had grown in his imagination unsought in vivid fragments. The new centre of interest in the novel was to be not the hero's character or adventures or accomplishments in themselves, but the visible link between his successive experiences and awareness of worthy models and his gradual achievement of a fully rounded personality and well tested philosophy of life. The theatre novel was to become a 'Bildungsroman'.

It was entirely natural that after seventeen years the idea of educating and improving society through the theatre should have lost its former appeal for Goethe. About the theatre and its influence Goethe had now few illusions, especially since he had unwillingly taken over in 1791 the general supervision for the Duke of the newly established Weimar Court Theatre. In time, with the inspiring cooperation of Schiller, and direct acquaintance with the work of a really great actor, Iffland, he was to acquire a new interest and take a full share in raising the art of the theatre in Germany to a new peak, but while writing the *Lehrjahre* he could only treat Wilhelm's idealistic efforts for the theatre with irony, as an episode in his education by personal experience. When Jarno, the *raisonneur* of the later books, asks Wilhelm: 'How are you getting on with your fanciful plans of doing something for art and morality in the company of gypsies?' Wilhelm recites a litany of disappointments with the personal deficiencies of his actor friends, only to be laughed at by Jarno for expecting them to be any better than men in general. He had been describing not the theatre but the world (VII, 3). What he had learnt specifically from the actors, together with their aristocratic patrons, was to become more fully conscious than he had been instinctively since early manhood of the human limitations of the section of society to which he belonged by birth, the commercial middle class.

The point at which the revised version, the *Lehrjahre*, first explicitly reveals itself as a 'Bildungsroman' is in the third chapter of Book Five, where Wilhelm firmly rejects the proposals sent to him by his business associate, Werner, for the re-organization of their firm after the recent death of Wilhelm's father. This is just before the middle of the completed novel, when Goethe has made use of about four fifths of the contents of his first version. Looking back and comparing, one finds that he has re-written the *Sendung*, changing it in many ways to suit his new conception. The result is that the theatre no longer seems to be for Wilhelm the one thing of interest in life, which he meets with in many different forms on his business journeys, and soon sets out to reform with all the self-confidence of a young genius. It is one experience among many, though still predominant, and Wilhelm learns from it, in his engaging, open-minded way, as he learns from everyone and everything, often noting down his observations for our benefit. His love of art and literature is no longer a sign of creative talent, expressing itself in revolt against a philistine and divided home, but an expression of the natural tastes of a young man from a well-to-do family, whose grandfather had been a discriminating collector of pictures and whose parents, though they sell the paintings to pay for a fine house, splendidly furnished, evidently take an aesthetic pleasure in it, for they hardly entertain at all, whereas their friends and later partners, the Werners, have their dark old house always full of guests. It is only young Werner who is a thorough-going capitalist, though still of an early type. He believes, like the merchants praised in the *Spectator*, that he is contributing to universal happiness by pursuing his own interest, and prudently observing the old-fashioned virtues, order, economy, perseverance, self-control. He lives, as he boasts, by other men's follies, and usefulness to him is his criterion for everyone and everything. His ruling idea is that his capital must be productive, not of human satisfaction but of more depersonalized wealth. So he proposes in his long letter to Wilhelm (v, 2) to marry Wilhelm's sister, as had long been planned, and to take her and her mother into his already over-crowded house, for what does a little inconvenience matter compared with the prospect of adding greatly to their capital by selling the Meisters' fine big house, always a useless luxury like the picture collection before it? He hopes that Wilhelm has not inherited the silly notions that had run in his family so far! He congratulates him on having made so many interesting and useful observations on his journey – Wilhelm, not daring to tell his father how he had really spent his time, had pretended to have been keeping a diary, as his father had recommended, and made up with the help of a friend pages full of statistics and technical descriptions to send home. Werner's letter convinces Wilhelm finally that the life of a prosperous merchant has no appeal for him now, and 'that it is only in the theatre that he can complete the "Bildung" which he desires for himself'.

In the following chapter we have Wilhelm's reply to Werner,

explaining, in conciliatory terms, how differently from Werner he now sees the world, and why only work in the theatre will satisfy him. It is tempting to take this letter as expressing the author's own views and to make it the key to the novel, but it is important to remember that it is Wilhelm who is speaking, long before his 'Bildung' is complete, and speaking in such a way as to make his adoption of values very unlike those of the normal merchant as palatable as possible to his future brother-in-law. He seems to make both the lessons he has learnt so far and the kind of satisfaction he hopes for in an acting career surprisingly external, but the changes that have already taken place in him go far beyond the improvement which he mentions in his physique, in his manner and bearing in society, and in his voice and speech. He has come to realize his limitations as a 'Bürger', the carefully brought up son of a good middle-class family, first of all through sharing the bohemian life of a group of actors. The contrast is complete. Instead of the 'sacred economy' of money and time, the love of order and a rationalized way of life excluding surprise and adventure, Wilhelm encounters what may sometimes seem to him idleness, waste and fecklessness, but is more often admired as the naive insouciance of genius, generosity, courage. He never quite loses his bourgeois prejudices, but he soon realizes that this almost totally opposite point of view can have its attractions for a free spirit. Though the actors are the paid servants of art, it is their naturalness that attracts him to them as individuals. At their best they have the charm of the spontaneous, at their worst they are merely human. Unlike the worthy Werner they can live in the moment, indulge their senses without shame and appreciate physical grace and dexterity. They teach Wilhelm to fence, to dance and to take people of all sorts for what they are, whether socially approved or not. They are spontaneous above all in their affections. Mariane, Mme Melina, Philine follow the heart and not the middle-class code. Listening to Mme Melina's open confession before the village judge of her relations before marriage with the man she already looked upon as her husband, Wilhelm 'formed a high opinion of the girl's character, while the officials wrote her down as a shameless hussy and the townspeople present thanked God that cases of this kind had either never happened in their families, or never been found out'. Wilhelm of course, like Werther envying the peasant boy his naive expression of passion, is of the age of Rousseau, and in his early manhood it is the winged god he worships, but already at the end of the *Lehrjahre* love has become the goddess of family life, the bond of a social institution. The love of order is too deeply engrained in Wilhelm to be completely dispelled at any time by the passing appeal of spontaneity in others. If Wilhelm is ever to become an artist, he, like Gustav Aschenbach (*Der Tod in Venedig*), or Goethe himself, will carry over into his new profession at least the love of orderly habits and the full use of time. But just as his infatuation with the theatre and with Mariane makes him blind to the tawdriness of the scenery and properties as he waits for his mistress in the wings, so the sight of her untidy bedroom, littered with scraps of finery, ribbons, hairpins, toilet articles bearing the signs of use, clothes and possessions of all kinds in dusty heaps, gives him a delightful feeling of intimacy, though his own room at home is a model of elegance and artistic taste. Similarly the gay friendliness of Philine, her careless generosity, her outspokenness and intolerance of humbug, her bright ideas for amusingly passing the time – these and similar traits in Laertes, Friedrich and the rest make him happy to forget, at least for a time, the claims of caution and restraint. Although Goethe does not conceal the danger of giving impulse and instinct free play, and sets off the generosity and grace of some with the avarice and stupidity of others, the immediate effect on Wilhelm of living with the actors is a kind of re-assessment of all values which confirms him in his unworldliness. In these chapters Friedrich Schlegel was given many a hint for his apology for idleness (in *Lucinde*), Brentano for his baiting of the philistine and the whole romantic myth of the artist's inherent superiority to the normal citizen was given a powerful impetus.

When he replies to Werner, Wilhelm has already had some experience of another way of living and thinking besides the theatre which is new and attractive to him as a 'Bürger'. The theatre itself provides an introduction for Wilhelm to aristocratic society, just as Goethe's literary distinction had given him the *entrée* to the court of Weimar. There is a certain logic in this transition, because if the nobleman was free through his inherited wealth and privileges, the actor became something of a free artist in Germany earlier, for instance, than the writer. So in the 1770s and 1780s, roughly the period of the *Lehrjahre*, the stage attracted middle-class boys with some education and artistic leanings, like Iffland and K. P. Moritz, as we have seen, and Wilhelm can plausibly put forward the idea that as an actor he will enjoy what matters to him of the freedom for which all envy the nobleman, the freedom to be himself, with the expectation of being appreciated for his personal qualities.

Having undeceived Werner about the misleading diary and told him that a life of money-making and mindless relaxation is not at all his own ideal, Wilhelm writes:

At the back of my mind, it has been my wish and intention since my youth to develop to the full my own self, the powers that are in me. My ideas have not changed, but I see rather more clearly now by what means I can realize them[...] If I were a nobleman, we should soon agree, but as I am only of the middle class, I must adopt a course of my own, and I want you to understand me. I don't know how it is in other countries, but in Germany it is only for a nobleman that a certain general development of his personality is possible. A 'Bürger' can earn his reward and at a pinch perhaps train his mind, but whatever he may do, his personality does not count.[2]

A gentleman, on the other hand, Wilhelm believes, values his individual personality in itself and expects others to do so, as his dignified bearing shows. Serlo, the accomplished actor, explains to him in detail later how difficult it is to imitate the manners of a gentleman, because they are mainly negative, and the result of long practice. He must never hurry, or betray his feelings, but maintain the same unruffled calm with everyone and in any situation. Goethe clearly has in view what Lord Chesterfield in his famous *Letters to his son* had called 'the lesser talents' – 'an engaging manner, an easy good breeding, a genteel behaviour and address'. We can only understand the emphasis he makes Wilhelm lay on these externals and Wilhelm's extraordinary expectation that as an actor he will, though a mere 'Bürger', find in displaying himself on the stage a similar satisfaction in his own all-round development as he attributes to the born aristocrat, if we take Goethe's attitude towards his hero as ironical, here as in so many other places. The reality behind the aristocratic mask has been clearly displayed in Book Three, and Wilhelm has himself been made to agree with the actors in the belief that only a comparatively poor man can appreciate the happiness of inwardness, and be capable of true friendship and fidelity (IV, 2). The troupe, accompanied by Wilhelm, had been invited by a count to his

37

mansion, to help to entertain a general of princely rank and his staff, and Wilhelm had gone gladly, full of the highest expectations and 'praising his genius' for leading him up to 'the higher regions' where dwelt the thrice blest favourites of fortune, who would surely, in their privileged position, have learnt discrimination, and directed their minds to the necessary, the useful, the true sooner than most – irony again of course on Goethe's part at Wilhelm's naiveté (III, 2). Seen at close quarters, the aristocracy are found to be just as full of illusions about themselves as ordinary mortals and everything about them is façade, like the beautiful but chimneyless fireplace in the unfurnished building where the troupe has to spend its first night. The actors find that their patrons, from the Count downwards, know little about art though surrounded by beautiful things. Literature and the drama are two forms of distraction among the many in their lives. All praise the Baron as poet and connoisseur, but he is quite evidently a vain poetaster. When an anonymous poem about him causes malicious glee among the actors, Wilhelm reproaches them for falling into the usual German blunder of running down the achievements of men of rank in the arts, but this is perhaps a cover for Goethe's expression in these verses of a feeling to which he himself, as a bourgeois poet at the court, was not a stranger:

Ich armer Teufel, Herr Baron,
Beneide Sie um Ihren Stand,
Um Ihren Platz so nah am Thron,
Und um manch schön Stück Ackerland,
Um Ihres Vaters festes Schloß,
Um seine Wildbahn und Geschoß.

Mich armen Teufel, Herr Baron,
Beneiden Sie, so wie es scheint,
Weil die Natur von Knaben schon
Mit mir es mütterlich gemeint.
Ich ward mit leichtem Mut und Kopf
Zwar arm, doch nicht ein armer Tropf.

Nun dächt' ich, lieber Herr Baron,
Wir ließen's beide, wie wir sind:
Sie blieben des Herrn Vaters Sohn,
Und ich blieb' meiner Mutter Kind.
Wir leben ohne Neid und Haß,

38

Begehren nicht des andern Titel,
Sie keinen Platz auf dem Parnaß,
Und keinen ich in dem Kapitel.*[3]

In the Utopian world of the later chapters, differences of rank are, as Schiller put it, treated as completely negligible when humane issues are at stake, though he wondered how the ordinary reader would accept a novel ending with three marriages which are all misalliances. In the third book however the social gulf is very real, even between two people as attractive in each other's eyes as Wilhelm and the Countess. They are described as exchanging meaningful glances across this gulf much as two outposts of opposing armies, separated by a river, fraternize with each other without thinking of the war in which they are fighting. There are hints of many fleeting love affairs at the castle which break down all barriers, but they are typical of the morals of the rococo age, painted here in all its heartlessness and charming elegance. There is a memorable description of the Countess dressed for a banquet. All about her is artifice, yet this supreme art has the effect of the natural. 'If Minerva leapt completely armed from the head of Jupiter, this goddess seems to have stepped out from some flower light-footedly in full array.' The picture of the Countess's *lever*, at which Wilhelm's reading of scenes from his play is interrupted by a succession of momentous trifles, has only one rival in German literature, the first act of Hofmannsthal's *Rosenkavalier*.

All this is of course to be regarded as a part of Wilhelm's aesthetic education, which is continued when the troupe leaves the Count's mansion, with Wilhelm now as its elected head. It is no longer the actor's life in itself which serves Wilhelm's further development, so much as his delighted exploration of the work of Shakespeare, first brought to his notice, as a dramatist really worthy of his study, by Jarno at the mansion. Wilhelm revels to begin with in the richness and variety of Shakespeare and lives himself into his characters, seeing

---

* I, poor devil, dear Baron, envy you your rank, your place so close to the throne, and many a fine piece of arable, your father's castle too, his shooting preserve and rents.

Me, poor devil, dear Baron, you envy, as it seems, because nature was a kindly mother to me even as a boy. I grew up with a cheerful temper, poor indeed, but not a poor dolt.

Now it seems to me, dear Baron, we'd better leave things as they are, that you should remain your father's son, and I my mother's child. Let's live without envy or hate, and neither seek the other's title, you claiming no seat on Parnassus, and I none in cathedral chapters. (Only the very blue-blooded were elected to these perquisites.)

39

himself as a kind of Prince Hal who finds pleasure for a time in the company of low companions. He even adopts a fanciful form of dress, wearing a bright silk scarf round his waist and a kind of ruff, made of strips of muslin sewn to his shirt. Goethe shows us how he gradually discovers more and more in Shakespeare, first in *Hamlet*, the play which made the deepest impression in the *Sturm und Drang* period, when Shakespeare was introduced by degrees into the repertoire of the German theatre, above all by F. L. Schröder in Hamburg, from 1776, after he had prepared the ground by producing a series of post-Shakespearian English comedy and tragedy. The domestic dramas of Lessing and his imitators and the strong stuff of *Sturm und Drang* had also helped to wean the public from French classicism and 'comédie larmoyante'. Erich Trunz has well brought out the novelty of the chapters about Wilhelm's enthusiastic reading and production, the interesting feature of which is not so much the particular interpretation of *Hamlet* which is offered, clearly in part a characterization of the hero himself, as the quasi-religious attitude of Wilhelm to the art of Shakespeare.

It is a way of experiencing art which was only fully developed in the age of Goethe. Art means something like this for Wackenroder's Klosterbruder too [in the *Herzensergießungen*] and for Hoffmann's Kapellmeister Kreisler (in *Kater Murr*). This way of seeing art only became possible in a world for which the Church had ceased to answer all men's questions, but where man stands before the Sphinx of life and the best interpretation that he finds is expressed as art. It has become a feature of modern education ('Bildung') that there is a way of experiencing art which reveals the world, but this recognition dates from the *Lehrjahre*. Theorists like Herder had spoken about it earlier, but here a poet creates for us someone going through the experience.[4]

It must be admitted that Wilhelm is not seen in the novel to derive any very clear revelations from Shakespeare about life and the world, but the plays and his own experience begin to throw light on each other. It is immediately after his realization of his own conceit and rashness in leading the actors by a dangerous route, where they were attacked and plundered by robbers, that he interprets 'The time is out of joint; O cursed spite, That ever I was born to set it right!' as an indication that Shakespeare wanted to show us 'a great deed laid upon a soul that is not capable of it', like an oak-tree planted in a flower-vase (IV, 13). Similarly we are reminded of his tendency to ascribe misfortunes passively to 'fate' which could well have been prevented, the bad habit of which three mysterious strangers on separate occasions try to cure him, when he says that it is left to fate to accomplish the revenge of which neither Hamlet nor the subterranean powers had been capable (IV, 15).

It is still from people, from personal relations, that Wilhelm learns most in the fourth book, which is about the motley company's fate after leaving the temporary security of the Count's mansion. Eventually all make their way to a large town where Serlo, a famous actor-manager already known to Wilhelm, runs his own standing theatre. Serlo is in all essentials modelled on F. L. Schröder, the German Garrick, in Hamburg. Wilhelm has long discussions about Shakespeare with Serlo and his sister Aurelie, whose talent is as outstanding as her brother's, though it is in emotional scenes that she excels, while he is a comic and character actor. Compared with Serlo, who has theatre blood in his veins and has learnt his art in an acting career of the utmost variety which began in his earliest years, Wilhelm will always be an amateur, but his idealism and poetic sensibility impress the hardened professional so much that, having trouble with his present troupe, he offers to take on all Wilhelm's friends if he himself will join them as *jeune premier*. Wilhelm does not immediately accept the invitation. For one thing, he has regained a certain interest in commerce through seeing new aspects of it in the big town and hesitates to give up all that it might provide him with. But his deepest desire, he admits, anticipating the fuller statement he is to make in the letter to Werner already mentioned, is 'to unfold and develop the capacities which may lie in him, whether in body or mind, for the good and the beautiful'. He is grateful and amazed that 'fate' seems to be giving him a second chance of realizing what he had dreamt of before Mariane's unfaithfulness, a great and beneficent career in the theatre. Perhaps the love of art had always been his strongest motive, and not merely the attractions of an un-philistine life?

Wilhelm's reference to Mariane suggests a closer look at the role played by women in Wilhelm's 'Bildung'. Is it true, as D. H. Lawrence once wrote to Aldous Huxley (27 March 1928), that '*Wilhelm Meister* is amazing as a book of peculiar immorality, the perversity of intellectualized sex, and the utter incapacity for any development of contact with any other human being, which is peculiarly bourgeois and Goethean'? The sentences which follow show that Lawrence was completely equating Wilhelm with Goethe himself, which is surely unjustified, a misuse of fiction. 'Goethe began millions of intimacies', it goes on, 'but never got beyond the how-do-you-do stage, then fell off into his own boundless ego. He perverted himself into perfection and God-likeness.' A very similar impression of Goethe himself had been conveyed by Max Beerbohm in the essay *Quia Imperfectum* of 1919: 'Of Goethe we are shy for such reasons as that he was never injudicious, never lazy, always in his best form – and always in love with some lady or another just so much as was good for the development of his soul and his art, and never more than that by a tittle.' This note is struck as early as 1850 by Walter Bagehot in his Shakespeare essay, where he says of Goethe: 'He moved hither and thither through life, but he was always a man apart ...In every scene he was there, and he made it clear that he was there, with a reserve, and as a stranger. He went there to *experience* ... No scene and no subject were to him what Scotland and Scotch nature were to Sir Walter Scott.' George Eliot, though she greatly admired Goethe, approved of this criticism, and similar remarks are to be found about that time in R. H. Hutton's review of Lewes's *Life of Goethe*, in Sarah Austin and in D. G. Rossetti.[5] This is an impression of Goethe which is understandable in Victorian English readers of Goethe's autobiographical writings, *Poetry and Truth*, where he is consciously reviewing the experiences which have made him what he is, and the *Italian Journey*, where his self-confessed seriousness, his determination to *study* art and life, as the very German Winckelmann had done before him, seems all wrong to readers who associate the thought of Italy mainly with holidays. One is reminded of Henry Sidgwick's alleged reply to a German visitor who said that there was no word in English quite corresponding to 'Gelehrte': 'Oh yes there is. We call it "prig".' This sums up the instinctive reaction of many of us to the whole notion of 'Bildung', of conscious self-development. But an attentive reading of *Wilhelm Meisters Lehrjahre* does not seem to me to justify Lawrence's criticism.

The affair with Mariane is such an old, old story that Goethe chose in the revised version to combine it with Wilhelm's interminable recollections about his first puppet-play and precocious interest in the theatre. Looking back in Book IV, as we have just seen, Wilhelm is not sure whether it was his wish to continue indefinitely the novel irregular life, into which a chance passion for an actress had plunged him, which had made him think of the stage as a career, or whether it was the pure love of art which had made him fall in love with an actress. In Book I (chapter 8) he had however told Mariane that his love of the theatre had indeed begun with the puppet-plays, and that in his teens, before his education by private tutors was over, it had been decided to put him into Herr Werner's counting-house to be trained for commerce, and then: 'My mind turned only the more decisively away from everything that I considered an unworthy occupation. I wanted to devote every effort to the stage and to find there my fortune and happiness.' It was then that he wrote the poem about a youth at the cross-roads which is mentioned several times, in which the muse of tragedy and a figure representing commerce had contended with each other for him. The collapse of his romance drives him into the arms of trade, but his deeper feelings are unaltered and assert themselves when, on his business journey, any form of acting comes his way. The official moral of the Mariane episode is put into the mouth of the stranger, really the first emissary of 'The Tower', we learn later, who talks to Wilhelm in the street just before his disillusionment with Mariane. The stranger urges him not to excuse his habit of following his inclinations by invoking 'fate', the will of higher beings,

giving chance a kind of rationality, to follow which is even a sort of religion[...] I have no joy in a man, unless he knows what is good for himself and others, and keeps his arbitrary impulses under control. Everyone has his own fortune under his hands as the artist has the raw material which he wants to form into a figure. But it is the same with this art as with all others. Only the capacity for it is innate, and it must be learnt and carefully practised.

For three or four years Wilhelm applies himself more seriously than ever to commerce, renouncing his old ambitions in poetry and the theatre and nursing his grief at his loss, 'convinced that it was the first and the last that he would suffer in his life and rejecting any comfort which suggested to him that these sufferings would ever end'. But then, on a business journey on horseback, he finds himself enjoying the fresh air and the fine hilly country, and soon he makes interesting contacts with people. In a small town he comes across Philine and Mignon almost simultaneously, the first members of the other sex to play any part in his life after Mariane. Philine, the actress, is as her name implies a sort of man's dream, detested by women. She is golden-haired, cheerful, sprightly and above all uninhibited, but she is a highly individual creation, not just a sex doll. Her levity is incurable, but she is recklessly generous, good-hearted and open, though well able to take care of herself in a crisis, for she has come through many. A born anarchist, who sees the state as a silly old man in a wig, she incorporates more than anyone else the attractions of bohemian freedom for the serious Wilhelm. She represents a constant temptation to let everything slide, and that is her function in the Bildungsroman. Almost at the end of the novel (VIII, 7) Wilhelm says: 'I loved Philine, but could not help despising her.' In Book v, 10, after Philine's characteristic song about the joys of night, Wilhelm tells the indignant Aurelie that he could account for every moment when Philine and he have been together, but the comedy with Philine's slippers that night shows that he is far from insensible, and in the wild night following his triumph as Hamlet, his mysterious nocturnal visitor turns out eventually to have been Philine, though next day she runs off with the equally irresponsible Friedrich, and marries him later.

Mignon, the mysterious girl in boy's clothes, who looks about twelve but is more childish than her age, shy and unapproachable, barely articulate in German and given to strange salaams and capers, arouses Wilhelm's compassion. He rescues her from the swarthy Italian acrobat's ill-treatment and treats her like a daughter, but in her devotion she soon seems attached to him in more than a childlike way, though the longing for a far-off home in her incomparable songs, which seem to express her nature as the Harpist's do his, never leaves her. She seems the very spirit of Romantic poetry and of Goethe's feeling for Italy, but in notes for the continuation of the novel he applies to her the phrase: 'madness through discordant relationships'. Her story, when at last we hear it, seems like part of a Gothic novel of horror.

Book III brings for Wilhelm the frequent sight of the Countess, a paragon of rococo charm married to an old eccentric. She has every attraction, rank, youth, beauty, elegance and a certain shyness.

She is not insensitive to a handsome, gifted young man, and they look at each other with interest across the yawning gulf of rank. The mischievous plot of the gay Baroness and Philine for bringing the pair together alone is foiled by the Count's unexpected return, to see himself, as he thinks, sitting in his dressing-gown, reading, a terrifying omen which makes him turn to Pietism. Wilhelm had been a very unwilling party to this intrigue, being 'by nature far removed from any empty gallantry', but when he was finally taking leave of the Countess, she rashly showed signs of her growing liking and he, emboldened, took her into his arms. Goethe contrives a sharp awakening to their moral lapse and an effective close to Book III by making the Countess, who had returned Wilhelm's kisses, suddenly tear herself away with a cry, put her hand to her heart and beg him, if he loves her, not to see her again. The author answers later his own question as to what strange warning of chance or fate tore them asunder. The diamond-studded portrait-medallion of her husband which she wore had been pressed painfully against her breast. Before long, in spite of her doctor's reassurance, she was convinced she had cancer, and like her husband took refuge in religion.

In Book IV, after the attack by armed bandits on the troupe as it makes its way to the big town, the wounded Wilhelm, left behind while the rest seek help in a village, is discovered near nightfall lying with his head in Philine's lap by a young lady, one of a party on horseback, followed later by several coaches. The Amazon, as she is always called later, makes the deepest possible impression on Wilhelm. 'He had fixed his eyes on the gentle, dignified, quiet, sympathetic features of the lady approaching. He thought he had never seen anything more noble and lovable.' In comparison with her Philine looked an impudent vagabond. Wilhelm's wound is dressed by a surgeon brought from one of the coaches, but soon the party is hurried on its way by the lady's uncle, eager to see his family in safer country. As he faints away again, Wilhelm has a vision as of a saint. The manservant left behind to look after him eventually finds quarters for the couple with a clergyman, but when Wilhelm recovers, he cannot find the Amazon's family from the information left by her man. In his memory she and the Countess are as alike as twins.

It is only in the last book that this thread is taken up again, and the Amazon is found to be indeed the Countess's sister Natalie, about whose virtues we have heard in Book VI, the 'Confessions of a "schöne Seele"', her aunt. But first there is one more possible partner for Wilhelm to be considered, Serlo's sister Aurelie, to whom Serlo tries to marry him to secure his services for his troupe. Aurelie is described in Goethe's formula as a case of 'stubborn self-torturing attachment'. Wilhelm, a good listener, hears from her the long story of her stage career and of her impressions of the stream of men who have made love to her, an indictment of the crude approaches of every possible social type. She could only keep sane by coolly observing their antics as caricatures of humanity, without surprise, because having lost her mother early, she had been brought up by a nymphomaniac aunt, and known her loathsome miscellaneous visitors. She is moved to tell Wilhelm of her experiences because she finds him so ignorant of human nature in the real world, though so perceptive a critic of dramatic poetry. 'Nothing gets in to you from outside. I have seldom seen anyone who knows so little about the people he lives with, so completely misunderstands them.'

All this time Aurelie had been entirely devoted to her art but, lacking encouragement from an intelligent audience, she had let her brother marry her to a dull but efficient young man whom he wanted as business manager, and she had fallen in with their wish to give their audiences what they wanted. At last, just before her husband's early death, she had met a man she could wholly admire, who understood her art and gave her a new motive for her work, a cultivated landowner who had served as an officer with Lafayette in the American war. It is the Baron Lothario who plays a leading part in the later books of the *Lehrjahre* and in the *Wanderjahre*, a man with many interests and many claims on his affections. Distraught with her hopeless love for him, overworked and filled with a sense of failure she vents her frustration one day on the hapless Wilhelm. Staring into his eyes she asks him whether he can say that *he* has never tried to win a woman's favours by deceptive arts and assurances. He can, he says, because his life has been simple and temptations few, and to show how he shares her feelings, he is ready to vow that no woman shall ever hear a declaration of love from his lips to whom he cannot devote his whole life. That he may never forget, she scores with her dagger the palm of his outstretched hand.

The first five books show us an eminently teachable young man in a natural sequence of situations into which he was led, in adult life, mainly by his passion for the theatre, in a world which is recognizably that inhabited by Goethe himself before the French Revolution. If we picture to ourselves the middle class, the actors and the nobility of the time with the help of the novel, we shall know them very much as they were, even though the facets of their life which are illuminated here are carefully selected to suit the author's purpose. This selection has to be much more rigorous in the later books, as Emil Staiger has pointed out:

The nearer Wilhelm Meister comes to his real goal, the more the range of his existence is contracted. No place in public affairs, no mark of distinction, no important office fall to his lot. The army, the government, the church, all general institutions lie outside the area over which the classical laws of culture hold sway. It is only in the circle of the family, with a few friends grouped around it, that the individual still appears as a human being with clear contours. But it must be a moderately well-to-do family. Its strength must not be used up in the fight for existence. Culture of the highest grade, moreover, presupposes a tradition that is not of yesterday. The group chosen must therefore inevitably be an aristocratic one. Within the nobility again certain types must be carefully avoided. The patriotic traditions, for instance, that were lively after the Seven Years War, have no place here. There are neither Prussians nor Saxons, only Germans, in fact not even Germans, but only men, citizens of the world, compelled indeed to live in space and time, but not bounded by space and time.[6]

The gradually increasing abstraction so well described by Staiger is principally, no doubt, a consequence of the shift in the central theme from a life in the theatre to the formation of a personality. Consciously or not, and it seems quite consciously, the revised version conveys a message, the particular conception of the good life we call Weimar humanism, the content of which is to be found also in many other works of Herder, Goethe and Schiller chiefly between 1785 and 1805. H. A. Korff has analysed the intellectual content of these works very clearly in his *Geist der Goethezeit*. The kind of ethical view he finds in Herder, for instance, he expresses at one point as follows: 'The ultimate meaning of our humanity is that we develop that higher human being within ourselves, which emerges if we continually strengthen our truly human powers, and subjugate the inhuman.'[7] This may strike us now as disappointingly vague and question-begging.

Herder's ethical views bear the imprint of his own experience and habit of life in an unpolitical age and country. In his maturity, at least, it is quiet family life that is the norm for his view of the good, as it was for Goethe's and Schiller's. The values of inwardness are to the fore in it, but political action, adventure and heroism are praised as virtues only for earlier ages.[8]

In the same spirit of goodness and kindness, undogmatic but still unconsciously Christian, Goethe brings before us an Iphigenie overcoming the curse of inhumanity, that had hitherto dogged her family, by her inner vision of a new ideal, one which, as Korff puts it, 'convinces us not by its utility but by its beauty'. The touch of the author of *Iphigenie* is clearly visible in the 'schöne Seele' and Natalie. In the life story of the schöne Seele, which is given by her doctor to Wilhelm to comfort Aurelie in her self-inflicted illness and constitutes Book VI of the novel, we have the reflexions on the growth of her own personality of one of the group of people most given to such introspection at that time, the unorthodox Christians who came to be called 'Pietists'. It forms an apt transition from the revised theatre novel to the openly didactic final section of the new 'Bildungs-roman', for in her dissatisfaction with the life of her class, her quietism, the concentration of all her energies on the salvation of her own soul, the schöne Seele forms a kind of feminine counterpart to Wilhelm. Her inner life, like his, soon outruns the means of expression available. She will not marry, any more than he will take up a normal occupation, at the cost of sacrificing her impulse to be fully herself. She is intelligent, sensitive and naturally religious but, as the daughter of a court official, she is for long surrounded by people 'without the least culture' who reject with contempt not merely blue-stockings, but any girl of good family who has intelligent interests, 'probably because it was thought to be bad manners to put so many ignorant men to shame'. Her old French tutor warns her not only against these cavaliers' subtle seductiveness, but also against the danger of infection from their touch. We witness a scene of amazing brutality in which she becomes involved at a private party in 'good' society. There is no idealization of the aristocracy here, any more than in the preceding books, but what surprised contemporary readers was Goethe's insight into the mind and heart of a deeply religious woman steeped in the quite special traditions of German Pietism. Goethe could not have written this section, as he wrote to Schiller (18 March

48

1795), if he had not earlier 'made studies from nature for it', a reference, as became clear later from his *Dichtung und Wahrheit* (II, 8) to his friendship in Frankfurt days with his mother's cousin Susanne von Klettenberg (1723–74). The extent of his own involvement in Pietism for a short time only became known through the publication (1922) of his letters to his Leipzig friend E. Th. Langer, and his 'Protean' ability to enter into the way of thinking of Catholic contemplatives too had been proved, not long before the composition of the *Lehrjahre*, by his friendship with Fürstin Gallitzin,[9] though there was really nothing surprising for sensitive readers of *Iphigenie*, as we have said, or of *Tasso*, with its portrait of the Princess.

The schöne Seele leads in her maturity a life of good works, prayer and contemplation like that of a sister of certain Catholic orders, and she is in fact a Protestant 'Stiftsdame'. Her rich uncle had secured her admission to a 'Stift' when it was clear that she would not marry, and it was this that enabled her to lead what she called the life of 'a Herrnhut sister on her own account', that is, without having to reside in a 'Schwesterheim'. Only blue blood, a specified number of 'descents', together with the ability to contribute a considerable sum to the funds of the community, qualified a lady for membership of a 'Stift'. After taking vows of chastity and obedience to the Superiors she was assured of a fixed income, a kind of annuity, for the rest of her life, if she chose to live outside the 'Stift'. But more remarkable than her obviously privileged position is her natural goodness and serenity, as one of those 'Glad hearts, without reproach or blot/Who do God's work and know it not', or what Schiller (in *Über Anmut und Würde*, 1793) had defined as one 'who may confidently leave his will to be conducted by feeling'. Goethe's schöne Seele sees no merit of her own in her uninterrupted moral progress, in the fact, as she says, that 'my actions continually draw nearer to the idea that I have conceived of perfection, and that I find it easier every day to do what I consider right, in spite of the weakness of my body...It is an impulse that guides me and always guides me aright; I follow my convictions and know as little of restraint as of remorse. Thanks be to God that I recognize to whom I owe this good fortune and that I can only think of these qualities with humility.'

Goethe wrote to Schiller while engaged on this book that 'the whole rests on the noblest illusions and the subtlest confusion of the subjective with the objective' and following a hint from Schiller makes Lothario, her nephew, say that the true schöne Seele is his sister Natalie. The implied criticism is that the aunt is over-concerned with herself, with her own salvation, that she has not the self-forgetfulness of the genuine saint, no adequate sense of the suffering in the world. This is one of the dangers of inwardness that we shall find also affecting some of our later subjects in their humanistic 'Bildung'. If the schöne Seele represents the Pietistic strain in eighteenth-century German culture, her uncle, described in her 'Confessions', stands for the complementary rationalistic move-ment. His character is summed up in his maxim: 'A man's greatest merit is to control the circumstances of his life as fully as possible, and to reduce their influence on him to a minimum.' Life itself is an art for him, and the highest of all. His house and estate are the perfection of order and good taste, the expression of his energy and practical ability. In his life there is no room for longing or for brooding over the power of destiny. Longing, according to one mouth-piece of the author, is to be converted into calm contemplation. Fate, as three different strangers have all told Wilhelm in successive books of the novel – he meets them all again at the end of Book vii, when he learns about the secret society, The Tower, which they serve, and which has been exercising a benevolent supervision over him – fate is a useless concept, an imaginary excuse for lack of self-control. A man's fortune is in his own hands, to be shaped by him as raw material is shaped by the artist. These thoughts are symbolized in various ways in the Uncle's house, described in Book vii, above all in the Hall of the Past, where Mignon, in one important aspect the personification of longing, dies and is laid to rest. 'Children, go back into life!' the funeral choir sings, 'Flee from night! Day and joy and duration are the lot of the living.'

The last two books are full of directly didactic passages like this, and the characters seem to be there mainly in order to speak them. These figures have nearly all been gradually brought before us first in the preceding books, and four of them turn out to be brothers and sisters, the four nephews and nieces of the schöne Seele, who have lost their parents early and been brought up in the house of the Uncle by a French Abbé. Natalie is the 'Amazone' of Book iv, Lothario is

Aurelie's lost lover in the same book, the Countess of Book III is a younger sister and Philine's boy-follower in Book II, strange to relate, is their irresponsible young brother. Eventually we learn that the Harpist and Mignon are the brother and niece of the Uncle's old friend, the Marchese, who also appears, and Wilhelm is finally taken into the family as Natalie's husband. The four brothers and sisters have been educated by their rationalistic great-uncle and their tutor the Abbé, whose origins are mysterious and who has certainly lost his faith, without religious instruction and on Rousseauistic principles. The first step in education, says the Abbé, is to discover a child's wishes and inclinations and enable him to satisfy them as soon as possible, 'so that the pupil, if he has been mistaken, may discover his error soon enough, and when he has found what suits him, may hold fast to it and develop in that direction with all the greater determination'. The children have been kept out of the way of their introspective aunt and she complains, not without reason, that the Uncle is more tolerant in principle than in practice. The results of this trial and error method of education have been good with two of the children, Lothario and Natalie, and not so good with the rather empty-headed Countess and the cheerful impulsive idiot Friedrich. Natalie, discussing her education with Wilhelm (VIII, 3), says that as far back as she remembers her chief interest has been in people and their difficulties, not in nature or art, and her unreflecting impulse has always been to help them, and not with money, but with the things they needed. But though the Abbé's method had suited her, she does not use it herself, and lets the many girls and young women she has around her find out everything by experience.

Anyone who does not help at the moment seems to me never to help, and anyone who does not give advice at the moment, never to advise. In the same way it seems to me necessary to formulate and make the children learn certain laws, which give a certain support in life. In fact I would almost go so far as to say that it is better to go wrong by following rules than by being driven this way and that by the caprices of our nature.

Lothario rather reminds us of Goethe's admiring description to Eckermann (12 March 1828) of the young Englishmen in Weimar, who are no cleverer and no better than other people, he admits, but unlike so many young Germans, 'they have the courage to be what nature made them. Nothing in them is misshapen and twisted, nothing half-hearted and perverse. No matter what kind of people they are, they are always complete human beings.' He puts it down to their tradition of personal freedom, national pride and above all a freer education and early development than most Germans enjoy. Byron of course fascinated him as the picture of untrammelled English genius. It is typical that in the last chapter of the novel, the old Count, whose memories are confused, greets Wilhelm as an English lord. Lothario is not a poet, but he combines the highest cultivation with the love of adventure in the cause of freedom – 'If an action was not surrounded by a thousand dangers, it did not seem worthy of notice.' His distinguished service as a volunteer with the French contingent in the American War of Independence has already been mentioned. It had cost him a great part of his fortune, and when Wilhelm first meets him he is busily improving his estate, convinced now that 'here or nowhere is America', i.e. an opportunity for useful activity. His utilitarian tendency is reflected in the unlovely additions he has made to his old mansion and in his impatience with medieval survivals such as the exclusive right of the nobility to own land and their exemption from land tax – the kind of thing that Freiherr vom Stein was soon to do away with. He also contemplates the freeing of his peasantry, but not over-hastily, and not to his own detriment. The death of the Uncle has brought him so much new land that he sells some to Werner and Wilhelm, and Wilhelm is to manage it as an investment – so in this region 'noble' estates can evidently be sold already to 'Bürger'. Lothario is also, we hear, keenly interested in public affairs and is in touch with leading figures. He is himself a born leader, who inspires and invigorates those around him. We hear that the Tower is to turn into a sort of international consortium for the protection of landowners against the risks of revolution, clearly a veiled reference to the plight of aristocratic refugees from the French Revolution, which is otherwise never mentioned. In the last chapter of the *Lehrjahre* Lothario puts forward the idea of a new 'Bund', an association of the old 'Tower' members and Wilhelm for the furtherance of 'worthy' activity for the public good. This is one of the bodies behind the emigration project in the *Wanderjahre*.

'A man is never happy until his unlimited strivings find their own limits' is a maxim of Jarno's (VIII, 5), and Lothario finds it true not only in his public activities, but also in love. To Aurelie, on his return from America, he seemed to be used to success with women. We hear of a farmer's daughter before her, and after her Therese and her supposed mother, living abroad, then Lydie and a discarded lady who persuaded her divorced husband to fight a duel with him. After all this varied experience, the type of woman he wants as a wife, a type personified in Therese, is a good housekeeper. There are several parallels in Goethe to the passage describing his ideal, in the *Zweite Epistel*, for instance, or in *Hermann und Dorothea*, and it seems to have been Goethe's own. Therese is in fact not only an excellent housekeeper but an expert in estate management, a woman with a career of her own. She has little imagination, but clear ideas and strong common sense. It is from her that we have perhaps the most illuminating comment on the character of Wilhelm (viii, 4). She finds him very like Natalie, with the same eagerness for something better, 'by which we ourselves bring into being the good that we think we are finding'. Wilhelm's life, she says, has been one of endless seeking and not finding. But it is not a futile seeking, but a wonderfully good-hearted seeking which makes him think people can give him what can only come from himself.

Lothario, Natalie and their friends are clearly meant to be taken as models of 'Humanität', as men and women who are 'noble' in the sense of Goethe's poem *Das Göttliche*:

> Der edle Mensch
> Sei hülfreich und gut.
> Unermüdlich schaff' er
> Das Nützliche, Rechte.*

The intellectual and moral foundation beneath these books is the ethical idealism of Goethe and Schiller at the height of their powers, the lasting importance of which for the best minds in Germany in later generations will be the main topic of all our later chapters. The thoughts and aspirations of Lothario and Natalie have a wider scope than those of their great-uncle. The Uncle walls off his estate, like a monastery of reason and art, from the chaotic world outside, but they have the cosmopolitan spirit of the younger generation. The idea of the Tower, so fantastic for a modern reader, does not seem quite so unconvincing a piece of literary apparatus, contrived for the sole

---

* The noble man should be helpful and kind, should tirelessly strive for what is useful and right.

purpose of imposing a kind of unity on the revised novel, if one looks into the history of secret societies in Goethe's day. High hopes were entertained for a time by people as cool-headed as Lessing from Freemasonry, it had a certain vogue for short periods in Weimar, and the Illuminati, the Rosicrucians and other secret societies had evidently a considerable following. Goethe's poem *Die Geheimnisse*, of which an impressive fragment was written in 1784, was inspired by similar hopes of a humanistic substitute for a vanishing religion. Pierre Byezukhov in *War and Peace*, reflecting a Russian continuation of the tradition, is still looking in the same direction for a key to the meaning of life. What was common to all these movements was the attempt to harmonize the conflicts due to religious, national and social differences.

Aesthetically the revised version of the novel, the *Lehrjahre*, is marred by the introduction of several other features, as well as the improbable secret society, which were well-tried attractions of the popular German novel of that time, an attack by robbers, a fire, motifs like abduction and incest, the linking-up of most of the characters as members of a single family and other incredible coincidences. As Max Wundt long since pointed out, Goethe's essential subject in the later books is the presentation of an ideal way of life and the hero's connection with it becomes more and more external.

It seems as if the author had not had the patience to show the ideals he has in mind emerging and ripening in Wilhelm himself, by making him discover them in active life and make them his own. At any rate he chooses the short cut of parading this ideal before him in living examples[...] The question is hardly raised as to how far he is capable of realizing these ideals in his own life.[10]

There is naturally a love interest. Several of the characters fall in and out of love with each other in quick succession and the loose ends are tied up in no less than four marriages, three of them of an aristocrat with a plebeian. Here one might perhaps speak of 'intellectualized sex'. These later books

do not strike home to our imagination. Natalie, for instance, is a completely ideal character, who educates and loses Mignon, who hears of Wilhelm's adventure with Philine, furthers his match with Therese, and ultimately marries him herself, with unaltered serene equanimity. Wilhelm's early life is full of the substantiality of experience; his later education is theoretical.

Hence we cannot help feeling that in his adventures with the troupe he was a real person among real persons, while in the later part, and in the *Wanderjahre*, he is an unreal ghost walking among other ghosts.[11]

However imperfect the form of the later books of the *Lehrjahre* may be, the view of life conveyed in them to the patient Wilhelm is, as we have said, the very essence of Weimar humanism, profoundly interesting as such even for a Marxist critic like Georg Lukács, who sees it all as part of 'the heroic struggle of great bourgeois artists against the hostility to their art of capitalist society', and the expression of the hopes for the renewal of human society aroused in Goethe's best contemporaries by the French Revolution. It is a picture of a Utopia, he says, but of one truly founded on elements from existing reality. It is like one of those rare communities spoken of by Schiller in the last of the *Letters on aesthetic education*, where 'conduct is not governed by the unthinking imitation of others' behaviour, but by the fineness of a man's own nature', his nature corrected by wise education, and by the self-corrective processes of experience of life. The leading idea of the theorists of the Tower is the inability of the individual to live happily for himself alone. For one thing he, like everyone else, will be gifted in some directions but not in others, so that in any civilized society there must be scope for all kinds of complementary activities. The division of labour on which middle-class society is founded is therefore reaffirmed, but the ideal of harmony is not forgotten, the harmony of mind and body in the individual (this more particularly in the *Wanderjahre* with its insistence on crafts) and the harmony of the diversified activities of a society. It is mankind that is infinite in faculty, not the individual, and a man's first aim should be to discover his true vocation. The Tower has allowed its protégé Wilhelm to do this freely, following the Abbé's principle, by experiment, a painful, fumbling process for those in whom there is most to develop, but the only way in which we get to know ourselves, namely by action. The Abbé's Rousseauistic ideas are not fully accepted by Jarno and Natalie, as we have seen, which means that Goethe presents his Utopia, Lukács says, with a certain irony. No one disputes however that the beginning of wisdom for Wilhelm is the discovery of Felix, the realization that he is a father, responsible for another now and in the future, necessarily one-sided himself, but a member of an enduring society which aspires to harmony. This is a new form of 'Bürgerlichkeit' distinguished from the old, as Korff says, by a higher spiritual awareness, a fuller consciousness of their citizenship, which gives their life a meaning unrealized by those who nurse their emotions, like Werther, or without talent, like the young Wilhelm, live for art. They find their satisfaction in real life, unlike those against whom the hard saying in Wilhelm's 'letter of apprenticeship' (vii, 9) is directed: 'A man who works only with signs is a pedant, a hypocrite or a botcher.'

Does that not really mean that this so-called 'Bildungsroman' is not quite what such a novel is generally supposed to be? The question was raised in an illuminating article by Kurt May in 1957, which brought out in a detailed analysis the full meaning of Max Wundt's much earlier criticism, already quoted. Wundt had said that Goethe, in the last books of the novel, only brings various complementary ideals before Wilhelm's eyes without asking how far Wilhelm is capable of realising them in his own life. May goes further and says that Goethe did not mean his hero to become finally a man of harmonious all-round culture such as Humboldt had envisaged in his famous youthful essay (see pp. 15–18), although this has always been assumed by critics in general, knowing Goethe's own reputation as 'uomo universale' in the Renaissance tradition. Goethe did indeed at various times show himself in his writings to be attracted by the harmonious personality ideal, for instance in the Winckelmann essay of 1801, but he says there that to realise such an ideal had been reserved for the Ancients alone. Schiller on the other hand had advanced the 'wholeness' ideal in the sixth letter on Aesthetic Education in 1795 with a passion similar to that of Hölderlin a little later in his *Hyperion*, but 'the Goethean "Bildungsroman", on the contrary, ends with the recognition that a man of his day could not develop the full harmony of his nature and would do better to aim at being, and to have himself educated as, a fragment, a single part'.[12] This does not mean that Goethe had failed in what he was attempting, but that he had never been aiming at what his critics have supposed:

It is only these numerous interpreters of Goethe's book who, in good faith, have seen a harmonious education as realized at the end of the *Lehrjahre*, not the author himself. It has been widely assumed that in this 'classical' novel the classical personality ideal must have been realized, that in an idealistic work of art the idea of man must surely be made to triumph. Goethe however, on the contrary, has shown Wilhelm as cultivating himself only in the measure permitted by his limited capacities and potentialities. The idea of man as such cannot be perfectly attained in a single individual[...]and Goethe has, in the *Lehrjahre*, written a novel round the belief that the modern humanistic ideal of harmonious 'Bildung' has to be abandoned.[13]

The realist Goethe recognized then that we must content ourselves in education with something less than 'restoring the totality of our nature', as Schiller had demanded. He left Wilhelm, at the end of the *Lehrjahre*, not already at the desired goal, but with the prospect of proving himself, in the company of his son Felix, his wife Natalie and her friends and through the acceptance of a limited task in civil society, a reasonably cultivated person, some time in the future. This made a continuation, such as Goethe eventually wrote in the *Wanderjahre*, an artistic necessity.

FRIEDRICH SCHLEIERMACHER:
MONOLOGEN (1801)

One of the attractions of the *Soliloquies* is that, apart from the light the book throws on Schleiermacher as a person, it presents in its five short chapters, some eighty pages in all, a number of the central ideas of German Romanticism, not in the form of the isolated aphorisms these writers favoured, difficult to interpret for lack of a context, but as part of a relatively clear and unified whole, a work expressing an individual mind at a particular stage in its known development. 'One man cannot offer to another any more precious gift', the author begins, 'than that which one has spoken to oneself in the innermost privacy of the mind.' The mind, in these confessions, is that of the most versatile humanist who became for German Protestantism a reformer second only to Luther. Even Karl Barth, whose general approach was so different, wrote that in any history of modern theology, the foremost name to be considered was and always would be that of Schleiermacher.[1] His great achievement was to restore the self-confidence of the Church and to make Christianity again a possible creed for intelligent men after the formidable philosophical, historical and textual criticism of the German Enlightenment. There had been a series of German thinkers since Leibniz who fully accepted, as he did, the best secular thought of their day, and still held on with a good conscience to what they saw as the essence of Protestantism. Schleiermacher was *the* thinker of this type in the age of Romanticism. 'Just as seriously as he wishes to be a Christian theologian', Barth says, 'he wishes in all circumstances to be a modern man.'[2] Like Herder before him, he could go a long way with the rationalists in their criticism of accepted doctrines, but he kept the heart of his faith intact as a truth known by direct experience, known as directly as Wordsworth knew God in nature, and something shared from his earliest years with those most dear to him, though the ideas he came to associate with religious feeling were much more complex in him.

In a letter written two years after the *Soliloquies* to Eleonore

Grunow, Schleiermacher says that he remembers clearly when he first became aware of what he calls religious feeling – which seems to mean in this context a complex of ideas and images, accompanied by feeling-tone, an intuition of a religious truth – when he was out on a walk with his father. Feeling, he says in the same letter, is something of which a child is not yet capable, 'the uninterrupted and as it were ever present activity of certain ideas', ideas which can only emerge when the imagination, as well as the intellect, has reached a certain stage of development. When this feeling had once shown itself his father did everything he could to develop it, but it had come spontaneously.[3] His father was a minister of the Reformed Church, like his own father before him, but he had not come unscathed through the Enlightenment and had only found peace of mind at last in the kind of Pietism practised by the Moravian Brethren, though he did not go so far as to leave the Reformed Church. When Friedrich (born 21 November 1768) was fourteen years old, he says in the same letter, his parents decided that he at least should be a genuine 'Herrnhuter' and be saved from his father's painful experiences. The father wanted to protect his son 'against the combined power of the world and of the sceptical intelligence which he did not fail to recognize in me'. Friedrich was received into the community by the brethren at Gnadenfrei in 1783 and finished his secondary education at their 'Pädagogium' at Niesky, proceeding after two years there to the Seminary of the Moravian Brothers at Barby, a training college for Herrnhut teachers and clergy.

Friedrich's early schooling had been rather irregular because of his father's frequent moves as an army chaplain, but his outstanding ability soon made itself evident and for the last two years before he went to Niesky he attended a good school at Pless in Upper Silesia as a boarder. Here a pupil of the great Ernesti passed on to him his love of the Classics and gave him a good start in Latin, encouraging him naturally to think of a scholarly career, but the religious atmosphere of his home remained still a stronger influence.

Religion was the maternal womb in the sacred darkness of which my young life was nourished and prepared for the world still hidden to it. In it my mind breathed before it had discovered for itself objects, experience and knowledge outside.

This passage from the *Discourses on Religion* is not the only evidence we have of the religious passion dominating the life of his family. There is above all the fact that his parents were willing to be parted from all their children at once for what they held to be their spiritual welfare, for in the same year they sought and obtained admission to the Community for all three. Friedrich went to the secondary school at Niesky, his brother Karl was accepted at the school for younger children and his sister Charlotte, three years older than himself, at the House of the Sisterhood, where she stayed for thirty years, and then joined her brother in Berlin to teach his children. Perhaps the state of Frau Schleiermacher's health had something to do with the break-up of the family, at any rate she died later in 1783; the father re-married and lived for eleven years longer, and during that time Friedrich never saw him again, though they frequently wrote to each other. Even allowing for the difficulty and expense of travel, and the resulting long separations between children at boarding-schools and their parents, the completeness of this break is surprising.

It was not very long before the father had reason to doubt whether he had acted wisely, because the supposedly sheltered environment had the unexpected effect of producing a conflict in his son of a most disturbing kind, which the father naturally misinterpreted.

He took for the activity of a vain heart, the fatal urge to plunge into the abyss of scepticism, what was simply the product of my feeling for truth, without any feeling of pleasure or pain about what would come of it.[4]

In its devotional aspect, life with the Herrnhuter was entirely to Friedrich's liking. Returning to Barby on a visit twenty years later, he still felt that there was no form of Christian church service 'which more nobly expressed and more surely aroused Christian piety than that in the Brotherhood'.[5] But it was a different thing with their theology and their attitude to secular knowledge and philosophy. Even before going to Niesky the young Schleiermacher, with his keen intellect and love of clarity and consistency, had spent sleepless nights worrying over points of doctrine. At Niesky he and one or two friends tried to forget their questioning of the naive fundamentalism of their teachers in heroic feats of study, reading everything available to them in Greek and Hebrew. At Barby however, which was near Halle with its university, it was impossible for the staff, with all the censorship and strict discipline they imposed, to prevent the brighter boys from absorbing the spirit of secular humanism which every year was gaining a firmer hold on the world of literature and learning in Germany. The year was 1785, when the *Allgemeine Literatur-Zeitung* began to appear in Jena. Even its first volume brought good reviews by Schütz of Kant's *Metaphysik der Sitten* and *Kritik der reinen Vernunft*, Kant's own long review of the first part of Herder's *Ideen* and many similar expressions of the most advanced theological and philosophical thought of the time. In the following year Reinhold wrote his famous letters on the philosophy of Kant for the *Teutscher Merkur*. These leading periodicals and many oddments of contemporary literature penetrated the defences of Barby and awakened in Schleiermacher and some of his friends what he calls in the *Soliloquies* 'the clear consciousness of humanity', that is, of humane modern feeling or 'Humanität'.

When Schleiermacher had been only a year at Barby, the undermining of his simple creed by liberal ideas had gone so far that he decided that he could not finish the course and become a Herrnhut teacher or preacher, as had always been intended, but it was several months before he could break the news to his father. The letters they exchanged early in 1787 are moving evidence of the prolonged mental suffering they both endured. Eventually the father agreed to his son's suggestion that he should be allowed to study for a year or two at Halle, where an uncle on his mother's side was a professor of theology. But although Schleiermacher always hoped that he would in time find his way back to the Church, it was not through the rationalistic theologians of Halle that he regained his peace of mind, but through philosophy, ancient and modern, in which he could now freely follow his interests, in voracious but unsystematic reading which made these two years for him, as he said later, 'like Chaos, before the world was created'. He had his uncle's complete support and Eberhard, the professor of philosophy, gave him just the help he needed. He encouraged his ethical bent and, along with F. A. Wolf, his love of the Greeks, while criticizing from a common-sense point of view the philosophy of Kant, which was quickly gaining adherents in all the universities and naturally made a profound impression on Schleiermacher. A further year's quiet work in a small town in the Neumark, Drossen, to which his uncle had now retired, having given up his chair to become a parish minister again, gave Schleiermacher time, living 'like a real Herrnhuter', concerned only about the ultimate questions, to think things out for himself.

He was just twenty-two when, in the autumn of 1790, he was persuaded by his uncle to sit the first theological examination in Berlin because, with this qualification, he might hope to obtain at least a tutorship. A letter to his friend Brinkmann reveals his state of mind: 'I fear my good genius will ominously flap his wings over my head and fly away, if I am to be questioned on theological subtleties which in my heart – I find ridiculous.' However, he was immensely intelligent, he had done his book work, and he passed. In the nine years which elapsed before he wrote the *Soliloquies*, at the age of thirty-one, he continued the perpetual exploration of himself on which that work lays so much stress, and greatly enlarged what was also essential to his mature view of life, his knowledge of other people. He was very fortunate in the family with which he obtained a tutorship, a post which was always for a young theologian merely stop-gap employment, and often a humiliating and unrewarding experience. Count Dohna, a retired general, and his intelligent wife, though they had the highest connections at the Prussian court, led by choice a patriarchal life with their large family on their estates at Schlobitten in East Prussia, about sixty miles south-west of Königsberg. They all liked this quiet young man, with his wide-hearted understanding of others, his lively imagination and great range of interests. Though he had probably seen very little of polite society, he seems to have had a natural dignity and an impressive sense of independence. In the same long letter about himself to Eleonore Grunow from which we have quoted above, he mentions with approval what some one had said of him as a student, that he had never cared in the least about his appearance or comfort, would sacrifice anything for a friend and liked to live with his own thoughts in solitude, but if he came together with people of rank and wealth, he seemed more at ease than anyone in the company. He still thinks he was right in what he instinctively rejected in those days, but he had not yet found all the best in life. 'I knew nothing yet about art or women. It was only in the domestic circle in Prussia that I came to understand anything about these latter.' As he writes in the fourth *Soliloquy*:

It was in the house of strangers that my eyes were opened for happy family life, where I saw that freedom alone refines and gives proper expression to the delicate mysteries of humane feeling, which for the uninitiated who respect them only as bonds of nature are for ever a sealed book. Mixing with the greatest variety of people and social groups I learned how to get behind appearances and to recognize the same human nature in every dress, translating for myself the diverse languages it acquires in different circles.

This passage, which incidentally reflects back on Schleiermacher's own home, seems to mean that the relations between members of a family, founded upon instinctive behaviour and serving a biological purpose, assume different forms in various social groups or classes according to their inherited traditions. 'Culture' is imposed upon 'nature', so that 'delicate mysteries' – romantic love, mutual respect and so on, can grow out of 'bonds of nature'. Schleiermacher probably came to see a much more positive value in the aristocratic tradition than he had previously imagined, much as Goethe did in Weimar. Refinement of feeling and charm of manner in women, like the Countess and still more her seventeen-year-old daughter Friederike, particularly impressed the young tutor. After mentioning Friederike by name, still in the same confessional letter, he writes: 'It was only by way of the feminine mind that I came to know true human values.' He got on well with the boys of the family too, but not so well with the Count, whose obstinate conservatism about the French Revolution, and also about teaching methods, got on his nerves after two and a half years and made him resign a post in which he had given of his best, earned liking and respect and acquired a deeper insight into human nature and the ways of society. For his future it was of the greatest importance that he had been encouraged to preach regularly in the chapel of the estate and discovered his outstanding talent in this direction.

The next three years (1793–6) are a relatively dull period in Schleiermacher's life. After some months with his uncle again, he spent a depressing winter in Berlin, glad to take temporary teaching posts and to live at the Orphanage. Early in 1794 he took his second theological examination and was ordained, having by now presumably decided that however unorthodox his religious views might be, he was sure of his calling as pastor and preacher, and felt that he had the roots of genuine belief within himself. Two years as assistant to a distant relative in the small town of Landsberg in Prussia, very near his uncle, gave him experience of the routine of a minister's life. He was glad when, in the autumn of 1796, still on the recommendation of Hofprediger Sack, the most influential man in the Reformed Church in Berlin and Schleiermacher's mainstay throughout these early years, he was able to return to the city as Reformed Church Preacher at the Charité Hospital. He looked after the religious needs of the patients along with a Lutheran colleague, who lived with him on the third floor of the hospital, near the V.D. ward. To judge by all accounts of the inefficiency of this huge overcrowded hospital at that time, burial services must have been frequent occurrences, but the two chaplains also preached on Sundays to the old and infirm who occupied the ground floor, and their friends, not a large or demanding congregation, so that something simpler and plainer was needed than the sermons Schleiermacher had given at Landsberg. He also preached sometimes at the Dom or the Parochialkirche, the two churches which the Evangelicals had to themselves, or at one of the other nine, like the Charité, which they shared with the Lutherans. His duties and the milieu in which he performed them sound grim indeed, but there seem to be no complaints about them in his letters, and there is only one mention of the hospital, which is surprising, because according to Dilthey, all reports speak of its lack of cleanliness even by the standards of that day. The veterinary school next door on the other hand was highly praised. In the one establishment, said the Berlin wits, men were treated like dogs, and in the other dogs like men. The lack of apparent special concern in Schleiermacher about social evils, which may in fact be no more than a reflection of our ignorance, might also be, like his own uncomplaining tolerance of poverty and discomfort, the other side of his passionate interest in the minds and hearts of his fellow-men, and in his own inner development rather than in external success.

In the new ideas and fruitful friendships these six years at the Charité brought him, they were the most memorable in his life. As he looks to the future in the fourth *Soliloquy*, he rejoices in his present opportunities: 'How many noble natures I can see at close quarters in whom humanity is developed in quite different ways than in me! How many men of knowledge I have around me!' The dreadful thought comes to him that he might at any time be banished from this fair world to 'bleak wastes, where it is impossible to keep in touch with other humane people, where a dull landscape pens me in on every side in an eternal sameness', by which he means, no doubt, some village in East Prussia, like Stolp (in Pomerania), where he did spend the years 1802–4. Schleiermacher's friends and acquaintances included many of the clergy, but he was still more interested in the intelligent men and women he met in lay society, especially in a few Jewish houses. He did not frequent the fashionable salons of the rich and well-educated Jewish hostesses who played so important a part in the social life of Berlin for ten or twenty years before 1806, but like Wilhelm von Humboldt earlier, he never tired of the company of Henriette Herz, to whom he had, already in 1793, been introduced by Alexander von Dohna, the eldest son of the Count. 'Something deep down in my nature', he wrote to his sister, 'makes me always more ready to make friends with women than with men. There is so much in my feelings that men seldom understand.' We have quoted above (p. 4) his explanation of the special role played by Jewish hostesses in Berlin society. Henriette Herz and her husband, the best doctor in Berlin, who gave private lectures on science, were much sought after by distinguished strangers, but Schleiermacher liked to go there to tea and to run away when others came. For years he visited them nearly every day, and he knew Dorothea Veit, Mendelssohn's daughter, also quite well even before Friedrich Schlegel came to Berlin in the summer of 1797. Friedrich Schlegel and he were quickly drawn to each other. Their enthusiastic letters about each other to other Romantics are well known. Soon they were sharing rooms, the better to exchange ideas and, through Schlegel, Schleiermacher was of course drawn into the circle and pressed hard for contributions to the *Athenäum*. Some aphorisms and reviews were the first result, followed in 1799 by his most famous work, *Über die Religion. Reden an die Gebildeten unter ihren Verächtern*, and at the end of that year by the *Monologen* (Soliloquies). Meanwhile Friedrich Schlegel had written and published his novel *Lucinde*, about which hardly any of his closest associates could find anything good to say, and now Schleiermacher who, out of kindness of heart, had helped Friedrich Schlegel and Dorothea most generously in their many difficulties in real life, published anonymously a far too generous

65

defence of the novel. *Lucinde* had of course a *succès de scandale*, in a small way not unlike that of *Lady Chatterley's Lover*, though its literary merits were much more dubious. Schleiermacher however was not strong in aesthetic criticism, even of literature, still less of painting or music. What really interested him in *Lucinde* was its author's rejection of the ethics of the rationalistic bourgeois, seen as a soulless and unthinking acceptance of rules and conventions, and he read into the book a presentation of humanity, approaching his ideal, in the relations between men and women.

It is not surprising that Hofprediger Sack warned Schleiermacher as early as summer 1798 that the company he was keeping might hinder his promotion.[6] At that time Sack was thinking of the Jewish salons, which Frau Unger had recently attacked in her *Briefe über Berlin*. His complaints grew more insistent when he heard about Friedrich Schlegel and Dorothea Veit, and finally about *Lucinde*. Though he did not yet know that Schleiermacher had written the *Vertraute Briefe*, his defence of the work, he wrote to him in 1801 about his intimacy with 'people of suspect principles and manners'. In the same letter he protested strongly against the views expressed in *Über die Religion*, which seemed to him pure pantheism. As this was the work which made Schleiermacher particularly important for the early Romantics, initiating a new phase in their thought and 'making "religion" almost a catch-word of the Jena circle' (Kluckhohn), we must remind ourselves of its central ideas to understand what Schleiermacher meant for his brilliant Romantic friends, and what conception of religion is presupposed in all the meditations of the *Soliloquies*.

Schleiermacher's own summary in the last paragraph of the second discourse, 'On the essence of religion', brings out well the novel features:

The usual idea of God, as a separate being outside and behind the world, is not the alpha and omega for religion, but only a seldom quite candid and always inadequate way of expressing it.

This beginning will now recall the controversy in this country about John Robinson's *Honest to God*, or perhaps the more radical 'theology without God' so much discussed in Germany in the last twenty years, but students of German literature will be reminded too of

Goethe's 'Was wär' ein Gott, der nur von aussen stiesse'* and similar rejections, common enough in that age, of the anthropomorphic view. It was because the Age of Reason had so thoroughly undermined orthodox Christianity that Schleiermacher gave his book the sub-title *Discourses to the cultivated among its despisers.* The readers he had in view were in the first place his intelligent and immensely well-read Romantic friends. He goes on to say in what way the notion of a personal God can be the reverse of candid – dishonest:

Anyone who forms such a conception in an un-candid way, because what he must have is a Being so constituted that he can make use of Him for his comfort and assistance, such a man can believe in a God of this kind without being pious, at least not in my sense, and I think not in the true and proper sense.

This is a rejection of petitionary prayer and the mental attitude it expresses, the desire that God 'shall guarantee their happiness from outside, and be a stimulus to morality for them'. Pleasure and pain are bound up with the physical world, a deterministic system, with which God does not interfere. If He did it would not promote morality, but the reverse, according to Kant's teaching, for moral action is only possible to free agents, moved by neither hope nor fear.

The idea of a personal God is however not necessarily 'uncandid', in fact it is almost impossible for most people to think of God except in personal terms, as Schleiermacher always remembered in his sermons, where he had to use the vocabulary of his congregation. So he continues:

On the other hand, if a man forms this conception, not arbitrarily, but because he is in some way compelled by his way of thinking, in that he can only hold on to his piety by this means, for such a man even the imperfections, which will always adhere to his conception, will not be a hindrance, nor sully his piety.

But the true source of religion is not in any kind of 'conception' at all, but in the experience of being in touch through direct feeling with the infinite that lies behind all the finite:

But the true essence of religion is neither this nor any other conception, but the immediate awareness of divinity, as we find it, as much in ourselves as in the world.

* What would be the use of a God who only pushed from outside?

As Schleiermacher has said earlier, 'Frömmigkeit', piety, religious experience, is a unique kind of awareness of reality, every bit as reliable as intellectual knowledge or aesthetic experience, but conveyed to us through a separate department of our being. It results from 'Betrachtung', meditation of a particular kind:

Meditation for the pious man means being directly conscious of the general existence of all the finite in the infinite and through the infinite, of all the temporal in the eternal and through the eternal.

'True religion', he says a little later, 'is a sense and taste for the infinite'. Spinoza was one of the masters of this kind of contemplation. 'He was penetrated by the sublime world spirit, the infinite was his alpha and omega.'

Schleiermacher was consistent in abandoning, along with petitionary prayer, the usual form of belief in immortality as personal survival. The passage on meditation in the second Discourse continues:

And similarly the aim and character of a religious life is not immortality, as many desire it and believe in it, or perhaps only pretend to do so; for their desire to know too much about it lays them very much open to this latter suspicion. It is not that immortality outside of time and behind time, or rather after this time, yet still in time, but the immortality which we can have directly in this temporal life, and which is a task in the solution of which we are constantly engaged. To become one with the infinite in the midst of the finite, and to be eternal in every moment, that is the immortality of religion.

We shall see in the *Soliloquies* how closely belief in an immortality of this kind is associated with the idea of 'Bildung', the self-moulding of which Wilhelm von Humboldt speaks, though its motive and its aim are easily distinguishable from his.

Of the three elements to which Christian doctrine was whittled down by the most advanced rationalists of Lessing's day, the 'Neologists', namely the beliefs in God, freedom and immortality, only freedom retains anything like its earlier sense in Schleiermacher's *On Religion*. Even Schiller, an avowed heathen, had kept two, in *Die Worte des Glaubens*, substituting the belief in virtue for that in immortality. What many other theologians have considered the very essence of Christianity, the idea of man's redemption through Christ's suffering, Schleiermacher had abandoned much earlier, together with belief in a special, supernatural, revelation. In his sermons, and in the *Glaubenslehre*, in which, in his maturity, he tried to formulate what, in his opinion, should now be taught as Christian doctrine, he continually uses traditional Christian language, but in Karl Barth's view he cannot avoid certain 'concealments and ambiguities' when there is a conflict between the Christian and the modern in his thought.[7]

The *Soliloquies* followed close upon the *Discourses* in 1799. They grew out of a sermon which Schleiermacher had given at Schlobitten on New Year's Day 1792, on 'The true estimation of life', elaborated on his uncle's suggestion about the time of his next birthday, 21 November 1792 (Dilthey has printed this version), and finally taken up with a view to publication seven years later on his 31st birthday. The book was written in four weeks and published, anonymously, in the first days of 1800; the new century, a still more striking turning-point in time than the earlier occasions which had jogged the author's thoughts on the proper use of time. He felt it was perhaps rash to reveal himself so fully, but he felt 'an uncontrollable longing to speak out, completely into the blue, without aim, without the least thought of effect'.[8]

Like Faust (ll. 1663ff., 'Aus dieser Erde quillen meine Freuden...')* Schleiermacher looks to his experiences on this earth, and not to any hopes or assurances of happiness beyond the grave, when he asks himself what makes life worth living, but unlike Faust, he is not disillusioned with the inner life. On the contrary, he rejoices in being one of the elect, for whom it means incomparably more than 'the vain fuss and bustle' of the man in the street:

In you I rejoice, sublime hint of the divinity within me, welcome invitation to an immortal life outside the realm of time, and free from its harsh laws! But those who know nothing of the call to this higher life, carried on the stream of fleeting feelings and thoughts, will find it no more readily if, without knowing what they do, they measure time and divide up earthly life.

The wordly, i.e. normal men and women, show that they are conscious of the passing of time on birthdays, for instance, or recurrent festivals like New Year's Day, but their thoughts bring them no comfort:

* From this earth my joys spring.

69

So time marks its runaway slaves with empty wishes, and brands them painfully with idle laments, making the worst like the best and catching these again as easily as those.

Not only the ordinary sensual man, but the artist and the moralist too, if they judge life according to the happiness or the success which fate happens to mete out to them in their external existence, 'sigh under the curse of time, which lets nothing endure'. Even their recent life is for them like the unmusical man's dim memory of a symphony:

a fleeting harmony, arising from the contact of the transient with the eternal; but man is a lasting work, an imperishable object for contemplation. Only his innermost action, in which his real essence consists, is free, and when I look within at this, I feel myself to be on the sacred soil of freedom and far from all ignoble limitations. It is on myself that my gaze must be directed, so that each moment may not be allowed just to pass by as a portion of time, but be lifted out as an element of eternity, and transformed into a higher freer life.

The great mistake of most people, he thinks, is to be over-concerned about external things, 'the world', as they call it:

World always comes first with them, and mind is but a petty stranger in the world, not sure of his place and his powers. For me mind is the first and the only concern, for what I recognize as world is its finest work, its self-created mirror.

Later he amplifies this last sentence:

What I hold worthy of the name of world is only the eternal fellowship of minds, their mutual influence, their reciprocal formation of each other, the noble harmony of freedom.

I take him to be thinking here of what is generally called 'Kultur', civilization, the continuing influence of the mind of earlier generations, and the 'Bildung' which this alone makes possible, a most precious gift. 'This world of minds I allow to change and develop the surface of my being, to influence me', he says, whereas of the 'corporeal world' he says: 'It has no influence on me, the influence is exerted by me on it.' We have already met with striking parallels to this proud claim, in Schiller's last letter to Humboldt (p. 28) and in the Uncle's maxim in the *Lehrjahre* (p. 50).

Schleiermacher holds, like the prophets of 'Bildung' in the Weimar circle, that the only true life is the life in the mind, assuming as axiomatic the freedom of the will and the supremacy of the mind over the body. The individual's debt to the civilization into which he was born, his moral duty to develop to the full his mind and personality, his expectation of lasting satisfaction from the inner life alone, all these ideas are further common ground. The influence of Pietism had always been perceptible in men of this temper, but in those we have studied it has been neutralized by rationalism. In Schleiermacher it is still very strong, but he has the serenity of the rationalists. Instead of constantly feeling the pulse of his piety, so to speak, like the young Anton Reiser, with trembling hopes and fears about the life to come, Schleiermacher is quite confident that introspection will reveal to him 'the Divine', and that already here below his thoughts may dwell with the eternal. What happens to him in life and whether or not he achieves his external ends is a matter of comparative indifference. In any case, 'my activity was still not empty; if I have only become more clearly defined and individual in myself, then through this development I have also formed [a bit of] world', that is, presumably, extended the knowledge of human potentialities. This idea is expanded in the second Soliloquy.

Towards the end of this first chapter there is a regular paean to introspection:

It is self-contemplation then, this great blessing, and this alone, that enables me to fulfil the sublime demand that man shall not lead his life merely as a mortal in the realm of time, but also immortally in the sphere of eternity, as a creature not merely earthly, but divine. My earthly activity flows in the stream of time, perceptions and feelings change and I cannot arrest any of them. The scene I have fashioned in my play flits by, and on the sustaining wave the stream bears me continually towards new experiences. Yet whenever I cast my eyes back into my inner self I am at the same time in the realm of eternity; I behold the working of the spirit, something no world can change nor time destroy, something that itself alone calls world and time into being. Nor does it take, say, the hour that divides years from years to call me to the enjoyment of the eternal, and to awaken the eye of the spirit, which may be asleep, even though the heart is beating and the limbs stretching themselves. He who has once tasted the divine life would fain lead it for ever: every activity should be accompanied by the glance into the mysteries of spirit, every moment a man may simultaneously live outside time in the higher world.

This is clearly the same man who in the *Discourses* had written: 'Self-contemplation and contemplation of the universe are interchangeable concepts', and in a later edition of that work replied to his critics: 'How could anyone say that I have described a religion without God, when I have presented nothing else than the direct and original existence of God in us through feeling?' In both works one is conscious however of a shift in the meaning of traditional terms, which may easily produce the impression of ambiguity mentioned by Barth. There is not only the conflict between modern and Christian of which Barth speaks, but Schleiermacher has his own way of being each of these. We may be reminded of Schiller's 'Das Ideal und das Leben':

> Werft die Angst des Irdischen von Euch,
> Fliehet aus dem engen dumpfen Leben
> In des Ideales Reich!*

but the aim is not just 'peace of mind' or 'reinvigoration' after the struggle of life, but a mystical quest for the divine in the depths of the personality, when a man has become, through contemplation, 'more clearly defined' and 'individual', more and more his essential self. It is a highly individualistic conception of religion which leads to a complete re-thinking of Christian ideas about the nature of God, about immortality and about the working of conscience. From two or three more passages we may at least indicate the direction in which Schleiermacher's thought is moving in this first Soliloquy:

Do not divide what is eternally one, your being, that cannot dispense either with action or knowledge of your action without destroying itself! Set all things in motion in the world and accomplish what you are capable of. Make manifest your individuality, and mark with your spirit everything that surrounds you; labour at the sacred tasks of humanity, draw friendly spirits to you, but always look into yourself, be aware of what you are doing and in what form your active depths are revealing themselves.

That sounds to begin with very like Schiller again, and the next few lines are clearly inspired by Kant and Fichte:

The thought with which they believe they are thinking of the Deity, though they never get so far, has still for you the truth of a beautiful allegory of what man should be. Through its mere existence spirit maintains for itself the world.

Traditional religion is apparently for Schleiermacher a species of poetry, but it suggests at least the ideal that man should strive after.

---

* Cast aside mortal fear, take refuge from narrow, stifling life in the realm of the ideal.

We are reminded of Goethe's poem, 'The Divine' ('Edel sei der Mensch, hilfreich und gut'), and also of idealist metaphysics. If our mind can remain conscious of itself as persisting unchanged throughout all our varied activities, then this awareness is immortality, 'for mind requires nothing but itself'. Immortality and the vision of the Divine are not something reserved, as is usually thought, for mortals after death, but attainable here and now, and the first Soliloquy ends with the writer assuring himself:

Even now the spirit hovers over the temporal world, and to behold it is eternity and the heavenly delight of immortal hymns. Begin your eternal life then even now in constant self-contemplation; have no care about what will come, weep not about what passes away; but take care not to lose your own self, and weep when you drift along in the stream of time, without bearing heaven within you.

The final words of the first Soliloquy might be interpreted as an expression either of human dignity or of Christian submission. Again a parallel in Schiller comes to mind – the passage at the end of the sixth of the letters *On the aesthetic education of man* where, rejecting the view, central to Adam Smith's *Wealth of Nations* (1776), that the fragmentation of human powers makes for progress, he says he cannot believe that nature intended man for any purpose whatsoever to miss being his full self. In the second Soliloquy again we find Schleiermacher appealing to the idea of 'humanity', and to that of duty based on religious sanctions, as the surest source of right action:

To contemplate the humanity in oneself, and having once found it, never to turn one's eyes away from it, that is the only sure means of never straying from its sacred ground...Behaviour [of others towards me] that is truly humane creates in me the clear consciousness of humanity, and this consciousness allows of no behaviour but what is worthy of humanity...It is always nonsense and a waste of time to lay down rules and to make experiments in the realm of freedom. A single free resolution is needed to be a human being: anyone who has so resolved, will always remain truly human; if he fails, he has never been so at all.

Schleiermacher's authority is again his own experience. He recalls how, as a young man, no doubt in the years at Niesky and Barby when modern humanistic ideas were dissolving his childhood certainties, he himself 'found humanity':

73

With proud joy I recall the time when I discovered humanity and knew that I should never lose it again. The high revelation came from within, produced by no ethical code and no philosophical system. The long search, not satisfied by either of these, was crowned by a moment of illumination; freedom resolved the dark doubts by action. I may say this, that from that time on I have never lost touch with myself. What they call conscience I no longer know; no feeling punishes me, and none needs to warn me. Nor do I since then strive for this or that virtue...In quiet calm, in unchanging simplicity I bear the uninterrupted consciousness of complete humanity in myself.

The mood expressed here is very like that of Wieland when he had discovered Shaftesbury, with his notion of a 'moral sense' that grew naturally in young gentlemen properly brought up, so that, to behave humanely, they did not 'stand in need of such a rectifying Object as the Gallows'. Wieland is full of the moral optimism of the Enlightenment and, strange as it may seem, he was Schleiermacher's favourite author in early manhood. Schleiermacher's manner was calm and unhurried like that of Wieland, and though he was a man of principle and devoted to his friends, it is hard to believe that one who could be so sure that all was well with his inner world and express so little concern about the dark side of life in general can often have experienced strong passions. He was however intensely curious about the complexities of human nature, and here in the second Soliloquy he advances more clearly than anyone before the view, later regarded as typically Romantic, that men are not all essentially similar in their make-up, as the Enlightenment had believed, but all unique, to everyone's advantage. For men who have realized that men are not just animals, and all share the same gift of reason, it is natural to think that they are basically alike. But the truth is more complicated:

If most men represent humanity only in its cruder elements, it is because they have never conceived the thought of their own higher existence. It has taken firm hold of me...And thus there dawned on me what is now my highest intuition, it has become clear to me that every man is meant to represent humanity in his own way, in a special combination of its elements, so that it may reveal itself in every possible way, and that in the fullness of infinity everything that can come forth from its womb may become reality.

It was nothing new in Germany for a writer to extol individuality as opposed to uniformity, the Sturm und Drang had been full of the idea, and Goethe had carried it forward, as we have seen, to *Wilhelm Meisters Lehrjahre*, although Wilhelm learns there from his friends of the Tower that only mankind is infinite in faculty. Schleiermacher does not insist, like the Abbé there, that the young should try many things, to find out what they are good at. He combines the idea of individuality with something like the Platonic principle of plenitude appealed to by believers in the Great Chain of Being, the notion often mentioned by Herder in the *Ideen* that everything comes into being that can.[9]

The idea of individual development put forward by Schleiermacher with religious fervour as a kind of mystical ideal was immediately taken up by Friedrich Schlegel and the *Athenäum* group. It combined readily with the anti-mechanistic currents of thought which had come down from Hamann and Herder and with the early vitalistic theories in biology like those of J. F. Blumenbach discussed by Goethe in his short essay headed *Bildungstrieb*, translating 'nisus formativus'. He sees the anthropomorphic nature of such theories, which 'were for Goethe no more than useful expedients, designed to facilitate discussion of natural processes without claiming to define them conclusively'.[10] Goethe in his maturity always associates self-culture with the formation and transformation which he sees going on in all living nature. Organic structures generally, he sees, are never entirely stable or completed, but always things trembling in constant movement. He sees men, like plants, constantly converting material from without into new growth of their highly individual selves, and after Italy he habitually thinks of living things if possible in their whole life-cycles, and even of landscapes or towns not as they are at one moment, but in the successive appearances known to him, of Venice for instance at low as well as high tide. The classical ideal of personality as an organic unity of fully developed, freely active human powers was taken over by the Romantics but extended by their fertile minds with little thought for observed reality. As Kluckhohn says:

They have gone to school with Fichte and have absorbed his idea of 'infinite progress', according to which totality is never fully realized in temporal life, but is capable of being raised to an ever higher and higher power to infinity. In this sense Friedrich Schlegel can say: 'Imagine a finite cultivated to an infinite degree, and you reach the idea of a man' (*Ideen*) and 'It is a characteristic of humanity, that it must raise itself above humanity' (*Ideen*) and Novalis: 'We have to be not merely men, but more than men. Man is in general as much as universe'.[11]

Along with this by no means common-sense view of human nature went the realization that the highest creative powers of man are largely unconscious and that he possesses supersensual capacities for communication with others and possibly with spirits outside time and space. Hamlet's 'What a piece of work is a man!' began to look outdated.

New ideals of 'Bildung' were the natural concomitant of these enlarged conceptions of human nature and destiny. 'Bildung' in fact, as Haym already saw, became a party shibboleth for the German Romantics, and the most extravagant statements were made about it, especially by Friedrich Schlegel, who calls it in the *Ideen*, one of his collections of aphorisms in the *Athenäum*, 'the supreme good and the one thing needful'. He began in the way that had become usual in Germany late in the eighteenth century for ambitious spirits seeking the highest culture, like Wilhelm von Humboldt or Goethe, but with more scholarly competence than either of these, with the most searching study of Greek literature and philosophy, with the aim of becoming its Winckelmann. For him, as for them, the good, the beautiful and the Greek meant very much the same thing, and no one could have too much of them. 'The study of Greece and Rome', he wrote in an unpublished preface to his proposed great work, which remained a splendid torso, 'is of absolute value, not just for this man and that, but for the whole age, for the whole of humanity.'[12] This was written just before Friedrich got to know Fichte and his heady philosophy, and before his extended study, along with his brother, of modern European literatures began to relativize his classical enthusiasm. From the beginning, as his letters show, his goal had been something wider than scholarship, a general philosophy of life at a time when all values seemed to be in question. The foundations of his ideas about personal culture at the time of the *Athenäum* (1798–1800) seem to have been those familiar from Humboldt and Goethe, the belief in free will and perfectibility and the identification of humanistic idealism with religion, or with all that could now be hoped for in its place. Following Fichte, however, he made the most extravagant claims for the powers of the human mind when freed, as

Goethe's Baccalaureus puts it, from philistine modesty:

Wer, ausser mir, entband euch aller Schranken
Philisterhaft einklemmender Gedanken?
Ich aber frei, wie mir's im Gieste spricht,
Verfolge froh mein innerliches Licht,
Und wandle rasch, im eigensten Entzücken,
Das Helle vor mir, Finsternis im Rücken. (Faust II, ll. 6801–6.)*

What Schlegel always stresses is the unlimited capacity of everyone to develop from within, to what he calls god-like heights: 'To become God, to be a man, to develop oneself are different expressions of the same thought' (*Athenäum* Fragments). Unlike Schleiermacher in the second *Soliloquy*, he does not at the same time remind us of the limitations given with individuality, of the sobering truth that only mankind as a whole is infinite in faculty. He sees that men need each other's stimulus for full development and praises the 'symphilosophizing', the perpetual discussion which was a Romantic habit, but he wants the individual to aim at universality, and even to be able to 'tune himself' at will as one tunes an instrument – but only our own time could have provided the image he required, of choosing any wavelength one wishes, 'philosophical, or philological, critical or poetic, historical or rhetorical, ancient or modern'.[13] When the Schlegels and especially their women-folk had finally got unbearably on each others' nerves in Jena and dispersed, and one literary venture of Friedrich's after another had failed, his ideas of Bildung seem to have became much less exacting, though he himself continued his conquest of the languages and literatures of the world, becoming a pioneer in the study of Sanskrit and Persian and in comparative philology. At the same time he became more and more attracted by the order, beauty and authority of Roman Catholicism, and he was finally received into the Church in 1808 with Dorothea, whom he had married in 1804. He had shed his ideas about Bildung as a religion, as an ultimate goal in itself, by about 1804, when he wrote in the introduction to a *History of European Literature* in praise of a literary education as a mental training for practical affairs, which was to be a very ordinary late nineteenth-century point of view.

* Who else but I freed you from all the bonds of philistine restrictive thought? But I follow freely my inner light as the spirit moves me, forward with speed, enraptured with myself, brightness ahead, and darkness at my back.

The quasi-deification of the artist and original thinker in some Romantic writings round about 1800 is one sign of a new pattern of thinking about life in general which was to prove persuasive to many throughout the century and is by no means dead to-day. It is all part of the revolt against rationalism with its certainties based on quasi-mathematical laws. Herder had argued that there was no single ideal in ethics or art or anything else that we should all accept, resulting from the accumulated wisdom of the ages, but that different ages and groups had their own ideals valid for them. Even Schleiermacher had spoken to Friedrich Schlegel about the immorality of all moral laws. With the decline of orthodox Christianity, the questioning of social and political authority in the age of the French Revolution, the spread of Kantian ideas about values as essentially subjective, the result of human choice, and the general implication of the primacy of the will in the writers, like Schiller, whom he inspired, it came to be more and more usual for ordinary people to be impressed by vehemence of assertion, heroic defiance of authority, imaginative eloquence and that kind of emotional appeal rather than by reasoned argument based on verifiable facts.

The third Soliloquy is a criticism of contemporary society in the light of Schleiermacher's ideal of true humanity. It draws the familiar contrast between the ends pursued by the ordinary man, directed chiefly towards the physical comfort and material prosperity of himself and his family, and the purposes which the man of cultivation, especially the moralist, sees as worthy of his efforts. It is not an age of genuine enlightenment, but 'a bad and dark time', in spite of its belief in progress. 'This perverse generation likes to speak about the progress of the world, so that it can think itself better than its forefathers and boast about it.' It is true that man can feel himself to be more truly than ever before 'the lord of the earth', because of his mastery of useful knowledge and techniques, but it is a humiliating thought that this should be considered the whole purpose of humanity. Like Herder in *Auch eine Philosophie* he cries:

Is man then merely a sensual creature, so that even the most intense feeling of life, of health and strength can be his highest good? Is it enough for mind that it inhabits the body, controlling its processes of growth and reproduction and conscious of itself as supreme? Their whole effort is directed to the physical, their whole pride founded on it. In awareness of their humanity they

78

have only got so far that they can rise from concern about their own bodily life and well-being to concern about the similar welfare of all. That is virtue for them, justice and love, that is their loud shout of triumph over mean selfishness, that is the end of their wisdom.

That even the comfortable minority lead spiritually impoverished lives is to be seen from their social institutions, which all reflect a low view of the nature of man. Schleiermacher considers in turn friendship, marriage and what he calls 'the state'. What is wrong with friendship is that so few are ready to accept their fellows as true individuals, valuable through their differentness. 'Many of the better sort of men go about therefore with the structure of their own being hardly discernable, pruned as it has been by their friends and plastered over with foreign additions.' Similarly with marriage:

In their dumb uniformity all these families are the bare grave of freedom and true life. Does she make him happy, does she live wholly for him? Does he make her happy, is he all amiability? Are both never so happy as when one can sacrifice him- or herself for the other? O do not torture me, vision of the misery that dwells deep behind their joy, of the approaching end that only conjures up before them, as usual, this last illusion of life.

What is lacking is the new common will which should arise 'out of the harmony of their natures'. As children come into being through the physical union of their parents, so in every institution, according to Schleiermacher's idealistic theory, the merging of individual wills, which he sees as its *raison d'être*, should give rise to actions expressing a common will, not a state of things in which first one and then another member asserts himself. In the political system of Germany in 1800 he naturally finds this mystical ideal unrealized:

Where are the old fairy-tales of the wise about the state? Where is the power which this highest stage of existence should give to man? the consciousness which all should share of being participants in its reason and imagination and strength? So far removed is this generation from any notion of what this side of humanity can mean[...]that all believe the best state to be the one that is least noticed.

This means that 'the fairest artifact of man, through which he should raise his being to its highest stage', is regarded 'as a necessary evil, an indispensable piece of machinery to hide his deficiencies'. There are hints here already of the organic conception of the state that

Schleiermacher was to put forward in later life, with its mystical theories concealing hidden assumptions.[14]

In spite of his dissatisfaction with the present state of society and with the process of ossification which, as he has observed, so soon sets in when any reform is successfully attempted, Schleiermacher does not despair, because 'divine imagination' gives him sure foreknowledge of a better future. 'Bildung' will develop out of barbarism and life out of the sleep of death. This he believes on the analogy of what has already happened in history, taking the long view. Man has at least conquered nature, as 'the soul of the seer' prophesied long ago, though his savage hearers can have had no conception of what he meant. True civilization will in time follow, through the persistent efforts of the few who, 'hating dead forms live for their own individual cultivation and thus belong to the future world'.

The fourth and fifth Soliloquies consist chiefly of musings on Schleiermacher's own personal hopes and fears for the future. In the fourth, 'Prospect', he congratulates himself on the calm and clarity of mind with which he looks to the future as his own, to be shaped as he chooses, except in so far as each choice is a renunciation of certain possibilities. Because of his initial choice of his calling and aim in life, 'the first act of his freedom', he is no longer free to do completely what he likes, but no one in his senses wants to be. 'I live in the consciousness of my whole nature. To become ever more completely what I am, that is my sole intent', a very Nietzschean one, as Kluckhohn observes, and this is by no means the only similarity between these two late products of Christianity. Later in the Soliloquy Schleiermacher confidently claims that the power of the imagination makes the spirit superior to any external force and any limitation:

The impossibility of doing a thing externally does not limit internal action [...]So certainly do we belong to each other that though we have never met, imagination can still transport us to our beautiful paradise.

This is said of the ideal wife he has spoken of as merely a dream, though it is already Eleonore Grunow he has in mind. In the real crisis which supervened later, his confidence in imagination was badly shaken. In the fifth Soliloquy he assures himself, with the same boundless subjectivity, that old age itself has no terrors for the free mind. The differences men show in their aging can only be a matter of will:

Who dares to assert that the consciousness of even the great and holy thoughts created by the mind from itself depends on the body, and awareness of the true world on the use of the physical limbs?

The last paragraph of all sums up the theme of Schleiermacher's reflexions in these lines:

The profit a man gains through introspection is that despondency and weakness may not come near him, for from the consciousness of inner freedom and its activity spring eternal youth and joy.

Schleiermacher's *Soliloquies* is not perhaps the sort of book to attract a modern reader, dipping into it without preparation. Its elevated, rather mannered language holds him at a distance and its obtrusive verse rhythms, consciously adopted by the inexperienced writer, are distracting and somehow inconsistent with his aim of presenting his soul *à nu*. How infinitely better Nietzsche masks himself as a prophet in *Also sprach Zarathustra*, writing also with pastors' blood in his veins and, consciously or unconsciously, with Luther's Bible as the model of models in his mind! But read with some knowledge of the author's life, the earlier history of 'Bildung' and the ideas of his Romantic friends, the book can be a revealing and moving document, helping us to understand many aspects of German idealism at the opening of the nineteenth century, not as a philosophical system but as a 'Weltanschauung', applicable to the problems of everyday life. As Haym says: 'Here an ethical ideal is set up of wider application than that of our great poets, of richer content than that of our great philosophers', and at least the attempt is made to suggest improvements in private and public life in the light of this ideal.[15]

Schleiermacher's discussion of Bildung continues in important respects, as we have seen, the existing German tradition, but it adds much to it that bears his own stamp and some features that can be seen as typically Romantic. From the beginning it is clear that he is an idealist through and through, in the sense that life means for him mental activity, almost to the exclusion of any thought of the physical. He never questions the control of the conscious mind over

81

the body, or the freedom of the will, though he does not follow the more extreme Idealist philosophers and represent human conduct as unpredictable and completely non-determined. He understands the growth of character too well for that, giving due weight to the influence of heredity and past choices, as well as that of a man's friends and associates, and of the cultural tradition into which he was born. The chief novelty in his picture of human psychology is the intensity with which he realizes the fact of individuality, his awareness of the unique combination of qualities, or at least of potentialities, to be discovered in every human being. He goes further in praise of originality than Goethe or Humboldt, laying the whole stress on 'Ausbildung', the unfolding of individual capacities, all apparently to be welcomed, and hinting at 'Anbildung', the enrichment of the individual from without, so that he 'knows the best that is known and thought in the world', only in what he says in the second Soliloquy about being frequently in the company of others, to study the endless variety of human nature and learn to appreciate the qualities one lacks.

The second key-word for Schleiermacher is 'humanity' ('Menschheit'), a concept he himself arrived at, it seems, as much from intercourse with humane people as from reading. At a certain stage, he had an intuition of true humanity which gave him an ethical tuning-fork, so to speak, far superior to conscience as usually understood, namely, it would seem, as our memory of the moral rules drilled into us as children. In the age of Kant morality could not be a matter of obeying rules, but in the absence of them, standards are all internal and hard to put into words. Haym contrasts Schleiermacher with Friedrich Schlegel, who makes morality analogous to art and writes: 'True virtue is the quality of genius.' It is a 'divine egoism' for him if anyone makes it his highest calling to develop his individuality, much as Gundolf tried to persuade us that Goethe's chief artistic creation was himself. It is in this mood that Schlegel and his friends make 'Bildung' their all in all, the antithesis of the utilitarian and the narrowly moral, One of Friedrich's *Ideen* runs: 'Do not squander your faith and love on the political world, but offer up your inmost being in the divine world of scholarship and art to swell the sacred fiery stream of eternal culture.'

Schleiermacher was quite free from this 'divine egoism'. A main source of his idea of the humane, as of Schlegel's, must have been recent German philosophy and literature, but his standpoint was always moral and religious, not aesthetic. He could not make very much, for instance, of *Wilhelm Meister*. There was too much 'negativity' in Wilhelm and in the characters generally, it was all aimed too much at readers of a particular class, one very important for Goethe's life but not for that of the time. The matters of general interest in it on the other hand all suffered from arbitrariness.[16] He had some contacts with Goethe but did not take to him. Goethe, according to Friedrich Schlegel, reading the *Discourses*, was at first delighted with the author's manysided culture, but as the book became more and more Christian and the style more careless, he changed his mind and ended up with a 'healthy and happy dislike'.[17] The religious basis of Schleiermacher's thinking keeps it, in spite of his preoccupation with self-culture, free from the self-centred narrowness even Spranger finds in Wilhelm von Humboldt (see above, p. 22). 'His ideal', says Dilthey, 'directs the will towards a highest good embracing the whole of humanity'.[18] He seems to delight in finding new developments of human individuality, much as poets like Brockes had greeted new beauties in a garden, as fresh evidence of God's goodness. It is true that in the second Soliloquy he expresses his determination to form himself within rather than to 'form works', the literary works which Friedrich Schlegel was so eager to see him produce, but this is only because he considered it impossible for anyone to be a serious writer and at the same time 'give humanity in himself a distinct shape and express it in action of all kinds', the task to which he was fully committed. What he had chiefly in mind was no doubt the formation of his moral personality by contemplation directed towards the sort of problems he was to deal with exhaustively a few years later in his *Grundlinien einer Kritik der bisherigen Sittenlehre* (1803), his study of ethics. Before he died at the age of sixty-five he was to produce 'works' in abundance, theology which 'initiated a new period in church history' (Neander), moral philosophy of lasting importance and a fine translation of Plato with commentary, all this while fully engaged in lecturing and preaching, always extempore, so that what we have of his lectures and sermons is almost all reconstructed.

Schleiermacher's feeling for the individual quality in other people as human beings struck Friedrich Schlegel as quite exceptional, far in excess of his own or that of anyone he knew. 'His whole being is moral', he wrote to his brother, 'and among all the outstanding men I know, it is in him alone that moral sensitivity outweights every other quality.'[19] But individualism in one form or another is of course recognized as one of the main characteristics of Romantic theory in France and Germany, and of Romantic practice everywhere.[20] Schleiermacher's unlimited sympathy with others and his trust in life are attractive youthful features in the Soliloquies, but looked at historically, the belief in and pursuit of individuality, especially in its political applications, may well be regarded as the starting-point of dangerous tendencies, as well as of intoxicating new hopes. The idea of individual uniqueness as a most desirable quality came to be applied, already by Schleiermacher himself in the third Soliloquy, as we have seen, to every form of social group from the family to the state. As Erich Franz writes:

The idea of individualism in Schleiermacher is not merely compatible with the recognition of the community, it may rather be said to demand it, and the two ideas form a closely woven unity. The full development of the self only takes place in the give and take of friendship, for all friendship is based, if genuine, on love of the individual features in one's friends. In friendship, marriage and relations with the fatherland this new type of man looks for more than any before, namely 'a furtherance and a complement to his own self-cultivation ('Bildung')', 'a gain in new inner life'. So together with the new personal individualism, the new individual and concrete conception of the state comes into being. At this point the contrast between Romanticism and both the Enlightenment and Weimar Humanism becomes particularly marked.[21]

Meinecke in his great study of the transition from cosmopolitanism to the nation-state in Germany makes no mention of this original contribution of Schleiermacher's, but he points to a very similar argument in Novalis, which was taken up by Adam Müller, the most influential political theorist of the time. Müller began his lectures in Dresden in 1808 on the *Elements of Politics* with this very idea of the personality of the state, which he missed in Adam Smith. The best way to think of the state, he said, was as a great individual comprising all the small ones.[22]

It seems almost paradoxical, Erich Franz says, that while carrying the ideal of the inward development of the personality to an unprecedented extreme, Schleiermacher should at the same time have discovered the notions of the people ('Volk') and the fatherland, long before Schiller's patriotic play *Wilhelm Tell* (1804) and Fichte's *Addresses to the German People* (1807–8). What it meant was that the old natural law conception of the isolated personality, still held by the Enlightenment and Kant after a development, mainly in Germany, of centuries, was replaced by the recognition of a connection between the individual and the community founded in their very essence. We shall come back to this important question of where German ideas of the state began to diverge from those of France and Great Britain, much discussed during and after the First World War, in the last chapter (see pp. 237–8) but it is interesting to note that Franz, writing in National Socialist times, distinguishes those believers in the unity of the state and the individual who lay the stress on personal development, like Schleiermacher, Fichte and later Lagarde, and those who lay it on the super-individual community, like Hegel ('The highest community is the highest freedom') and the nationalistic 'folk'-enthusiasts of his own day like Ernst Kriegk. He quotes in a note, in self-defence, that even Kriegk considers the individual to represent 'an autonomous whole'.[23]

Franz finds the root of Schleiermacher's individuality ideas in the homely piety of the Herrnhut Brotherhood. These Pietists had the keenest interest in each other as persons and in the state of each other's souls, they delighted in intimate letters, confessions, diaries, psychological self-exploration, and they were always conscious of the separateness of their group of converted souls from the wicked world. The group and the individuals who made it up really had an 'organic' connection like a body and its members. Long before Schleiermacher's time the process of secularization had set in, with educated pietists and their families, and originally religious attitudes had come to be transferred to friends and lovers, nature and literature. The literary results of this transference in men of genius are well known. Gradually more abstract objects were found for these generous impulses, in social and educational work in particular, notably in Halle, through Francke's foundations, and at the end of the century, it seems clear, one important source of emergent nationalism was this same reservoir of feeling for something outlasting and transcending the individual. Gerhart Kaiser has brought together evidence of a connection in a number of well-known figures between originally pietistic ways of thinking and feeling and the earliest expressions of patriotism in German literature. Not just single ideas and images but whole systems of them were involved, passed on by 'patriotic heirs of Pietism' like F. C. von Moser, Klopstock, Lavater, Herder, Novalis, Schleiermacher and Steffens. 'The heirs of Pietism transfer the basic principles of its religious life, emotionalism, subjectivism and spiritualism to an imagined ideal fatherland. They are "preachers of patriotism" (Novalis) announcing their mystic visions of an "inner fatherland", a sort of eschatological idea very different from the political realities in Germany.'[24] Such men tended thus to deceive themselves about the actual state they lived in, explaining its faults away instead of trying by political means to correct them. Kaiser brings out too the connection between the Lutheran doctrine of Christian submission to the state and German political theories, about the essence of freedom consisting in accepting the law as one's own will, summed up in Hegel's phrase: 'Freedom is insight into necessity.' It is not surprising to find Schleiermacher preaching patriotism after Jena and taking a prominent part later in recruiting volunteers at the beginning of the War of Liberation.

Schleiermacher was a great and good man, in public and in private life, but looking back after a century and a half and remembering the calamities that have resulted for the world from the excesses of German nationalism, one cannot help questioning some of the views he put forward in all innocence. If what is regarded as most important in men's development, taking them singly, or in groups and nations also interpreted as persons, is individuality, richness in novel features, then provision must somehow be made for the 'harmony' or 'proportion' included, as we have seen, in the recipes of Humboldt and Goethe, otherwise the uniqueness on which these individuals pride themselves is bound to lead to conflict in a crowded world. Historicism, the full appreciation of the uniqueness and claim to consideration of every nation and civilization thrown up in turn by history, combined with Romantic irrationalism, the idea of self-dedication to an ideal, no matter what, as the value of values, seem to us now, in the light of experience, to have been a wonderful stimulus for emergent nations, but ultimately a great danger to the peace of the world. Schleiermacher's political ideas are of course only present in germ in the *Soliloquies*, but he returned to them later in various lectures, in which too he is 'not purely descriptive but bases his argument on assumptions which he never makes explicit, and of which he was possibly unaware'.[25] One such assumption in the *Soliloquies* seems to be that all original development in himself and others is good, a piece of optimism which he perhaps unconsciously justified by his religious belief in the omni-presence of God. In practice he supported the Prussian monarchy through thick and thin, as the product of history and not something 'created by man himself proceeding from a theoretical model', which would always be useless.[26] He did not conceal his belief in constitutional government, however, and after the July Revolution in Paris, there were rumours current in Berlin in 1831 that he was one of the leaders of the newly founded democratic party. They were quite unjustified, and Schleiermacher put out a public statement which is a good example of the authoritarian way of thinking to which we shall find many parallels in later German writers. It ends with these words:

Since the Peace of Tilsit [1807] we have made rapid progress, and that without revolution, without a parliament, more, even without freedom of the press; but always preserving the unity of the people with the King and the King with the people. Should we not have to be robbed of our sound senses to imagine that from now on we should make better progress with a revolution? Therefore I for my part am very sure that I shall always be on the side of the King if I am on the side of the wisest men of the nation.

4-2

GOETHE: WILHELM MEISTERS
WANDERJAHRE (1829)

Thomas Mann considered *Wilhelm Meisters Wanderjahre* to be, as we shall see (p. 246)

a wonderful anticipation of German progress from inwardness to the objective and political, to republicanism. It is a work that is far more complete in its humanity than the German 'Bürger' thinks if he understands it merely as a monument of personal culture and pietistic autobiography. It begins with individualistic self-development through miscellaneous experiences and ends in a political utopia. In between stands the idea of *education*[...]It teaches us to see the element of education as the organic transition from the world of inwardness to that of the objective; it shows how the one grows humanly and naturally out of the other.

Searching in the early days of the Weimar Republic for support in the German classics for the new political attitude he had come to regard as necessary at that time, Thomas Mann could indeed find in the *Wanderjahre* some of the leading ideas he mentions. In times of crisis, there have always been Germans who have turned to their classical writers in search of illumination and wisdom, notably after 1848, 1918 and 1945.[1] Wilhelm Mommsen, however, who has examined Goethe's political and social views perhaps more impartially than these writers, finds that they, with a host of others, have tended to read into Goethe a message for their times, inevitably coloured by their own political convictions. He brings out in his sober assessment of Goethe as a political thinker the essentially eighteenth-century view of society that Goethe continued to hold all his life, and explains why it is hopelessly misleading to apply modern labels to the opinions about society and the state expressed by Goethe and other Germans in the early decades of the nineteenth century, when in their country there were no political parties in the modern sense and the pattern of political and social thought was indescribably complex and shifting.[2] In any case, it is always dangerous to use imaginative works as evidence of a writer's real opinions, for any ideas about the actual world which may be expressed in them are put into the mouths of fictional characters with a primarily aesthetic appeal. With late works of Goethe's like the *Wanderjahre* or *Faust II* such a procedure is especially hazardous, because characters and events in them are seldom what they seem at first sight, but often a symbolically coded, perhaps very obscure expression of the poet's playful thoughts and fancies.

In the opening chapters of the *Wanderjahre* there is a good example of this poetic ambiguity. At the beginning of the main narrative we are told how Wilhelm and Felix, moving through mountainous country, fall in with a group of people who look just like the Holy Family in old paintings of the Flight into Egypt, then, in the first of many novellas interrupting the main story, we learn how this apparent reincarnation has quite naturally come about. One plane of imagined reality is suddenly merged, as it were, into another, as happens today in the cinema, and a minimum of straight narrative forms only one element along with short stories, descriptive reports, letters, diaries and collections of aphorisms. Characters seem to wander out of the interposed stories into the main narrative and back, and in the seventh chapter of the second book, set on Lake Maggiore, we meet 'the painter', who is eagerly seeking out and painting pictures of the home background in Italy of the dead Mignon, of whom he can only have heard by reading *Wilhelm Meisters Lehrjahre*. This is in short a thoroughly Romantic work in the way in which it combines all possible forms and mingles the 'real' with the symbolic. 'Inwardness', to revert to Thomas Mann, is allowed so much scope that we are never sure that we can take anything as 'objective and political' statement, and not rather as the uncommitted theory or fantasy so common in German literature.

Before testing Thomas Mann's statements about the *Wanderjahre*, it may be helpful to remind ourselves of the well-authenticated reports we have about Goethe's political and social opinions as expressed in conversations with Eckermann, Riemer, Chancellor Müller and Luden. On this evidence Goethe was a conservative individualist to the marrow, the sort of man who greatly prefers the *status quo* to any new form of state or society constructed from a blueprint. Benthamism, for instance, he firmly rejected, Soret says, 'because the good of the great mass of the people is not for him a principle, but a result'. For illustration Goethe pointed to his own work as a writer, in which he had simply tried to tell the truth and say what he thought, without considering the interests of the masses, but from which good for others had resulted, though not his original aim. There might be something to be said for principles like Bentham's in legislation, but that was none of his business and he gladly left it to others. Anyhow, in his view, it should aim at removing evils rather than at positive improvements. Everyone should keep his place and work according to his lights.[3] Similarly he had said to Eckermann six years earlier that he saw troubled times ahead, but that the sensible thing was for a man to carry on with the job he had learnt to do in his own station in life, and to leave others to do theirs. Let the cobbler stick to his last, the peasant follow the plough and the prince learn how to rule. For that was also a job that had to be learnt, and no one should lay claim to it who did not understand it.[4]

There is a similar natural order for states as for individuals, Goethe told Falk. They grow, flourish or decline through the influence of geography and climate on people with their own particular endowments, and theories do more harm than good in the process.[5] Pückler-Muskau found that political systems and constitutions did not greatly interest Goethe. 'He kept returning to his favourite idea, that everyone should only be concerned about working on with faith and love in his own sphere, great or small, and then good would not fail to result, under any form of government.[6] It went without saying for Goethe that what any state most needs is a firm government with unquestioned authority. Immediately after Prussia's defeat at the battle of Jena Goethe said to Riemer:

When St Paul says: 'Let every soul be subject unto the higher powers, for there is no power but of God; the powers that be are ordained of God' [Romans xiii, 1], he is giving expression to a very high culture, and one that it had not been possible to reach by any path until Christianity showed the way. It is a command which, if all the conquered now observed it, would keep them from all wilful and ill-advised behaviour, which will do them no good.[7]

Goethe is invoking the divine right of kings, that is, in support of the French invader! It is in the same spirit that he spoke of the Holy Alliance to Eckermann with the highest praise: 'Nothing greater and more beneficial for humanity has ever been conceived.' He had no patience with the eternal faultfinders who attacked it, people, he said, who had vented their spite on the great Napoleon in his day.[8] He did not see in such criticism a laudable independence but a lack of that respect for other people which had been instilled into him in his youth. Sometimes he blamed the vogue of Rousseauistic ideas in education, speaking to Boisserée for example about the conceit and impudence of the small boys he had seen in the Pestalozzi-type school at Wiesbaden, 'who were not afraid of any stranger, but more likely to frighten him'.[9]

Goethe sometimes admitted that there was something in his individual nature which made him luke-warm on political questions and inclined to keep out of conflicts of any kind, but he thought too that this was typical of the German Bürger of his time. 'I have never in my life wanted to set myself up in vain opposition to the strong current of mass opinion or of the ruling principle. I have always preferred to retire into my shell and live there as I wished.'[10] One can suggest many explanations of the political and social indifference of the mass of the middle class in Germany in the eighteenth and early nineteenth centuries – separatism and centuries of authoritarian rule, even in the so-called Free Towns like Frankfurt am Main, the survival of the medieval system of rigid social estates, along with traditional economic forms and techniques in agriculture and guild industry, the Lutheran habit of obedience to the established authority in secular matters, and so on. An important factor in Goethe's case, as Barker Fairley has pointed out, was that the French Revolution happened when he was already forty years old, 'at the very time when he was least willing to concern himself with it and, if for no other reason, least able to learn from it'.[11] It was natural that as a cosmopolitan, who shared Schiller's view that 'it is the privilege and the duty of the philosopher and the poet to belong in mind to no nation and to no people, but to be in the full sense of the words the contemporary of all times',[12] he refused to write war poems in 1813, when a great many expected it of him. 'I go on being my natural self and try, not following the way of the world, to conserve, to bring order and to explain. And so too I try to urge the friends of scholarship and art who stay at home like me to keep alight, if only under its ashes, the holy fire which the next generation will need so badly.'[13] Comparing notes with Thomas Mann in the Shades, he will certainly agree with him that extreme nationalism is barbarism and a fatal thing for writers to succumb to, the sin against the Holy Ghost (see p. 249).

They will also agree in rejecting German conceptions of national freedom when they go beyond the reasonable ideal of independence among equals. 'One never hears more talk about freedom than when one party wants to suppress another.'[14] It is not the refusal to acknowledge anything above us that makes us free, Goethe said to Eckermann, but the capacity to respect what is above us. He resents therefore the bad manners of north German merchants in claiming equality by sitting down uninvited beside him at his table in an inn.[15] He is no 'prince's lackey' because he gladly serves a prince whose whole life has been one of service. Order is impossible without a social hierarchy.

W. Mommsen shows conclusively that Goethe retained to the end typically eighteenth-century German ideas about the relationship between a prince and his subjects. It would be misleading to call him reactionary, for he still believed that in the course of time, political and social institutions inevitably grow oppressive and unbearable, 'reason becomes nonsense, blessings turn into plagues', as Faust had said. But just as in geology he preferred Neptunist gradualism to Plutonist theories of violent upheavals, so in the political and social sphere he could see no good coming from violent uprisings of the ignorant masses, like the French Revolution as he always saw it, ignoring the dominant part played by his own class, the bourgeoisie. Reform from above, timely adjustments initiated by enlightened rulers and their experienced advisers were his prescription, for the kind of government he always had in mind was like the one he knew and had once shared responsibility in, the paternal 'Conseil' of the Duchy of Weimar, consisting of the Duke and three advisers, which had administrative and legislative functions of the utmost variety but, since Weimar was so small a state, virtually no concern with maximisation of the state's military and political power, the question which in Prussia was always of supreme importance. After 1806 Goethe was quite happy to see Weimar in the 'Rheinbund' and to call Napoleon *his* Emperor, for he looked upon him as the protector of German and even European culture. It was culture that really mattered, the freedom of the creative individual to fulfil himself and thereby to contribute to the 'world-literature' which he saw coming, or to its counterparts in the other arts and sciences. After 1815, Metternich's policy of restoration seemed to him the safest course, and he had no sympathy with the progressives who called for freedom of the press, the abolition of the censorship, popular representation and written constitutions. The existing political and social order had worked too well, he thought, to be rejected in favour of mere theories, which neglected what was for him the basic truth, that 'we are all only free if we fulfil certain necessary conditions. The Bürger is as free as the nobleman, as long as he keeps within the limits assigned to him by God, when he was born into a particular state of life.' What freedom had he enjoyed himself that winter, except the use of one small study and the adjoining bedroom? It is enough for anyone to be able to live in health and to follow his calling.[16]

The prevailing idea about property, it is unnecessary to add, was that it too should be distributed as it always had been, according to one's inherited status, with a wide range from rich to poor. Though foreigners like Mme de Staël and even Howitt (c. 1840) were still struck by the slow pace and calm continuity of German life, Goethe noticed a new social mobility in his old age. He wrote to Zelter:

Young people are stimulated far too early and then swept away in the whirlpool of the times. Wealth and speed are what the world admires and all seek[...] It is a century for capable, wide-awake, practical people who, with their nimble minds, feel themselves superior to the crowd, though their own gifts may not be equal to the highest tasks.[17]

These words were written just at the time when Goethe was beginning the revision of the first, shorter version of the *Wanderjahre* which had appeared in 1821, to produce the final one of 1829.

The re-writing carried out when he was almost eighty years old was almost as extensive as that which had been necessary to transform the *Theatralische Sendung* into *Wilhelm Meisters Lehrjahre*, and here again the re-shaping had the effect of giving the original central idea of the work more universal expression by shifting the interest from Wilhelm himself to a group of characters pursuing a similar but more definite aim, association with whom contributes towards making him more mature in character. The novel about Wilhelm's undefined wanderings becomes one about emigration with clear social aims in view, though the title more fitting for the earlier version is retained. The groups concerned and the background in which they move are chosen to illustrate social problems of Goethe's later years, European rather than purely German. The apparently secure foundations of the age of the Rococo, depicted in the *Lehrjahre*, have been shaken by two revolutions, the political French revolution of the bourgeoisie and, more stressed in the *Wanderjahre*, the economic revolution still in progress, the commercialization of agriculture by the 'improvers' and the gradual encroachment, on guild forms of craft industry and local trade, of new forms of industry and trade based on the replacement of the strength of human muscles by machines, powered first by water or wind and then by steam. It was in the nature of these new forms to involve larger and more impersonal units at each stage, to move away from local trade and guild industry to the provincial, national, world organization of these activities, and from the aim of producing for each traditional grade of society the consumable goods etc. that had 'always' been considered fitting towards unlimited production for profit in a world market. In a word, modern capitalism was beginning to transform even the backwaters of Europe, at a different rate of course in the various countries, and in the regions and cities of each.

In the *Wanderjahre* the process has gone at most as far as what Sombart for instance calls 'early capitalism'. The general conditions of life are those of an agrarian country, like Germany until well after Goethe's time, one where only a minority live in towns, and most are engaged in agriculture, cattle-breeding etc., some on large estates like those of the Uncle or Makarie and some as peasant proprietors. The region described is not named, but it is upland or mountainous country like much of southern Germany and Switzerland, where a great deal of the land is unproductive, so that the peasantry are glad of part-time work in their homes, like the spinning and weaving described in the fifth chapter of Book III. Lenardo's diary tells in great detail of a so-called domestic industry such as Goethe would remember vaguely from his Swiss journeys but which he asked his artist friend Heinrich Meyer to observe specially for him on a holiday visit in 1810 to his home near Zürich, a weaving district. Goethe follows this report closely, often word for word. Domestic industry is an early form of capitalism in which the manufacturer usually has no factory, but supplies a number of workers, perhaps widely scattered, with raw materials, and often with tools, such as a loom, so that they can perform the work he requires, like spinning and weaving, in their own homes at their own pace. They take back the finished product to him, are paid by the piece and receive further supplies of wool etc., while he markets what they have made.

The other industries mentioned are all crafts, organized in guilds, and the planners of the two ideal communities which are to be established, one in America under Lenardo and one in Germany under Odoard, both lay much stress on the strict observance of guild rules. They hold on in fact to the guild 'mysteries' which in real life were in Goethe's lifetime being more and more replaced by technologies based on the application of scientific discovery, so that the transmission of technical skill from generation to generation and from place to place was no longer so completely dependent on the personal element. The idea of knowledge as a valuable personal possession best protected by secrecy determines even the framework of both parts of *Wilhelm Meister*, which are at bottom the story of the philanthropic secret Society of the Tower and the privately organized 'League' which succeeds it and combines forces with Lenardo's party of emigrants and Odoard's company of settlers for under-developed land in Europe. The activity of these philanthropists takes anachronistic forms. Though the craft guilds in a state of decay lingered on in Germany well into the nineteenth century, they had largely been replaced in most of western Europe by some form of capitalistic organization aiming at unlimited production and profit, instead of the slow and careful making of articles in a traditional style, to order or for a local market. In real life in Germany, the first demand of a manufacturer trying to establish a new industry was for freedom from guild restrictions, 'Gewerbefreiheit', and states eager to promote industry, like Prussia under Frederick the Great and later, had commonly granted licences to such firms, which imposed certain safeguards but removed the manufacture from the control of the guilds. Nothing of this kind is mentioned in regard to Lenardo's and Odoard's enterprises. Their efforts seem to be directed towards restoring a lost harmony in industrial society by a reversion to medieval practices, and the leaders are influenced by ethical and humane considerations rather than by the capitalistic ideal of efficiency and profit-making. It is true that new competition in the textile industry from firms using 'machinery', to be understood, no doubt, as looms driven by water-power, is twice briefly mentioned in

Lenardo's diary of his travels (*Wanderjahre* III, chapters 5 and 13). Together with over-population – due in real life to a reduced mortality in infancy and the absence of earlier checks like famine, now that the potato was an established crop – this competition is a growing threat to full employment among the hand-loom weavers. There had indeed been a large-scale emigration in 1816 and 1817, mainly because of the failure of the 1816 harvest, and there was a steady trickle of emigrants caused by growing uncertainty among the peasantry about their future, a trickle which was to become a flood at times in the 1830s and 1840s and particularly after 1848, so that there were plenty of precedents in real life for Lenardo's scheme. Odoard's plan reminds us more of eighteenth-century resettlements like those carried through by Frederick the Great of Huguenots and German peasants, particularly from the south, on newly-drained land in the Oder valley and so on. Friedrich List was to advocate a similar inner emigration, to what he considered a possible German Hinterland on the lower Danube and the Black Sea etc., in his *National System of Political Economy* of 1841.

A surprising feature about the plans of Goethe's aristocratic idealists to establish completely new communities on undeveloped land, where the old moral values will be maintained in a truly humane society of craftsmen, is that no mention is made of the aspect of economic reform most hotly debated among great landowners, questions of land-tenure and agricultural techniques. We are not told how the new land is to be distributed among the settlers, nor how its cultivation is to be planned and carried through for the good of the community. In real life the capitalization of agriculture had preceded or accompanied the industrial revolution in western Europe, through enclosures, land drainage, the use of better farm machinery and the rotation of crops, including new crops like turnips and clover, providing foodstuffs for cattle which made possible their more productive use. All these changes were inspired by the profit motive rather than the aim of maintaining traditional forms of life and work as sacrosanct through their age, and alone conducive to peace of mind. The aim, as in industry, was unlimited production for profit, instead of subsistence farming. There is no hint of these developments either in the *Lehrjahre* or the *Wanderjahre*. Lothario (*Lehrjahre* Book VII, chapter 3) has ambitions as we have seen for the improvement of his extensive estates, which he has already made much more productive than they had been in his father's time. When he inherits his uncle's estate (chapter 9) he buys more land to round off certain portions, by amicable arrangement with Werner, Wilhelm's business associate, who is evidently investing in land as a speculation, but all Lothario's estate management remains shadowy in the extreme. So also does that of the Uncle in the *Wanderjahre* who, like the other uncle in the *Lehrjahre*, is rooted in the Enlightenment, 'the age of the Beccarias and Filangieris, when the maxims of universal humanity exercised their influence in every direction'. Though eminently practical, he was rather pleased when reproached with not making his estates pay as well as they should. 'The amount of income which I fail to make, when I could, I look upon as an expenditure which gives me pleasure, because in this way I make the life of others easier. I do not even have the trouble of giving this money away myself, and so everything comes to the same in the end.' Nothing could be further from the point of view of the capitalistic 'improver', yet the Uncle and his circle believe it is right for them to hold on to and increase their inherited wealth, as untouchable capital.[18]

It was not through ignorance of the reform of agriculture that Goethe omitted any mention of it, as we see from his conversation with Soret of 3 June 1824, when he was not entirely surprised to learn from this tutor in the ducal household that people at court seemed to know nothing about Albrecht Thaer, whose jubilee as a land reformer was just being celebrated in Berlin. Goethe had written a poem for Zelter to set to music for the banquet to be held on Thaer's 73rd birthday on 14 May 1824, which he summarized in a letter to Zelter (11 March). Thaer's first book (in 1795) had been about English agriculture, which he had been able to study while physician-in-ordinary to George III. His ideas had been taken up in Prussia, where he founded the Mögelin agricultural institute, later part of the University of Berlin, in 1804. In Goethe's poem *Zu Thaers Jubelfest* he interprets Thaer's theories as an illustration of his own conviction that all things are in flux, a central idea in the *Wanderjahre*:

> Nicht ruhen soll der Erdenkloss,
> Am wenigsten der Mann.*

---

* No clod of earth must be allowed to rest, and man still less, i.e. hard work, ploughing and the rotation of crops will increase the yield.

The Uncle had been born in Philadelphia of a Quaker Family, early settlers in America, but coming to Europe as a young man he had preferred its ripe culture to the unlimited opportunities of America. His nephew Lenardo, on the other hand, after making the Grand Tour, desires nothing so much as to return to the family estates in America, where inherited traditions will count less than personal initiative. Through Wilhelm he hears of the project of the Tower to organize a body of emigrants, and joins forces with them. The activities of the Pedagogical Province, where Wilhelm's son Felix is educated, and even those of the mysterious Makarie, two focal points of the novel, also make their special contributions to the combined plan, so that in the final version of the novel a slightly less tenuous link holds together the various groups of characters than earlier when, as the sub-title 'The Renunciants' indicated, they had been presented primarily as exemplifying various kinds of renunciation, symbolized by their rule that they must be continually on the move, 'wandering'.

Wilhelm Meisters Wanderjahre is still a 'Bildungsroman', but it is far less concerned with the development of individual personalities than with that of man in society. Even the young Felix is educated in a boarding-school of unprecedented extent, the Pedagogical Province, the description of which is an essay in educational theory, though there are also incidents enough in the main story to bring out his personal character. The inadequacy of Wilhelm's old gospel of all-round development and self-expression is first suggested to him early in the novel when in the mountains he comes across Jarno, now, surprizingly, a dedicated geologist. Wilhelm is told (1, 4) that though manysidedness had been a good aim in its day, the time has now come for specialization. Following up the Abbé's already mentioned idea that not the individual, but society is infinite in capacity, Jarno uses the obvious analogy of the orchestra to suggest how the individual can fulfil himself while performing a useful social role. 'Make yourself a first-rate violinist, and you may be sure that the conductor will gladly find a place for you in the orchestra. Make yourself competent in one thing, and see what position society ['die Menschheit'] will assign to you in the life of the whole.' The idea of harmonious co-operation leads up to one of the dominant themes of the *Wanderjahre*, the glorification of craftsmanship as a model for human activity.

It is everywhere necessary to work one's way up by useful service. It is best to restrict oneself to a craft. For the least gifted it will remain a craft, for higher capacities it will become an art, and the best, in doing one thing well, do all, or, less paradoxically, in the one thing well done they will see a symbol of all that is well done.

Wilhelm is compared by Jarno to a staff which grows green in any new ground where the wanderer plants it, but never takes root. How much better, his previous analogy of the charcoal pile suggests, is wood that has become charcoal, by being allowed to smoulder but never to blaze. Education, that is, by disciplined work, vastly increases a man's usefulness to society, and this, not Romantic self-expression, is the proper criterion.

The rejection, in the *Wanderjahre*, of the ideal of all-round cultural development is thus consistent with the re-affirmation in the last chapters of the *Lehrjahre*, but with a new spiritual content, of the middle-class philosophy of life, though the leaders are still aristocrats, Lothario, Lenardo and Odoard, who voluntarily take upon themselves the burden of organizing the proposed new settlements which they, rather than the settlers, have initiated. The undeveloped land which they will colonize in America belongs to Lothario and Lenardo, and they are acting on the principle of the Uncle in the *Wanderjahre* (i, 6), who considers himself to hold his possessions in trust for the community:

A man should hold firmly to possessions of every kind, making himself the centre from which common property can proceed. He must be an egoist in order not to become one, must hold his wealth together so that he can be a generous giver.

The idea is of course that if the capital remains intact, there will be all the more interest on it to give away. Control remains firmly in the hands of the owner, a benevolent capitalist, but certainly no socialist. Similarly Odoard's scheme for the full utilization of lands belonging to the prince he serves is a piece of enlightened despotism quite in the spirit of Frederick the Great. In his uninspiring speech to his company of settlers (iii, 12) he explains that the land has been surveyed, the position of roads, inns, villages determined and plans drawn for the buildings. Although it is apparently to be a mainly agrarian province, nothing is said about land-tenure, assignment of holdings, proposed crops and agricultural practice, but great stress is laid on the proposal to declare from the moment of arrival that all crafts shall have the standing of arts, of 'strict arts' as opposed to the free arts of the sculptor, painter or writer. To conclude, Odoard hands round copies of a settlers' song in which the authoritarian note is unmistakable. The old will be assured of rest and dignity and young men will be given work and a wife, while land will be generously allotted for cultivation to the new arrivals, strangers though they be. The song ends ominously with the refrain: 'Heil dir Führer! Heil dir Band!', hailing the future leaders, Odoard and Lenardo.

These vague indications can be supplemented a little from other scattered hints about the political aspects of the ideal communities which are to be founded in Europe and America. In Jarno's discussions with the wise and saintly Makarie and her astronomer (iii, 14), the contrast between natural science and what might now be called political science is touched upon. In science and scholarship there must be absolute freedom of enquiry, because its results will concern not just the world of to-day and to-morrow, but the unlimited future. On the other hand

State and Church may have good cause to proclaim their authority as unquestionable, for they must deal with the unruly multitude, and if order can be maintained, the means are a matter of indifference.

Similarly in the aphorisms 'from Makarie's archives' we find such pragmatic items as no. 67:

What right we have to rule, we do not ask – we rule. Whether the people has the right to depose us, that question does not worry us – we simply take care that it is never tempted to do so.

This is the view often expressed by Goethe about the French Revolution, for instance to Eckermann (4 January 1824). He had hated the French Revolution at the time, because of its horrors:

All the same I was no friend of unbridled autocracy, and I was completely convinced that any great revolution is never the fault of the people but of the government. Revolutions are impossible so long as governments are continually just and continually vigilant, so that they forestall them by timely reforms and do not resist change until what is necessary is obtained by force from below.

In the long discussion of the plans for the American utopia between Wilhelm and (of all people!) Friedrich, which are summarized in III, 11, political institutions play a small part. They agree that it must be a Christian colony, but Christian in an undogmatic way. Children are to be taught first 'about the great advantages Christianity has brought us' as the basis of our civilization, but not till much later about its origins. Jews are to be excluded, 'perhaps pedantically', because they deny these origins. Ethics are the chief subject of the rather desultory conversation, which has a markedly 'bürgerlich' tone. There is great insistence, for instance, on the future community's obligation to make full use of every moment of time, helped by a profusion of clocks, which strike the quarters, and even by pressing the visual telegraph into service to indicate the time, when no messages are being transmitted. Cool-headed practicality is the principle to be followed, the same adjustment of desire and emotion to the demands of reality which is implied in the idea of renunciation ('Entsagung') proclaimed by the sub-title of the *Wanderjahre*, and illustrated particularly in the 'Novellen' which make up a good third of the text. In the main story too noblemen give up their wealth and privileges, their wives and sisters devote themselves to educating their own sex – a social task greatly neglected in the real world of the time – and Wilhelm himself renounces the many-sided development of his own nature, his aim in the later part of the *Lehrjahre*, in order to train himself as a surgeon and be capable of playing a useful practical role with the emigrants. The reader is told to imagine the lapse of a few years, between chapters seven and eight of Book II, to allow time for this training and for the education of Felix, whose life Wilhelm is able to save, at the end of the novel, only through his surgical skill. To appreciate how greatly Wilhelm's final choice of a calling would surprise contemporary readers one must remember that the very beginnings of modern surgery in Germany date from 1818 (the Heidelberg clinic), and that surgeons only ceased to be counted as greatly inferior to academically trained doctors ('Ärzte') from about 1860. In Goethe's day they learned their craft empirically as apprentices, and it was precisely a craft that Goethe wanted his hero to take up, in accordance with the ideas put forward early in the novel by Jarno about the new age of specialization. (Cf above, p. 98.)

Apart from the daily discipline of their crafts, all the guidance that the new settlers will normally need, Wilhelm and Friedrich agree, is the spirit of mutual respect and cooperation prevailing in the patriarchal families to which they belong. The only public instruction will be that in the three Rs, to be organized by the Abbé, and in self-defence, by Lothario.

On the legal and political institutions proposed for the new settlement very little is said, and only in the vaguest terms. In the real world, any such colony would have needed a clear understanding with its American neighbours about its political status, and it would presumably either have taken some form of German law with it, or adopted that of its neighbours. As virtually every state had its own law in Germany, the choice was difficult, and Goethe avoids it by saying: 'We are not thinking about justice, but we must have some form of police.' The police chiefs are to keep a constant watch, in shifts, and 'if they find it necessary', to call a jury together. If the jury proves to be equally divided on some issue it shall be decided by lot, and not by giving the chairman a casting vote, 'because we are convinced that when opinions are divided, it is always a matter of indifference which is adopted'.

This conveniently pragmatic attitude is typical of the complete neglect here of the really difficult questions of power and political machinery. The authoritarian presuppositions unconsciously made reveal themselves in such phrases as: 'A state's greatest need is courageous leadership', or 'About the majority we have views of our own. We acknowledge it indeed in the necessary course of affairs, but in a higher sense we have not much confidence in it.' In one of the collections of epigrams originally printed in the same volume as the *Wanderjahre* Goethe's opinion about majorities is stated more explicitly:

Nothing is more repulsive than the majority, for it consists of a few strong leaders, of rogues who adapt themselves, of weak men who assimilate themselves, and of the mass that troops after them all, without knowing in the least what it wants.[19]

There is no suggestion in all this that the leaders of the new community will be oppressive, rather the contrary. Laws, it is said, will be lenient, that they may be more surely obeyed, and may be tightened up later if necessary. It is suggested however that the

102

leaders, if they know their business, should be allowed to get on with it without interference. Wilhelm and Friedrich confess themselves rather chary of establishing a capital city, though they foresee where the greatest congregation of people will come about. The same attachment to the looseness and division of political authority familiar to them from their homeland comes out perhaps in the suggestion that there shall be no centre of government but an itinerant authority, as in the medieval German Empire.

It is hard to know how much of all this the author expects us to take seriously, for so much seems to be the product of passing whims and personal prejudice, as when we learn that as the settlers should aim at taking with them only the *advantages* of civilization, there shall be a ban on the sale of spirits – and on circulating libraries! or that no church bells shall be allowed, or drums in the armed forces. It is the bell of Faust's old neighbours' chapel which particularly annoys him, it will be remembered, and Mephistopheles is made to say:

> Jedem edlen Ohr
> Kommt das Geklingel widrig vor,
> Und das verfluchte Bim-Baum-Bimmel,
> Umnebelt heitern Abendhimmel,
> Mischt sich in jegliches Begebnis
> Vom ersten Bad bis zum Begräbnis.*

All in all then it seems that Thomas Mann has somewhat exaggerated the 'political' element to be found in the *Wanderjahre*, and that of his 'republicanism' it is hard to find a trace. Yet Goethe is undeniably feeling his way in this work towards defining an 'objective' goal for human effort. However utopian his imagined settlements may be, they are not for his hero just figments of the imagination, not new provinces of thought to be explored within his own mind, but communities of his fellow-men whose general well-being is the goal of his efforts and of those of his associates. If the author pictures them still as strongly authoritarian and patriarchal in their ethics and institutions, and if his ideal colony seems in some respects to reflect his own desire to put the clock back, to return for example to a guild system for which the economic pre-conditions no

* No man of breeding can bear to hear that tinkling sound, that damnable ding-dong that darkens the evening sky and gets into everything that happens from baptism to burial. (Barker Fairley's translation.)

longer existed in actuality, that is because the imagination of even a Goethe is limited by external historical conditions to an extent which we, with our hindsight, tend to forget. He had however, in the course of writing the two parts of *Wilhelm Meister*, shifted the aim of 'Bildung' from the extension and elaboration of one's own mental life, the conversion of as much as possible of the world outside into inner experience and the moulding nearer to perfection of one's own personality – the kind of effort we have studied in Wilhelm von Humboldt – to work for the material and spiritual good of a specific group of one's fellow-men.

Thomas Mann does not in any case claim too much when he says that in the *Wanderjahre* it is education which effects 'an organic transition from the world of inwardness to that of the objective', and makes 'the one grow humanly and naturally out of the other'. Goethe's treatment of education and religion in this work has been so fully discussed, even in England since Carlyle, that it is only necessary here to consider the passages particularly relevant to our purpose. We learn here better than anywhere else what kind of 'Bildung' Goethe towards the end of his life held to be essential for his countrymen in the post-revolutionary world. It is a process which, while allowing for the free development of the individual's nature and capacities, does not fail to make him aware of the debt he owes to the past, of his duty to society in the present and of the dependence of all men on immeasurable, imperfectly known forces.

Goethe's educational thought is linked of course with that of both predecessors and contemporaries, most obviously with Rousseau and Pestalozzi. His rejection of extreme Romanticism is no less evident than his debt to the great European humanistic tradition. His religious thought continues what Troeltsch has described as the typically German development first evident in Leibniz, who combined deep reverence for inherited forms of religion with the desire to be abreast of modern knowledge, 'aware of the universe revealed by science in all its grandeur, beauty and harmony'. At the same time Goethe's expression of a sense of dependence reminds us of Schleiermacher.

The Abbé's first principle of education is Rousseauistic, as we have seen, but read along with other thoughts of Goethe in the *Wanderjahre* it appears to be at the same time a conscious revision of the

Socratic 'Know thyself!' The pupil is encouraged to follow his bent without guidance, perhaps at a high cost, until he has found out what he can best do, when his natural desire to be active will keep him on the right path. The Socratic reference comes in the second aphorism in the 'Betrachtungen im Sinne der Wanderer':

How can one get to know oneself? By introspection [Betrachten] never, but certainly by action. Try to do your duty, and you will at once know what you have in you.

This is supplemented immediately by no. 3:

But what is your duty? What the day requires of you.

In the emphasis laid here on action, and still more in the many recommendations of the craftsman's form of activity as a model, Goethe is probably influenced by Pestalozzi's reaction against exclusively intellectual ideals in education, against the attempt to initiate 'a golden age through knowing a little about everything'. Starting with practical efforts to improve the life of the Swiss peasant, Pestalozzi had made vocational training the foundation of his system – and Rousseau already had made Emile learn a trade. Pestalozzi's aim was to introduce his pupil through normal crafts to 'the whole freedom of truly developed powers', satisfying mind and heart instead of making a man into 'a living machine'. Thus 'the goal of industrial training became the development of many forms of human excellence'.[20] In Goethe of course the emphasis is different, not on ways of ensuring a contented and industrious rural population but on curbing the reckless individualism so common in the Romantic age, and encouraging self-discipline and concentration of effort. Here again aphorisms such as these from the 'Betrachtungen' may be quoted to sum up Goethe's thought:

Activity of any kind without limitation always ends in bankruptcy. [21]

Everything which increases our intellectual freedom without giving us self-control is harmful. [65]

It is an important deviation from Rousseau that the education of Felix is entrusted not to a private tutor, but to a large boarding-school, where for years he is one of a community drawn from many nations and various classes of society. It is only within limits too that the Abbé's Rousseauism is followed here. The pupils' attention is still directed towards things, not words, and they are encouraged to discover their inborn bias by experiment, as in *Émile*, but not to the same extent as the Abbé's first pupils, Lothario and his sister and brother in the *Lehrjahre*.

They are shielded much more from dangerous errors and above all, principles of conduct with a religious basis are instilled into them by stages, in connection with their studies, from their earliest years, and called to mind repeatedly by the symbolic gestures with which they salute their teachers – one is reminded of the Boy Scouts' three-fingered salute, intended as a perpetual reminder of the three-fold Scout's Oath! These gestures are of course the first thing to catch Wilhelm's eye when he first enters the Pedagogical Province and sees boys at work in the fields. When one of the staff approaches, the youngest boys fold their arms and look up with a smile to the sky. Wilhelm is soon told what this means by the Three, the heads of the Province, a rather mysterious trinity whose unanimous opinion is apparently always expressed by one member, but attributed by Goethe always to the Three, so that it sounds as if they spoke in chorus. The Three consider it their main duty to 'unfold' the gifts bestowed by nature on their pupils, as on every healthy child, though 'often they unfold themselves better of their own accord'. But one important thing is not inborn, the thing 'which makes man in every point a man', namely a sense of respect, of reverence, and this they *demand* of all pupils, in the first place for their teachers and elders, or put more generally, 'for what is above us'. Reverence for what is above us implies the acknowledgment 'that a God exists, who is represented and revealed in parents, teachers, superiors'.

The doctrine of the Three Reverences is partly, it seems, a corrective to the child-worship which had already sometimes resulted from Rousseau's idea that the individual has a right, even in childhood, to develop according to his nature, because the theory maintains, if his latent abilities are properly drawn out and he is shielded from the harmful influence of a perverted society, the result will certainly be good. The disturbing impression made on Goethe by the small boys he saw in 1815 at a badly run Pestalozzi school has already been mentioned. They seemed to think themselves 'little gods of independence'. There were students full of Romantic notions from

Fichte and others, who also, as we see from the Baccalaurius scene in the Second Part of *Faust*, seemed to Goethe absurdly self-important in their claim that their generation alone was truly emancipated: 'Die Welt, sie war nicht, eh' ich sie erschuf' (The world did not exist until I created it). Liberalism in fact in post-war Europe then, as so often since, easily went to the heads of the immature and if it took political forms, as in the Burschenschaft movement, evoked a backlash of repression like the Carlsbad Decrees, of which the nervous bourgeoisie completely approved. Goethe's calm insistence on the inclusion of a capacity for reverence or respect as a requirement in education for a humane society is no doubt in part a response to these special circumstances of his time, but it has deep roots, as we shall see, in his religious thought.

The second type of reverence, for what is under us, is an expression of the religious aspect of Goethe's Work as a naturalist. It implies a sense of piety, in the Roman sense, towards the earth and the foundations of our life as physical creatures, exposed to accident and suffering and doomed to die. We shall come across something like it again later in Friedrich Theodor Vischer's 'two-storey' metaphysical theory, which we shall compare to the 'three-layer' theory of the neo-Hegelian Nicolai Hartmann.[21] Man, with his mind, all three writers teach us, is a product of mindless nature, and owes respect to what produced and sustains him. What is 'under us', in Goethe's phrasing, does not refer of course to people, though that has been a common misunderstanding of the passage. The symbolic gesture expressing this second reverence is to stand with arms behind one's back and to look down at the earth, and this is the form of greeting or salute required from boys in the middle school, so to speak, who have reached this degree of understanding of nature in their studies.

The pupil is not kept over-long at this stage, only until his teachers think the lesson has sunk in. 'But then we bid him take heart and, turning towards his comrades, align himself with them. Now he stands upright and brave, not selfishly isolated. Only in combination with his fellows he squarely faces the world.' The third gesture or attitude expresses reverence for what is equal to us, our fellow-men and humanistic culture. These older boys, to give their salute, line up, dress by the right and stand to attention, looking straight ahead. What would be needed in the coming century, Goethe implies, when orthodox religion had lost its hold and the spread of revolutionary ideas threatened the cohesion of society, would be bold, responsible action by reasonable men for the common good. It was not enough to cultivate the mind, and engage in uncommitted theorizing. So in the Province, intellectual training is combined as much as possible with practical work in the open air. The agricultural pursuits with which all pupils begin (and which Felix is to find so boring) are combined with instruction in singing and in the three Rs. All (except the artists, who need complete concentration) sing at their work, some very beautifully in harmony. At the next stage, when the boys move on to horse-breeding and training, modern languages are taught. The details are obscure. To break up the national groups, it is a rule that for a month at a time, all speak a particular language, the next month another, and so on – though Felix learns only Italian. The grammar of the current language is taught in odd hours by mounted grammarians, 'bearded and unbearded centaurs', who share the active life of their charges. The point of all this is to suggest that practical work and the acquirement of skills can quite well be combined with 'lessons' in the ordinary sense – an idea which has no doubt done much to inspire German experiments like the 'Landerziehungsheime' – the *Odenwaldschule*, *Salem* and the like, all of which have aimed at furthering 'the transition from the world of inwardness to that of the objective'. It is noteworthy that though lyrical poetry, music and dancing, epic poetry and the plastic arts are fully provided for, these last in close association with the crafts concerned in building, the drama and theatre are banished, because the inhabitants of the Province have no wish to appear to be what they are not, and there are no idlers to provide an audience – learning which, Wilhelm sighs for the time he has wasted!

Reverence, according to the Three, is something which the ordinary man can only learn from the wise. It is 'a higher sense, which has to be added to man's nature. It is only in specially favoured men that it develops of its own accord, and such men have therefore always been considered to be saints, or gods.' In all Goethe's references to religion, from his early letters to Lavater to his last conversations with Eckermann, he speaks of saintliness as a special gift, comparable with artistic or philosophical talent, which has been granted to some men and women in all ages. The religions of the world he thinks of as resulting from their intuitions of the Unknowable, as poetry is created by the imagination of poets who are also men. In the Pedagogical Province the boys are taught that the great religions at the root of the the three civilizations on which our own is chiefly based, Judaism, Hellenism and Christianity, can be fittingly associated each with one of the three different kinds of reverence, for each had its own particular approach to the holy, which can still be of value to us to-day. Goethe's proposed scheme of education has obviously a grandiose scope, even if some of the details are obscure. It is not easy, for example, to see why, after describing the Three Reverences and their associated gestures in the order 'above, below, equal', the Three go on to speak of the corresponding historical religions in the order 'above, equal, below'. The religions said to have been concerned with that which is above us are the 'ethnic' or 'heathen' religions of both Palestine and Greece, beliefs governing the public life of whole peoples. The pupils are taught about these from their earliest years. The religion concerned with that which is equal to or like us is the 'philosophical' religion preached by Jesus on earth, a religion for the individual in his private life. This religion of the heart and spirit is reserved for thoughtful pupils as they grow up. The religion of reverence for what is below us, finally, is the religion of redemption through suffering, centred on the Passion and the doctrines associated with it in the Christianity of the Church. This, with its reverence for suffering and death, for what horrifies and revolts us, is imparted to each pupil only as he leaves, in case he should ever have need of it.

Instead of a chapel the Province has a sanctuary, adorned with pictures illustrating the three kinds of religion. The greatest 'ethnic' religion, Judaism, is represented in a series of murals from the Old Testament, the story of the most irrepressible, the 'toughest' of all peoples, while smaller pictures in the frieze above point to parallels from Greek mythology. In a second gallery come stories from the New Testament, of the life and miracles and parables of Jesus, regarded as the history of a private life, with lessons for all men as individuals. The pictures of the Passion are in a third gallery, normally closed and not seen by Wilhelm. Erich Trunz has put forward the helpful suggestion that the three religions are presented in the order in which the pupils, as they grow, become psychologically able to cope with them, so that the one which lays stress on the problem of evil and suffering comes last.[22] It is the history of civilization rather than religious instruction that Goethe seems to have in mind, and there is no mention of any ritual, though we hear at the end of chapter 8 of Book II that the Superior (Der Obere), as the head of the staff is called, is 'teaching and blessing' in the Sanctuary.

The religious sentiments of the staff of the Province and of the mysterious Makarie, the saintly lady who is in charge of what was probably intended by Goethe to be a similar establishment for girls, but characteristically never grew to be anything more than a school of domestic science, are presumably what the Abbé (II, 7) in a letter to Wilhelm calls 'Weltfrömmigkeit', as opposed to the 'Hausfrömmigkeit' admired by Wilhelm in one of the centres of domestic industry he has visited. The 'piety of the home', of family life inspired by godliness in the Protestant tradition, was a splendid thing, the Abbé wrote, a sheet anchor for the individual and the basis of social stability, but it was not enough for the new life which their colonists under Lenardo would be facing. 'We must rise to the conception of a piety to the world, we must give our sincerely humane sympathies a universal practical application and think of the good not only of our nearest and dearest, but of the whole of mankind.'

The Abbé's formulation suggests a religion something like that which Tolstoy ascribes to the Freemasons round about 1800, in his description of Pierre Byezukhov's activities and beliefs in *War and Peace* (Vol. II, parts 2–4), an enthusiastic moralism centred in universal benevolence and conscientious striving after self-perfection, but without the Masonic odds and ends of doctrine and ritual, a religion without dogma for humane cosmopolitans. Erich Trunz sees it as parallel to the beliefs of Kant, Schiller and Hölderlin:

not the Greeks' upward glance to the Gods, and not Christian humility, but a further development from both, a picture of man as finding within himself the way to the Absolute, which shows itself to him in analogies in the world[...]The more a man listens to his deepest self, the more surely he finds himself directed to the God above us, finds himself associated in his dependence with the earth beneath us and allied morally with his fellows. Reverence for oneself is reverence for the God in us and the mystery of life.[23]

If that is a correct interpretation, it would seem to pre-suppose a degree of trust in introspection which goes beyond most human capacities, but we have found something very like it in Schleier-macher's *Monologen*.

Even more remarkable than this difficult doctrine is the saint of the new religion we are evidently invited to see in Makarie, Lenardo's aunt. Through Lenardo, Wilhelm comes to visit her at her country mansion and in what she says to him about the family he has just left he finds such penetration that it is as if a mask had been removed by her from their inner nature. Her discussion about mathematics with her resident doctor-astronomer is the first indication of her special interests, but with Wilhelm she talks only about people. In a tower of the house the astronomer has his observatory, and here on a clear night Wilhelm is overwhelmed by what he sees. His reflections recall Kant's words in the *Kritik der Praktischen Vernunft* about the two things which unfailingly fill the mind with admiration and rever-ence, the starry sky above and the moral law within. He answers his own question: 'What am I in comparison with the universe?' with the thought already expressed by Goethe in one of his finest later poems, 'Was wär ein Gott, der nur von aussen stiesse' (about 1812), about the inner universe 'revolving round a pure centre', equally valid with external nature as a revelation of the divine.

On first introducing us to Makarie (in I, 10) Goethe hints at the Makarie myth without departing from probability in the narrative. Wilhelm, resting so that he may see Venus in full glory just before sunrise, has a dream about Makarie in which, seated in her familiar chair, now golden like a throne, she seems to rise with clouds at her feet like a saint ascending, till presently a star shines out where her face had been, and joins the heavenly constellations. At that moment the astronomer wakens him, to see the morning star blazing from the sky. A little later Wilhelm finds papers in the house about 'Makarie's peculiarities' and before leaving he learns from Angela, her steward-ess, that the astronomer, sceptical at first, believes now that she not only 'bears the whole system of the sun within her, but moves in it in spirit as an integral part,' so full and accurate is her knowledge. When this story is repeated in more detail near the end of the novel (III, 15), in the last communication about Makarie, it is described (perhaps by analogy with current Bible-criticism?) as a document written from memory, some time after the information contained in it had been received, and therefore 'not to be regarded as fully authentic'. Goethe is ironically protecting himself, but he apparently feels that no religion can dispense with an irrational element of myth, which he still associates with the heavens, empty though they may be, in a playfully scientific way, reminiscent of Romantic 'nature-philo-sophy'. The elderly lady whose soul is said to make these siderial excursions, but who keeps them a secret for all but her closest confidants, is also the wisest and most sympathetic of counsellors. We repeatedly hear of her in this role in the course of the novel, and at the close many of the emigrants she has helped visit her to take leave and receive her blessing before they embark.

The framework story in the *Wanderjahre* is concerned with religion, education and important problems of life in society. It is too closely packed with ideas to be any longer a novel in the normal sense, but the serious main narrative is relieved and illustrated by a series of encapsulated short stories about love and friendship and family life, which we take on a first reading to have been introduced haphazard, but which prove on closer examination to be related to the central theme of renunciation. Sometimes, as we have seen, they link up with the main story directly through individual characters. Critics have been reminded of the free form of Beethoven's late quartets. On the whole, characters and plot are outweighed by ideas, but the ideas of a poet-sage, who puts his thoughts forward non-committally through imagined characters, blurring the boundaries between fantasy and objective statement. The educational and moral ideas are the most impressive, an experienced and good man's testament, but the political and social ideas, we have suggested, are largely those of the author's time and social station, nostalgic rather than prophetic. The book has the Romantic charm of an old and wise poet's dream.

ARTHUR SCHOPENHAUER: APHORISMEN
ZUR LEBENSWEISHEIT (1851)

In the introduction to the *Aphorisms on wise living* Schopenhauer admits that it is only possible for him to attempt a guide to a happy life, which is what he means by his title, by compromising with his philosophy proper, as expounded in *The World as Will and Idea*, in the second part of which he had declared (chapter 49): 'There is only one mistaken belief that is innate in us, namely that we exist so that we may be happy.' True wisdom consists rather, we learn there, in realizing that only suffering and death teach us the truth about life, that it is a 'process of purification'. He cannot expect everyone to follow him all the way in this view of life and in the *Aphorisms* he is coming down to the level of the majority of his probable readers and speaking from a merely empirical point of view, which in his system is presented as an illusion. The practical wisdom he has acquired in the course of his life is offered to the reader in the hope that it may be of value to him in his own, whereas in *The World as Will and Idea* he had produced at the age of thirty an interpretation of life in which everything was related to a single dominant idea derived, he claimed, from the philosophical analysis of experience, 'a decipherment of the world'.[1]

The first chapter of the *Aphorisms* surveys under three heads the most important factors contributing to human happiness. The first is: 'What a man is, personality therefore in the broadest sense. Accordingly this includes health, strength, beauty, temperament, moral character, intelligence and its development.' The second is: 'What a man has, so property and possessions in every sense.' And the third is: 'On what people think of a man'. This means of course what he is in the minds of others, so really how he is thought of by them. Their opinion of him falls under the headings of honour, rank and fame.'[2]

As a philosophical idealist in the Kantian tradition, Schopenhauer naturally considers a man's personal qualities far more important in their effect on his life than his material circumstances or his standing in society:

He is only directly concerned with his own ideas, feelings and acts of will. External things only influence him in so far as they give rise to these. The world in which everyone lives depends in the first place on his conception of it[...] Everyone is stuck inside his consciousness as in his skin, and lives directly only in it. Therefore he cannot be helped very much from outside.[3]

Schopenhauer expounds most eloquently the all-importance of the inner life, a theme common to all the authors we have considered, developed here however with special insistence on the good fortune of those who happen to have been born intelligent. Those who have not are predestined to be philistines, 'thrown back on sensual enjoyment, intimate and cheerful family life, low companionship and vulgar amusements', which is very bad luck, 'for the highest, most varied and lasting pleasures are those of the mind'.[4]

Separate chapters of varying length set out in more detail the author's reflections on each of the three sets of conditions governing human happiness. Under the heading 'About what a man is' Schopenhauer writes with great warmth and imaginative insight about what had evidently been for him, despite all his official pessimism, a continual source of delight, the intellectual life. His early inclination towards it had not been encouraged by his father, who had been mainly concerned with ensuring for him a safe livelihood in the future. When the boy, born in 1788 in Danzig, was about to enter the Gymnasium there at fifteen, his father persuaded him to give up the idea of preparing for the university and to serve an apprenticeship with a merchant instead, with a view to a business career, after first, by way of compensation, accompanying his parents on a long journey to several European countries, a trip which lasted over eighteen months. Even when his father died the boy, now seventeen, felt himself bound by his promise, and it was only when his mother, after two further years, realized how desperately unhappy he was, and learned from friends in Weimar that it was still not too late for him to think of studying, if that was where his bent lay, that he was able to begin the serious study of Latin and Greek. The phenomenal rapidity of his progress, his subsequent omnivorous reading at Göttingen and Berlin, leading to a doctorate at twenty-five and the completion by 1818, when he was only thirty years old, of *The World as Will and Idea*, were ample proof of his intellectual brilliance, and the incidental references in his work to the classics and to half a dozen modern literatures indicate in themselves not only massive learning, but a discriminating love of letters. When Schopenhauer in 'About what a man is' sings the praises of 'inner wealth, the wealth of the mind', he is writing of what he knows. After an intelligent and active mind the greatest gift, according to Schopenhauer, is bodily health: 'In fact nine tenths of our happiness depend on health alone. With it, everything becomes a source of enjoyment, whereas without it, no external blessing brings any joy.' Even the gifts of the mind lose much of their value without health, and in its absence no one can be cheerful and good-tempered, a precious gift often denied to supremely intelligent and sensitive natures. Of course it did not need a Schopenhauer to teach us these commonplaces, but they are of interest here for their autobiographical reference. This is how the great pessimist really was, possessed, like everyone else, by the will to live, more sensitive than most to the good things in life and for that very reason less easily contented, much as he admired asceticism – in others. Like Kant he recommended, and followed, a common-sense regimen, daily exercise out of doors – two hours of fast walking – and the avoidance of all excesses. Nothing is said here about personal relationships, for this man is a solitary, whose deepest wish is to be self-sufficient. He half envies, half despises the cheerful people he sees in the streets and at his *table d'hôte*, and thanks God for the carefully husbanded capital left to him by his father, which makes him independent. The kind of life he recommends as the happiest available to men is obviously only possible for the very small minority, in a peaceful world, who in addition to sufficient means have ample leisure, and the temperament and mental abilities required for the inward life. Schopenhauer never claims that these conditions are anything but exceptional:

Fate is cruel and men are pitiable. In a world constituted like this, a man who has much in himself is like the bright, warm room of a merry Christmas party, surrounded by the ice and snow of a December night. So the happiest earthly lot is without any doubt to possess a superior, rich individuality and in particular very high intelligence.[5]

The climax of this chapter is the splendid passage describing the delightful activities open to the man of cultivated intelligence. Schopenhauer leads up to it by reminding us of some of the central ideas in his philosophy. The powers with which man is equipped by nature, as tools of the will to live, are chiefly employed in an unending struggle with difficulties and dangers. 'But when there is a respite in this struggle, then his unoccupied powers become a burden to him. He must therefore now *play* with them, that is, use them without any end in view.' Otherwise he will fall a prey to boredom, the plague of the leisured classes. Schopenhauer does not follow Schiller and say: 'A man is only then fully a human being when he is at play', for there are men and men, just as with Schiller there are nations and nations, each revealing its character in its favourite recreation.[6] According to Schopenhauer, what people reveal through their choice of leisure occupation is the kind of psycho-physical type they belong to. He distinguishes three. There is one in which the physical processes, the qualities in which men are most like plants, predominate. In their free time such men will eat, drink or sleep. (Presumably the spirit of the time prevents the author from adding, as he would now, 'or make love'.) The second type is characterized above all by animal strength and agility – this Schopenhauer calls 'irritability'. Its members will walk, wrestle, dance, go in for sport or athletics – or let off their surplus energy in hunting or war. Schopenhauer finds the 'really human qualities' only in the third type, with its marked sensibility, found at its highest in men of genius. These in their leisure will contemplate, think, feel, write poems, paint or make music, read, invent, philosophize and so forth. The ordinary man of the first two categories, Schopenhauer continues, only really cares for something which calls his will into play, and thus acquires a personal interest for him. That is why card-playing is so much the vogue in 'good society'. It appeals to the players' will to win and this excitement of the will is accompanied, like every other, by a certain pain, but in this case it is only a slight and momentary pain, a sort of tickling of the will. The passage continues:

The man in whom the intellectual capacities predominate, on the other hand, can take and in fact requires the liveliest interest in things, but purely through the desire to *know*, without any intervention of the will. This interest transports him to a region to which pain is essentially a stranger, into the atmosphere of the carefree gods. The lives of others are passed in a daze, their every thought absorbed by the petty concerns of their personal welfare, by mean trifles of every kind, so that intolerable boredom assails them as soon as there is a pause in their occupation with such aims, and they are thrown back on themselves, only the wild fire of passion being capable of stirring the stagnant mass. But the man endowed with predominantly intellectual powers, on the other hand, leads a life full of thought, variety and meaning; he is occupied with worthy and fascinating objects whenever he can give himself up to them, and he possesses a source of the purest pleasure in himself. He is stimulated from outside by the works of nature and by the human scene, and further by the diverse creations of the most gifted minds of all times and countries, which only he can fully enjoy, because only he can understand and feel them. It is for him that these choice spirits have therefore really lived, it is to him they have really addressed themselves, whereas the others only by chance pick up and half understand a fragment here and there. It is true that he has through all this an additional need, unknown to the others, the need to learn, to see, to study, to meditate, to practise, and consequently also the need for leisure. But just because, as Voltaire rightly remarks, 'il n'est de vrais plaisirs qu'avec de vrais besoins', this need is the pre-condition for enjoyments to stand open to him which to the others remain denied, because to them the beauties of nature and art, and intellectual works of every kind, even if they heap up such things around them, at bottom mean no more than courtesans to an old man. A man enjoying these privileges therefore leads, in addition to his personal life, a second life, that of the mind, which gradually becomes to him the real aim of his existence, to which he regards the first life as only a means, whereas to the rest this shallow, empty and miserable existence itself has to serve as an end. That intellectual life will therefore take up most of his attention, and it acquires, through continuous growth in insight and knowledge, an integration, an ever increasing intensity, wholeness and perfection, like a work of art in the making. To this the merely practical life, directed towards a man's personal welfare, forms a sad contrast, capable as it is of extension only in length and not in depth.[7]

There are obviously close similarities between this passage and some of the earlier expressions of the idea of self-development discussed above. The most striking is the contrast drawn between two kinds of life, one of struggle and suffering in the world and one of happy contemplation, which immediately recalls Schiller's poem 'The Ideal and Life'. In his main work, twenty years earlier, Schopenhauer had already opposed the life of 'will' with that of 'idea' in a similar way, as we shall see. A difference between the two writers which is inescapable is their attitudes to active life. Schiller, in the spirit of Kantian ethics, praises full participation in the struggle and no avoidance of duty with its risks and pains. Living in the ideal world of the imagination in calm interludes, one can also attain to a kind of secular form of salvation, a life in the eternal in the midst of earthly life, as Schleiermacher was to put it. A. W. Schlegel saw Schiller's meaning quite clearly, as his review shows: 'Holding life at a distance, man must fill his imagination with ideals of human nature; yet without allowing himself to be lulled into passivity in real life, as if he were already in possession of the unattainable because he can imagine it.'[8] Schopenhauer on the other hand praises the intellectual life, the life of culture, as a deliberate withdrawal from miserable and shameful enslavement to the unconscious Will in active life. He does not represent this withdrawal as open to men in general, but only to those whom fate has endowed with brains. The ideal of wholeness and harmony in the cultivated personality, familiar from Schiller and Humboldt, is echoed in the latter part of the quotation from Schopenhauer, about the growth of wholeness and perfection like that of a work of art in the making, but there is none of Schleiermacher's insistence on individuality for its own sake as an element in the total revelation of humanity, and nothing of his religious attitude in general. Instead there is complete pessimism about the life open to the normal man. Only for the elect who have been blessed at birth with high intelligence there is hope of a new kind of salvation, as in earlier pagans from Schiller onwards, in the life of the mind. There is no hint here that the individual has any duty to society or any responsibility for its ills – all blame is shifted to the metaphysical plane – but the fortunate are recommended to make the best of what has fallen to them, which may be something much more tangible, as we shall see, than intellectual distinction.

After the chapter 'On what a man is' come two less strikingly original chapters on the other two principal factors on which happiness depends, first a very short one, 'On what a man has', and then one eight times as long, 'On what people think of a man'. The longest chapter of all is the fifth, which consists of 53 numbered paragraphs of 'Recommendations and Maxims' of varying length on the art of living. Chapter VI finally is a short tail-piece 'On the different ages of life', in which, at an age approaching sixty, Schopenhauer reflects on the gradual change that has taken place in his attitude to life, summing up his experience in disillusioned aphorisms like this:

118

If the character of the first half of life is unsatisfied longing for happiness, that of the second is apprehension of unhappiness.[9]

Or:

Of course, when one is old, one has only death ahead; but when one is young, one has life ahead; and it is an open question which of the two is more of a menace, and whether, all in all, life is a better thing to have behind one, or ahead.[10]

From pithy and often witty remarks like these one has the impression, for all the pessimism of the message, that the author is enjoying his skill in formulating it so memorably, enjoying his kind of work, as we shall find Friedrich Theodor Vischer saying (see p. 160). Life is a desperate business, but one can be very happy thinking and writing about it in peace, and so the author of *The World as Will and Idea* can quite sincerely praise the intellectual life, as in the long passage quoted. This paradox of the happy pessimist, Schopenhauer might say, illustrates the truth of his contention in his main work that in spite of our enslavement, with all life, to the Will, which keeps us 'perpetually on Ixion's revolving wheel', there are moments for some – artists, poets, philosophers – when they can put their driving force, the will, as it were into neutral gear, and simply contemplate disinterestedly, as Kant puts it, what is before them. This famous section 38 in the third book of *The World as Will and Idea* again reminds us of Schiller's poem. It culminates in the following description of the escape into 'the Ideal', into the aesthetic attitude or pure knowing:

But when some external occasion, or internal mood, lifts us suddenly up out of the endless stream of Willing, wrests knowledge free from enslavement to the Will; when our attention is no longer directed to the motives inspired by the Will, but conceives things as freed from their relation to it, disinterestedly therefore, without subjectivity, purely objectively, concentrated on them purely as ideas, not as motives – then the calm which we long for while subject to the Will, but always in vain, is suddenly there of its own accord, and we are completely content. It is the painfree condition praised by Epicurus as the highest good, the life of the gods: for we are released, for that moment, from the base drive of the Will, we celebrate the sabbath from our penitentiary labour in its service, the wheel of Ixion stands still.[10]

Thomas Mann, in his excellent essay on Schopenhauer, is by no means blind to the philistine element in the philosopher's political conservatism, his tendency to look upon the state as 'an institution for the protection of property', in his fears for the safety of his all-important private income, but he reminds us that this lack of political and social concern, this quietism, is the other side of the objectivity which, in Schopenhauer's view, alone makes art and philosophy possible:

For Schopenhauer, productive genius is nothing else than objectivity, that is, the capacity to adopt a purely contemplative attitude, as nothing but a percipient subject, 'a clear eye open to the world'[...] Philosophy, Schopenhauer declares, does not ask about the whence and whither and why, but only about the what of the world[...] Art and philosophy have not the least wish to change anything, but only to contemplate.[12]

The regrettable but inescapable truth that even great philosophers cannot for long completely forget their subjective hopes and fears, their 'will to life', soon impresses itself upon us as we read the *Aphorisms*. Every page conveys the impression of a very distinctive personality, and this, whatever we may think about the author's demand for pure objectivity in the artist, constitutes one of the book's greatest charms as literature, even though the character traits revealed are often in themselves repellent. Towards the end of 'On what a man has', for instance, after drawing attention to the relativity of human wishes which, in that static age at least, caused everyone to have his own horizon of hopes and wishes, so that the poor were not disturbed at the sight of the vast possessions of the rich, but the rich, if disappointed of some of their ambitions, found little consolation in all they already had, Schopenhauer concludes his common-sense and rather bourgeois remarks about money by admitting that no one is free without it, and that for a highly gifted man it is a special blessing to inherit a sufficiency,

For then he is doubly endowed by fate and can now live for his genius. But he will pay off his debt to humanity by doing what no one else has been able to do, and creating something which benefits it as a whole, and even perhaps redounds to its credit.[13]

Few passages can be so readily interpreted as pure autobiography as this, but the cumulative effect of many slighter indications of decidedly personal attitudes and tastes is very great. The author seems to speak as a middle-aged – or by the standards of that age elderly – man (he was fifty-eight when the book was published) of quiet, scholarly habits, who detests the idle *beau monde* of the courts, and expressly contrasts himself with Goethe in this respect,[14] yet admits to being no Diogenes or Spinoza. He is very glad to be a better-class *Bürger*, who does not need to waste time on uncongenial work and is accustomed to comparative independence. Gwinner tells us: 'His bearing was always that of an aristocrat; he always appeared fully dressed – black frock coat, white tie and shoes', and he made no concessions to prevailing fashions to the end. He led a solitary life, being unsociable from taste and principle.[15] Unlike Schleiermacher, he feels no need or desire to meet many types of men to enlarge his conception of humanity. Man is an open book to him, and he is not at all concerned about the government's problems or community affairs. The masses are nothing to be proud of in any country:

Concerning national character, since the term refers to the multitude, there will never be much good that one can honestly boast of. No, human narrow-mindedness, perversity and baseness take a different form in every country, and this is what they call national character[...] Every nation ridicules its neighbours, and they are all quite right.[16]

Like most of his fellow-countrymen at the time of writing, he is honest enough to say that he has no national feeling, knowing that 'every poor wretch who has nothing in the world to be proud of, decides as a last straw to be proud of the nation to which he happens to belong.' He himself leaves it to the democrats and 'German brothers' to prate about patriotism.[17]

Though he has strong links through his mother's friends and through his education with Weimar in the great days, he emphatically does not 'think nobly of man', and still less of woman. His views about women come out in the section on 'sexual honour' in the chapter 'On what people think of a man', and they are expanded very forcefully in chapter 27 of the second part of the *Parerga und Paralipomena*, 'On women', an essay from which Nietzsche must have derived many suggestions for his notorious speech of Zarathustra 'On old and young wifies'. Chapter 44 of the second part of *The World as Will and Idea* ('Metaphysics of sexual love') had explained in detail Schopenhauer's conception of men and women as the unconscious tools of the will to life, fulfilling the need of the species to survive and not, as they imagine, exercising their purely individual choice in mating. It is of course the central idea of Shaw's *Man and Superman*, and as in that play, it is the woman, in Schopenhauer's view, who is most completely absorbed, and therefore most cunning, in serving the purpose of nature. 'I have not counted in "What a man has" his wife and children', we read at the end of the chapter of the *Aphorisms* with that title, 'because it is he, rather, who is had by them.' In the following chapter, where every kind of honour is made to rest on utilitarian considerations, women's honour is explained away as their ideological defence of marriage. Their sex

stands as one woman, drawn up in marching order facing, as its common enemy, the whole male sex which, through its preponderance of physical and mental powers, is by nature in possession of all earthly goods.[18]

Schopenhauer had once had thoughts of marriage himself. From Italy, where he was relaxing after *The World as Will and idea*, he had written to his sister Adele about a wealthy Venetian woman of rank who was ready to follow him, but it came to nothing. He had grown accustomed since early manhood, Gwinner tells us, 'to looking upon sexual love only from its mercenary side'.[19] So we read in the *Aphorisms* that a man in his sixties experiences a natural, instinctive urge to live alone:

The thing which most strongly drives men to be sociable, the love of women and the sexual impulse, is no longer effective. The sexlessness of old age clears the way in fact for a certain self-sufficiency, which gradually absorbs the social impulse completely.[20]

The presence of women prevents serious conversation anyhow,[21] and so, apparently, does that of most men, for in company they talk about nothing but 'what is everyday, trivial and common[...] So it is an aristocratic feeling that feeds the tendency towards self-withdrawal and loneliness. Scoundrels are all sociable, lamentably so.'[22]

All these are clearly the views of one who, in the eyes of most people, is a selfish old bachelor and eccentric, disappointed in life, irritable and in no way superior to the average male, in what corresponds for Germany to the Victorian age, in his attitude to women and sex. He is equally cynical about average human nature. No one can count upon other people's fairness, gratitude, faithfulness or sympathy, so it is advisable to work rather upon their fears.[23] It is best to show them that you can do without them, and to make no display of affection:

But if somebody is really very dear to us, we must keep the fact from him, as if it were a crime. That is rather horrible, but it is true. Even dogs can hardly stand too much friendliness, let alone men.[24]

It is not surprising to learn that Schopenhauer preferred the company of dogs to that of men. What he wanted above all was to be left to himself, because 'the true, deep peace of the heart and perfect calm of mind', these supreme blessings, after health, are only to be found in solitude.[25]

But a solitary life is not for everyone. It becomes bearable and even desirable only if one's own self is 'big and rich', and of this he has no doubt as far as he is concerned. He speaks throughout as one fully conscious of his own exceptional gifts, his genius. He sees himself as proud, but not vain, the difference between the two being:

that pride is the already fixed conviction of one's own surpassing value in some respect, whereas vanity is the desire to arouse such a conviction in others.[26]

Schopenhauer is rightly convinced that he is one of the men 'endowed with predominantly intellectual powers' who are destined for the intellectual life, which he cannot help regarding not merely as the best kind of life for people like himself, but as the best absolutely. We should like him better if he showed a trace of humour, of the capacity to see himself as others see him and sometimes even laughing at himself. He certainly had wit. Combined with abundant malice, and the terse, laconic style that matches his superb intellectual grasp of complex phenomena, it is this above all which makes his observations about society and human nature memorable, though often unjust through over-simplification. He is not ashamed of the malice. He calls it 'gall' and finds fault with the Germans (in 'On authorship and style' in *Parerga und Paralipomena* II) for having too little of it. They will not think for themselves and condemn where they should: 'They have no gall, like doves: lack of gall is lack of intelligence, which always secretes a certain *acrimonia*.'[27] His bitterness is partly explicable from his perfectly justified feeling that his work had been unfairly neglected, but it is chiefly a matter of temperament. When he was nineteen and still at the Halle Gymnasium, he wrote satirical verses about a master which evoked a long letter of reproach from his mother, including these words:

All your good qualities are put into the shade and made useless for the world by your conceit, just because you cannot control your mania for always claiming to know better than others, finding faults everywhere except in yourself and trying to correct and override others.[28]

Johanna Schopenhauer was in her son's eyes of course too eager to be accepted by fashionable society as a wit and an entertaining writer – she eventually enjoyed considerable success as a novelist – and he could not stand her parties and her literary friends. Their equally self-centred natures were so incompatible that they quarrelled soon after this and never saw each other again in the twenty-four years she had still to live. The worst features in his mother's character, seen through very unfilial eyes, no doubt supplied part of the caricature he was so often to draw of 'das Weib', woman – he never used the politer 'die Frau' if he could help it. Not much is known about Schopenhauer's love-life, but it looks very much as if his imagination revenged itself in his image of woman for the humiliations suffered by an intellectual who despised sex but for long could not do without it. Far from overcoming in later life his passion for proving that he knew everything better, Schopenhauer felt himself justified by his published work in counting himself among those 'educators of mankind' of whom he speaks, when discussing the inevitable loneliness of those 'whom Prometheus had shaped out of better clay':

But as to the great spirits, it is natural that these real educators of the human race should feel as little inclination to mix frequently with the rest as pedagogues do to join in the play of the mob of children around them. For they, who have come into the world to steer men on the sea of their errors towards the truth, and to draw them up out of the abyss of their coarseness and commonness towards culture and nobility – they must indeed live among them, but without really belonging to them, and they feel themselves therefore from their youth on to be creatures noticeably different from the others. It is only gradually, as the years pass by, that they arrive at a clear understanding of the matter, and from then on they see to it that the distance between them as minds is marked by physical separation, and no one may come near them, unless he is already more or less exempt from the general taint of commonness.[29]

It is obvious that many of the attitudes we have discovered in Schopenhauer were not peculiar to him as an individual, but correspond to deeply-rooted German traits which we shall find, for example, in Stifter too. The first of these is the willing acceptance of paternalist, authoritarian forms of government and of social institutions generally. Thomas Mann puts very effectively his criticism (in 1938) of this aspect of the philosophy which had so deeply impressed him as a young man:

It seems to us that it is no contribution towards the improvement of human life as a whole, of which social and political life is a part, if the philosophical petty-capitalist ironically refuses to intervene in any way in this sphere, if intellect refuses to be moved by any political passion, following the motto: 'I thank God every morning that I have not to bother my head about the Holy Roman Empire', a motto that might suit the state very well. It expresses complete philistinism and shirking of responsibility, and one can hardly understand how an intellectual fighter like Schopenhauer could ever adopt such a device.[30]

Schopenhauer uses the same Faust quotation in his anti-Hegelian essay 'On university philosophy' in a paragraph in which he admits that the state needs its university-trained experts, but not that the state is the whole aim of human existence, 'the absolutely perfect ethical organism', as Hegel said. In other places, especially in the late essay 'About jurisprudence and politics' (in *Parerga und Paralipomena*, II), he is more specific in his authoritarianism, having been frightened, like Stifter, by 1848. He is convinced that questions of power are not to be solved by theorizing while human nature remains as it is:

A constitution incorporating merely abstract rights would be a splendid thing for another sort of beings than men really are, but the great majority of them are selfish, unjust, inconsiderate, mendacious, sometimes even malevolent, and at the same time very limited in their intelligence. These conditions make necessary a power answerable to no one, concentrated in one man, standing above law and rights, a power to which all submit themselves and which is regarded as a being of a higher order, a ruler by the grace of God.[31]

The ultimate sanction even in a modern society, Schopenhauer insists, is physical force, and it is the masses who dispose of the greatest force, but they are ignorant and stupid. 'The first task of statesmanship in such difficult circumstances is therefore to make physical force subject to and at the disposal of intelligence, mental superiority.'[32] The intermediate authorities who serve as leaders and advisers of the ignorant mass are such people as 'judges, ministers of state, officers, civil servants, priests, doctors, scholars, philosophers etc.' and it is only right that they should lead comfortable and privileged lives.[33] Schopenhauer is completely on the side of established authority and can find no words too bitter for the 'demagogues' of mid-century, the early socialists who, as enemies of Christianity, are optimistic about human nature and about leaving a society to develop in freedom. The result of the unlimited progress they preach would be: 'All would be able without let or hindrance to eat, drink and reproduce themselves to their hearts' content, and kick the bucket.'[34] The folly of their theorizing is evident in their campaign for trial by jury, 'the worst kind of criminal court', on which 'the butcher, the baker, the candlestickmaker' sit in judgment instead of 'scholars and experienced criminologists'.[35] The trouble with the Germans is that they 'look in the clouds for what lies at their feet'.[36] The upshot of Schopenhauer's plain thinking is to leave the inherited semi-feudal system as it is, so that philosophers may get on with their thinking in peace, suitably protected by the state.

All the leading ideas of the progressives of his time are similarly reviewed by Schopenhauer, with more assertion than argument. The best solution of the question of German unity would be for the imperial crown to go to Austria and Prussia alternately, for the life-time of the monarch, who should be given real power. The parody of the British constitution which has been adopted by all the petty German princes is a farce, simply a matter of fashion. If he is asked for his own utopian solution, he comes up with something foreshadowing Nietzsche's Superman: 'The despotism of the wise and noble of a true aristocracy, a true nobility, the ultimate product of a system of breeding, of mating the most noble-minded men with the shrewdest and most intelligent women'.[37] Apart from their indispensable role in breeding, Schopenhauer has not much use for women in his later years, and he entirely rejects the idea of their emancipation. For outspoken misogyny, his chapter 'On women' in *Parerga und Paralipomena* II has few parallels. It is only 'the male intellect clouded by the sexual impulse' that could ever call these little broad-hipped creatures the fair sex, for 'their whole beauty lies in this impulse'.

Schopenhauer goes on to deny women any capacity for the arts and to declare that modern Europe is greatly mistaken in putting woman on a pedestal, instead of acknowledging, like the Ancients, her obvious inferiority to man, and he concludes:

The European lady herself is a creature that should never exist, but there should be 'Hausfraus' and girls who hope to become them, and are therefore educated not to be arrogant, but domesticated and submissive.[38]

an opinion which he supports by a quotation from Byron's *Journals*. In another place (in 'About Jurisprudence and Politics') he declares that women never really come of age and should always have a male guardian – father, husband, son – or the state, as in India. They are so unreliable that in court, for instance, the witness of two men should be given as much weight as that of three or four women.[39]

Schopenhauer's opinions are often so outrageous that it is hard to take them as seriously meant, but they were consistent, in the fields we have considered, with the conscious or unconscious prejudices of important sections of German society in his day, and much later. For him, as we have seen, there are not only 'two nations' in German society, but the sexes are in a similar relationship, one fully and one under-privileged. Among males, finally, there are the men of genius, capable of the highest order of generality in their thinking and least enslaved to the Will, and the rest. Speaking as a genius, Schopenhauer expects to be regarded by many as unsociable, even repellent, and inevitably as arrogant, for modesty in a genius would be *contradictio in adjecto*. He is not a genius unless he is quite sure that he is right, as Schopenhauer had been since the time when his mother had rebuked his conceit. 'All in all', to quote Thomas Mann once more, 'the atmosphere surrounding him is that of a certain German middle-class way of life, only too familiar, only too like home.'[40]

ADALBERT STIFTER: DER
NACHSOMMER (1857)

Like Risach, the central figure of *Der Nachsommer*, Adalbert Stifter came from a village high up in the Bohemian Forest. Like him too he lost his father in adolescence, but was accepted at a good school, in his case that of the Benedictines at Kremsmünster, and maintaining himself from about the age of sixteen by coaching, went on to study at the University of Vienna. But whereas Risach decided early to enter the civil service, and rose in it to great heights, Stifter made good in quite a different way. At school he had proved to possess not only high intellectual ability but marked artistic gifts, which found expression in sketching and writing. After abandoning the study of the law he continued to maintain himself by giving private lessons, now in the families of the aristocracy of Vienna, including finally that of Metternich himself, but he devoted his best efforts to painting and story-writing. At the time of his marriage, at the age of thirty-two, he applied for a teaching-post at a school of forestry which he might have obtained but for an untimely illness, and after this gradually drifted into a literary career, though it was a long time before he looked upon himself as a professional writer. His aim was chiefly, he always maintained, to satisfy himself and to live up to the high ideals of authorship he had learnt from the great Germans of the eighteenth century, above all from Goethe. Even at his monastery school he had come under the influence of Leibniz-Wolffian thought, which had spread to Catholic Austria through the South German universities. The idea of human perfectibility, and the Wolffian interpretation of the good, the true and the beautiful as different reflections of the one divine source – ideas which many trace back anyhow to Scholastic philosophy – had been welcomed as a tolerable response to the pressure of Josephinism even in Jesuit and Benedictine schools.[1] They are the basis of the convictions which make themselves apparent in all Stifter's work. As he wrote himself:

In Kremsmünster I heard for the first time the thesis that the beautiful is nothing else than the divine presented in the garment of grace, that the divine however is manifested in man only in a limited degree, but in the Lord of Heaven completely. It is nevertheless his innermost essence and strives everywhere without fail to unfold itself as the good, the true and the beautiful in religion, in science, in art and in conduct. This statement struck me with force in the very centre of my being, and all my subsequent life, my twenty-two years in Vienna, my attempts in art and scholarship, my human contacts, my official duties, have led me to the same conclusion.[2]

Born as he was more than half a century later than Goethe (in 1805), in an environment different not only through the political and social changes brought by the early nineteenth century but by the fact of being an Austrian, surrounded by the scenery and immersed in the traditions of the Catholic south, Stifter cannot be expected to resemble Goethe at all closely in his work, for all his admiration of him as a writer. There is often something homely and slightly provincial about it, as there was, according to contemporaries, about his person and his conversation. He continued all his life to speak his native upper Austrian dialect and to look, as Clara Schumann wrote in 1847, 'by no means poetic'. 'His dialect too', she continued, 'does not sound very poetic, but in a conversation of any length his intellectual distinction is unmistakable.' In his writing however he always aims at the highest he knows. The High German literary language which he wrote was for him, as Hohoff says, 'an almost ceremonial abstraction' which does not flow naturally, but has to be consciously constructed, sentence by sentence, following as principal model the style of the older Goethe. In the same spirit he seems to delight in the punctilious politeness of his characters in *Der Nachsommer*, in the formal visits they pay to each other, in suitable costume, while staying in the same house. The severe restraint which marks every phase of the love story in the novel is clearly a product of the same attitude of mind in the author. He does not want to be merely natural, but to improve on nature with the help of freely accepted conventions, the value of which he has proved in his own experience. 'Bildung' has made him what he is, and he feels himself to be a missionary of true 'Bildung'. In his letters, when at the height of his powers, to friends and especially to his publisher, Heckenast, Stifter frequently speaks about his aims and achievements with a perhaps rather excessive self-confidence, though some of his writing, particularly his early contributions to *Wien und die Wiener* (1844), show that he was not quite so humourless as he sometimes sounds. To Joseph Türck he wrote (22 February 1850):

My books are not only literature – as such they may be of very temporary value. But as moral revelations, as human dignity preserved with strict seriousness, they have a value which, alongside the wretched, frivolous writings of to-day, will be more lasting than their poetic qualities.

Stifter often speaks of the German classical writers as an inspiration to him in his endless task. Reading the Goethe–Schiller correspondence he finds some comfort in the thought that these great men too had contemporaries who had little understanding of their problems, though he also envies Goethe the generous patronage which he repaid with master-pieces. He continues:

I am not a Goethe, indeed, but one of his kin, and the seed of the pure, noble, simple goes out to men's hearts from my writings too, I have proofs of that. Who knows whether they will not some day help to confirm a great genius in his goodness who is higher than Goethe, Schiller and all of them, and draw him away from the odious, disgusting nihilism around him towards peace and simplicity, to create all the sooner works which will be the delight and wonder of the world.[3]

It is hard now to take these solemn clichés at their face value, especially as we often find them combined with an obvious nationalistic bias, as when he writes about Hebbel, his pet aversion, who lived in Vienna from 1845 until his death eighteen years later, though Stifter left it for Linz in 1849. There is for instance a letter to Heckenast where he says:

It would be strange if despised Austria[...] which has saved Germany several times from political downfall, were destined to save it too through those strong and sincere hearts from literary madness. It would indeed be strange! It is striking that the only poet living in Austria who is grotesque, morally distorted and unnatural in the extreme is not an Austrian.[4]

Behind outbursts like this, as behind many of Stifter's positive claims about the ethical basis of his art and his hopes for its future influence, many readers to-day would be inclined to suspect some unconscious bias, perhaps an over-correction of a sense of inferiority. The preface to the work just preceding *Der Nachsommer*, the collection of stories called *Bunte Steine* (1852), is the best direct expression of his mature view of the relation between his writing and his ethical philosophy, which turns round what he calls here 'the gentle law[...] by which the human race is guided'. It is not the violent changes due to storms, volcanic eruptions and earthquakes that do most in the end to model the landscape and affect the course of life on earth, but the unceasing slow effects of water, wind and weather. To use the terms of Goethe's day, Stifter is not a Vulcanist in political and social affairs, but a Neptunist, an advocate not of revolution but of gradual reform, inspired by 'the law of justice and morality'. He does not here appeal to specifically Christian principles, but presents this law as the product of centuries of human experience of life in society, which teaches that men cannot survive without fairness and sympathy, almost literally Herder's definition of 'Humanität'. Stifter speaks of the 'gentle' law which guides man and nature, not only because moral cultivation makes 'gentlemen' of the uncouth, but because he thinks of goodness as intrinsically attractive, as had always been the contention of the Enlightenment. He stresses the essentially peaceful and reasonable nature of man, the 'sociability' achieved by man, as Pufendorf had claimed in the late seventeenth century, with the help of his fellows and his social inheritance, his culture. What still interests Stifter particularly is man's humanity as opposed to his animality, his capacity to control his passions and develop his mind and sensibility, a capacity he finds present, as Tolstoy did in Russia, not only in the privileged and educated, but in simple country people unconsciously moulded by a civilizing Christian tradition. He presents the characters in his 'Novellen' as individuals who, for all their uniqueness, seem to grow out of their environment as its natural product. Johannes Aprent, a master at the Linz *Realschule* who knew Stifter particularly well and collaborated with him when he was a school inspector, says:

What gives these stories their beautifully harmonious effect, which calms and satisfies the reader so completely, is that his characters are never set down arbitrarily like lay figures in some set of natural conditions, but that they themselves grow up naturally out of those conditions, so that the sisters in *Der Hochwald* are only the fairest flowers of the woods, and the boy in *Das Haidedorf* is the moorland's noblest product. That is why Stifter was firmly opposed to all those petty regulations, by which officials try to keep their hands on everything.[5]

131

There is no other German novelist in whose work description is so prominent a feature, description not so much of the appearance or character of people – Stifter has no liking for analysis – as of their natural or man-made surroundings, particularly any evidence of the skill and taste of earlier generations revealing itself in concrete form. In wild nature there is always for Stifter the suggestion of a divine presence, and similarly in houses and gardens, villages and estates there is what Hegel would have called 'mind objectified', the reflection of human choice and effort in the past. Like Balzac, Stifter liked to describe a room, for instance, which has become a symbol of the character of the person who lives in it, and to leave it to us, as Staiger says, 'to guess at the workings of the mind'. 'He is chary of revealing, still more of explaining, the movements of the soul, because no mortal eye can see into its depths.'[6] It is largely for this reason that three-quarters of the text of *Der Nachsommer* is description and only one quarter concerned with human actions, Staiger points out.

In spite of Stifter's obvious preoccupation with the idea of culture, Staiger would have us compare *Der Nachsommer* with *Wilhelm Meisters Wanderjahre* or Plato's *Republic* rather than with *Wilhelm Meisters Lehrjahre* and the 'Bildung' novels descended from it, like Mörike's *Maler Nolten* or Keller's *Der grüne Heinrich*, true novels with romantic plots, full of interest above all for the impressions they convey of clearly distinguished social classes in the actual world of their time. *Der Nachsommer* is much more of a utopia, 'an ideal world that never was and never will be'.[7] In its construction it breaks away entirely from the picaresque tradition and is more like a nineteenth-century Austrian version of *Hermann und Dorothea* than of the *Lehrjahre*. The idealization practised by Goethe throughout his short epic poem is based on his conception of something quintessential in human character and behaviour, what Viktor Hehn later called 'the natural forms of human life', which can be exemplified from any age. The theory of a modern classicism worked out by Goethe and Schiller in the 1790s had of course been based on this conception, which reflects their ambition to rival Homer and Sophocles in the handling of eternally human themes.

In reading *Der Nachsommer* one is frequently reminded of these Weimar theories, not only by Stifter's treatment of the central characters, but also by the views on art put into the mouth of Risach.

Speaking to Heinrich about his library, for instance, in the chapter 'Die Erweiterung', Risach is made to say about the poets:

They are the priests of the beautiful and as such, amidst the constant changes in prevailing views about the world, the human lot and even the divine, they keep us in touch with that in us which is everlasting. They present it to us in the garment of grace, which never ages, appears just as it is and neither judges or condemns.

Never losing sight of Goethe as his model, Stifter continually suggests that for Heinrich, who is made the narrator of the story, its heroine Natalie (the name comes of course from the *Lehrjahre*) shares something which he divines in the marble statue on Risach's stairway – a genuine Greek work found by him in Italy – and finds again in Nausicaea as he reads the *Odyssey*. All three seem to be fused for him into one ideal of beauty, with close affinities to the style in which women's heads are carved in his father's Greek gems. It is still among modern 'Bürger' that Stifter, like Goethe in *Hermann und Dorothea*, sees at least hints of 'noble humanity', but they are not simple, healthy citizens of a small market town or farmers' daughters, but peasants' sons who have through their own efforts, in trade or in the public service, raised themselves to a way of life in retirement resembling that of a country gentleman. To bring to us 'in the garment of grace' that which lasts for ever, to fulfil, that is, his highly abstract ideal of beauty, Stifter has to imagine a group of people quite as carefully chosen and as remote from normal reality in his day as the handful of characters in Goethe's poem. Almost all that Staiger says about Goethe's selection of detail applies equally here:

The number of figures he introduces is limited. He has to refrain from mentioning by name[...] great personages of German history in the past or present. Even the family names of his citizens would be incompatible with the style in which he is writing. That they are Christian in their way of life may only be unobtrusively indicated, without any reference to dogmatic beliefs...The real must be discreetly arranged into the beautiful. Whatever resists this arrangement is dropped.[8]

The effect in *Der Nachsommer*, as in *Hermann und Dorothea*, is to concentrate attention on family life, but the monotony is relieved here by far-ranging discussions between Risach and Heinrich about cultural matters. They are the readiest means of doing what German novelists since Goethe or even Wieland have always desired, to convey ideas while telling a story, but the reflective passages do not arise so naturally from the narrative as in the *Lehrjahre*, where the author provides his hero with a wide experience of life in contrasted social circles. In spite of the difficulties always presented by a story overloaded with thought, serious German novelists down to Stifter's time and far beyond it continued to feel that as artists, and not merely entertainers, it was part of their business, in Jakob Burckhardt's words, 'to make the things of the mind attractive to a large and varied public'.[9]

One effect of Stifter's preoccupation with general ideas is to make the love story, around which any action the novel may be said to have turns, extremely slow-moving. It seems as if the 'retardation' which Goethe and Schiller, in their theorizing about epic and dramatic style, found essential to the epic, is made doubly important here because of Stifter's wish to illustrate again the working of 'the gentle law'. Passion, even in the sense of a normal feeling for the opposite sex, has to be subjected in this utopia to deliberate rational restraint. Risach and Mathilde, frustrated in the natural fulfilment of their deep love because of the woman's intense resentment of the man's refusal, out of consideration for her parents' feelings, to defy the world and win her, find an autumnal happiness mingled with regrets in their 'Indian summer without a real summer first'. Reunited in friendship, their chief desire is that Natalie, Mathilde's daughter in her loveless marriage with a husband now dead, may by a happy marriage 'find the happiness which eluded her mother and her fatherly friend[...] When I first saw you standing at the garden fence of my house', Risach says to Heinrich, 'I thought, that is perhaps a husband for Natalie. Why I thought so I do not know. Later I thought the same again, but I knew why.' ('Der Rückblick', near end.)

That is almost the whole of the plot. The first two chapters of the novel are devoted to the development of Heinrich in childhood and youth, watched over and guided at every step by his father and surrounded by the loving care of mother, sister and devoted servants. It is soon evident that in this 'Bildung'-novel, unlike most, the hero is not to learn through his mistakes. It is a singularly harmonious family, no member of which ever seems tempted to take any step without the most unselfish and affectionate regard for all the others. The father, whose name is hardly ever mentioned, is a

merchant in comfortable circumstances, whose way of life is typically that of a good 'Bürger' in a capital city, here evidently Vienna,
though it is never named, at a period, also not stated, when his class
still enjoys general respect and can think of its activity as wholly
beneficial to society in general. Public and private interests work so
well together in this novel that one is reminded rather of the ideal
merchant in the *Spectator* and the German Moral Weeklies than of any
individuals known to history. The traditional virtues of the middle
class in the age of reason are much in evidence, a high regard for law
and order and a good name among one's fellows, for economy of time
and money, with due provision for the future and for accidents, a
liking for well-ordered, clean and uncluttered surroundings at home
and outside, a willing observance of accepted decorum in every
feature of social life, and so on. As in the *Lehrjahre*, the type of
merchant the author has in mind is what Sombart calls 'der wägende
Kaufmann', the cautious merchant of the inland towns, rather than
'der wagende Kaufmann', the adventurous merchant of the ports,
and amongst these cautious ones it is the older generation, like
Wilhelm's father and Werner's, and not the younger Werner, obsessed by the aim of making his money productive, of *having* the cake,
as Keynes used to say, and not eating it. But Heinrich's father has not
only, from small beginnings, made a considerable fortune in trade,
but at the same time, as we learn in the late chapter, 'Der Einblick',
used every opportunity on his travels to extend his knowledge of old
pictures, and denied himself many pleasures in order to lay the
foundations of a collection of his own. He was well aware that there
was no better way than this of insuring oneself against future losses.
Almost the first things he tells his children about his old pictures is
that they are very valuable. 'He said that he had only old ones, which
have a stable value, always available if one is ever forced to sell them.'
('Die Häuslichkeit'.) The same was true about his Greek gems, his
antique furniture, old weapons and armour, and so on. All these
possessions were a delight for him to behold, but genuine aesthetic
appreciation was indissolubly combined in him with the true Bürger's
feeling for economy, order, cleanliness etc. as sacrosanct. One is
reminded of Goethe's father, who did not approve of spending money
on things to be immediately consumed, but 'was not mean about
acquiring things which combined intrinsic value with a good outward

135

appearance', like the golden box with figures in relief, studded with jewels, which he promised his wife to mark the end of the Seven Years War.[10]

One feature of which Heinrich seems to speak with admiration in the first chapter, his father's strict observation of fixed rules in handling his treasures, which is carried still further at Risach's home, the Rose House, with its richer collections, would seem to most modern readers to be pedantic fussiness. A room must never look as if it had been lived in, but rather as if it were a place for display, where nothing in use is left lying about. Herr Drendorf (as we finally hear he is called) had a good library and was fond of reading, but he would only read sitting at a special old carved table in his library, and made it a rule to put the book back in its place after use, in one of the glass-fronted cases with green silk curtains which concealed the books from visitors – and no doubt also protected their bindings from sunlight. In the Rose House too books are put back immediately after use, and there is a further rule that they must be read in an adjoining reading-room, not in the library itself: 'The books acquired importance and dignity, the room is their temple, and you do not work in a temple.' ('Der Besuch'.) This arrangement is also praised as 'an act of homage to intellect', one expression, one might say, of the reverence for intellectual creativeness which is one of Stifter's deepest feelings. With the formal speeches and ritual changes of clothes which are obligatory even on family visits, humour and informal talk are incompatible in this far from permissive society, where all take themselves and their friends and relations very seriously, and seldom question inherited customs and attitudes.

The type of formal education planned for Heinrich by his father and the views on education put into the mouth of Risach later remind us in general of the later Enlightenment period, with few modifications dating from later than Goethe. The discovery and development of the pupil's innate aptitudes in the manner of *Émile* is the basic theory implied, clarified here by the thought of the age of Goethe. 'A man is not here in the first place for the sake of society, but for his own sake. And if everyone is here for his own sake in a proper way, society benefits too.' ('Die Häuslichkeit'.) That is of course pure Goethe or Humboldt doctrine, as we have seen. But both Goethe and Stifter, while declining to put society first, accepted consciously or unconsciously certain social assumptions of their time, for example that the right to exist for one's own sake does not belong to women in the same measure as to men, and not to all social classes alike, but mainly to the aristocracy, at least to that of intellect. The French Revolution might never have taken place for all the effect it seems to have had on the society of *Der Nachsommer*, and Romantic ideas about the emancipation of women have also left no trace. Even when Heinrich's family no longer lives in the old-fashioned way in a town house which served also as warehouse and office, but had moved out to a spacious villa in the suburbs, his mother 'devoted herself more busily than ever to domestic matters', and his sister, after sharing with him the same teachers for her elementary education, carried only one or two subjects further and 'had to be gradually introduced to domestic duties, so that she would some day be able to follow worthily in her mother's footsteps'. The point is emphasized later ('Die Erweiterung') when Klotilde, the sister, wishes to take up landscape-painting and Spanish with her brother, and her mother insists that she must not spend too much time on these diversions, 'for a woman's first duty is her home'. Mathilde, in spite of her higher social standing and very independent character, takes essentially the same view, that the role of women is a secondary one. Her promising son, Gustav, must be given every opportunity to prepare himself for the highest that life can offer, she tells Heinrich, but 'as for herself and Natalie, the life of women is always a dependent and supplementary one, and it feels in that fact reassurance and support'. She implies that as a widow, she is not entirely happy to have to decide so much for herself on her large estate. ('Der Bund'.)

The pronounced paternalism which is evident in all the chapters about Heinrich and his family, the entire neglect of the political element in life, the unquestioning acceptance by all alike of the existing social order and the absence of any expression of concern about the lot of the peasantry and the working class, all these features make on us now the impression not, as so many German critics have said, of a timeless utopia, but rather of an idealized recollection of an earlier, simpler stage in Germany's own history, a vision to which Stifter turns with relief after his experiences in Vienna in 1848. It is interesting to note how many of the central features of Stifter's ideal society correspond to those singled out by Ralf

137

Dahrendorf as characteristic of the solidly based opposition to a modern parliamentary democracy which persisted, according to him, well into the twentieth century:

German society remained illiberal in its structure and authoritarian in its constitution throughout the decades of industrialization. Although the absurd but effective combinations of old and new in the politics and society of Imperial Germany had lost their foundations in 1918, the Weimar Republic diverged seldom and timidly from the old models. Especially in times of crisis the longing for them grew strong.[11]

If this is true, it is a consideration of some importance when one tries to explain the rapidly growing popularity of *Der Nachsommer*, after long neglect, precisely in the difficult years which followed the First World War. Staiger sees this renewal of interest in Stifter as connected with the new understanding of the works of Goethe's old age, of Hölderlin and also, in music, of Johann Sebastian Bach (as well as of Bruckner as opposed to Wagner). This all represents a reaction, he thinks, against what had grown out of the older liberal humanism (Humanität), namely the belief in unrestricted self-assertion, a devil-take-the-hindmost struggle for money and power; and a new understanding for the element of reverence in the *old* Weimar humanism, which was a central feature still of Stifter's philosophy. Sociologists like Dahrendorf understandably find it difficult to divorce such attempts as this at a purely intellectual explanation from the conservatism in political, economic and social matters which was typical of most of the academic literary historians and critics who were behind the Stifter revival in the 1920s. J. P. Stern has illustrated from Stifter studies 'the peculiar paradox typical of much of German criticism. By and large, Stifter is regarded as the non-political writer *par excellence*, while at the same time many of the criticisms of his work follow more or less closely the course of German political history.'[12]

It was natural enough that Stifter, shocked by the chaos he witnessed in Vienna in 1848, and fearful for the future of his country if the irresponsible demand for freedom were to spread unchecked, should give his utopia a setting recalling what seemed to him best in the fast disappearing old Austria where, as he persuaded himself, everyone had known his place and been content with it. Stifter makes it easier for himself to produce this illusion by choosing as his

138

principal characters men who have either retired from the active pursuits of their maturity, like Herr von Risach, or are approaching retirement like Heinrich's father, never seen at work but only in moments of leisure with his family, or again young people still preparing themselves for active life, like Heinrich, and Mathilde's children, and not restricted through any lack of means by vocational requirements. It is important that they all happen to be by nature very likeable people, equable in temperament and carefully brought up to be full of consideration, especially for their own families. The merchant families in *Wilhelm Meisters Lehrjahre*, for instance, were far less shining examples of the domestic virtues. Stifter accepts the risk of dullness, which even in his day threatened the novelist who would not, in Chekhov's words, 'soil his imagination with the dirt of life'. Heinrich is shown to us therefore leading a completely happy boyhood and adolescence with a father, mother and sister who seem to have no problems which father cannot solve, and to be almost completely unaware of any problems in contemporary society. There is just a hint that in the more sophisticated household of Herr von Risach at the Rose House they are aware of social changes going on around them. Heinrich notices that there the family are not joined at meals by the servants, whereas at home his father's shop assistants still live with him in the old-fashioned way of the guilds and share family meals, except in the evening. Risach would have preferred, he says, to follow the old country custom, which tended to make faithful servants into 'good men and women, who are closely attached to the house in simple piety, as if to an immutable church, and to whom the master is a reliable friend', but the ever widening gulf between 'the so-called cultivated and uncultivated' has broken up what was formerly thought of as one family. Goethe, it will be remembered, had hoped for a 'piety to the world' to take the place of this 'piety to the home'. In *Der Nachsommer*, the brief mention of this problem is a sign of humane consideration on the part of the Drendorfs and Risach for their social inferiors, but it is almost the only expression in the novel of anything approaching the crisis of conscience about their social privileges which troubled so many of the gentry in Russia at that time. The social problems of Stifter's day in Germany already acute, receive no more mention in the novel than the political ones. As Hein pointed out already in the first full life of

Stifter, the main characters of the novel live 'for their own sake' in a kind of 'opalescent world of magic' while 'obliging gnomes' apparently do the hard work.[13] Towards his social superiors like the Princess ('Die Erweiterung') and her brilliant circle, Heinrich's attitude is very respectful, like Stifter's to Fürstin Schwarzenberg, but free from snobbery.

Following Risach's advice 'to acquaint himself with life around him' and acquire general impressions of the world outside his actual studies, he joins a club frequented by educated people interested in the arts, and we learn in one short paragraph that he visits places of popular resort, to see 'the real populace' at its pleasures, and learn something of its varied customs and manners, but these seem to remain only an object of curiosity to him. These rather superficial contacts with people unlike himself are evidently made in response to Risach's criticism of his too early specialization in one branch of science, and the ideal suggested is, as at the end of the *Lehrjahre*, the man who becomes a master in some particular field of activity after sampling a great many. As Risach puts it: 'In youth we should try out our powers in an all-round way in order, as men, to be competent in one particular field.' This advice is given to Heinrich on his fifth visit to the Rose House ('Die Erweiterung') when he must be about twenty-two years old.

Up to this point Heinrich's education has been highly systematic, though in the later stages he has freely followed his interests. He has been privately educated and not been sent to any university. This again is a striking reversion on the author's part to much earlier times, before the great improvement of the German universities and before the radicalization of a considerable number of students in the reactionary decades after the Carlsbad Decrees. Taught by good tutors, at first along with his sister, he has become eager to devote his life to scholarship from pure interest in natural science. As an inspector of schools, Stifter of course had his own well-informed views on higher education as it should be in mid-century. After a thorough grounding in Latin and Greek Heinrich occupies himself intensively, by his own choice, with mathematics, while his sister turns, as we have said, to domestic subjects and the usual accomplishments, but both continue their physical education through gymnastics and riding. This is all perfectly normal, but a novel feature is that from the age of eighteen, Heinrich is given limited control of his share of the money left to the children earlier by a relative, and this freedom is gradually increased until, when he is twenty-four, it is complete. He is encouraged to learn the value of money, even without taking up an independent profession, by being asked to pay rent for the rooms he occupies at home – he prefers this to seeking other quarters – and to re-invest some of his income. All these details make Stifter's ideal young man appear as a prudent *rentier* rather like Schopenhauer, glad to enjoy his inherited privileges but careful with his resources and quite unlike the cultivated and generous, but so often feckless and extravagant young noblemen who abound in Russian literature, the best of whom are 'conscience-stricken gentry'.

In Stifter's account of his young hero's efforts to educate himself, when he feels that tutors can no longer help him, there are still traces of the universalistic tradition of 'Bildung' in Humboldt's time, but the aim is one that would have been approved of by Goethe's Abbé, to make sure that he samples a whole range of studies before deciding which shall finally claim him. The order in which they are taken is not then so important – it is different for Heinrich from that followed by Risach in educating Gustav ('Der Besuch'). From the age of eighteen, after what corresponds to school studies of classics and mathematics, he is sent away by his father each summer to learn something at first hand about the world outside. At first he stays with a friend of the family in a country house not far out of town, to get used to being separated from his family, who visit him often. Next year he goes to a farmhouse much further away and learns about farming and primary production, as well as something about the various ways in which wood and other raw materials are manufactured into useful articles, in factories run by water power for instance, close by. These are of course object lessons ('Anschauungsunterricht') on a grand scale. It is only after this that he takes up natural history, which becomes a subject of inexhaustible interest to him. Botany and geology, the collection of specimens on long walks in the woods and hills, and close study of the subject in books, lead on next summer to zoology and the exploration of more mountainous country, and these interests again to attempts to record what he sees in line and colour, and to understand the geology of the landscape. It is an entirely concrete study of nature, rising from the particular to the general, very much in the manner of Goethe himself in actual life and to some extent of Stifter, with scarcely a hint, in this particular work, of the mystical 'nature philosophy' or the meticulous painting in words which we find in so many of Stifter's stories. Heinrich describes himself to Risach, when he takes shelter in his mansion with its rose-covered main wall, as 'an ordinary rambler' of independent means, but Risach does not take him at his word. He sees that geology understood genetically, as the history of the earth, Heinrich's central interest, is an extremely wide field, and that collecting material is only the first stage of a genuinely scientific inquiry, such as he shows himself to have begun in many subjects, meteorology for instance, by keeping his eyes open on his estate.

It is only through Risach that Heinrich comes in full maturity to some knowledge and appreciation of painting, sculpture, literature and drama. He is not a poet or artist by nature, like the young Wilhelm Meister, and though surrounded by good pictures at home, he has not been moved by them or by the Greek gems in his father's collection, nor has he shown any sign of going beyond a purely scholarly knowledge of the classics. History, ancient or modern, does not seem to have been allowed any place in his curriculum at all. In an age so obsessed by history as that in which Stifter had lived, this omission is striking, and must mark his desire to emphasize the timeless, the idea that in spite of what everyone was saying around him, the clock could indeed be put back and the simplicities of an earlier age recaptured. So although Heinrich's boundless curiosity has made him eager to know at first hand and to understand his external physical environment and the material culture created by human labour and ingenuity on this basis, he has shown no particular interest in his country's history or legends, or in the development, still less the present problems, of its society. Risach, though he has played a great part in his country's recent history, never speaks of it, but he does develop Heinrich's aesthetic sense. His drawing and painting have only been used to record things observed, as one now uses a camera. It is only when he has begun to paint landscapes and not just objects that, on his fifth visit to the Rose House, he learns from a long conversation with Risach and the designer Eustach something about atmosphere and the use of the imagination in painting. 'The eye should be exercized and taught', he hears, 'but the soul must create, helped by the eye.' ('Die Erweiterung'.) A little later Risach discourses too on the poets as among the greatest benefactors of mankind, 'priests of the beautiful', expressing, as we have seen, Stifter's own view of literature. It is at this point that he advises Heinrich to take a holiday from science and see more of ordinary life in town and country. When he next goes home, Heinrich discovers that his father has always had a deep love of the arts, and now that his own understanding of them is beginning to ripen, much later than his interest in science, they have long talks about books and pictures, and the son realizes at last what unnoticed treasures have always surrounded him. Through Risach he learns to see revelations of the mind of departed artists and craftsmen in his antique furniture and the church monuments he, like Stifter, delights in restoring.

There is no suggestion in all this of any possible conflict between science and the humanities, for culture is one and indivisible, and as model for Heinrich, Stifter must have had someone like Alexander von Humboldt, explorer and author of *Kosmos*, in mind, a widely cultivated man if ever there was one, rather than the great scientific specialists, like Liebig, Wöhler, Bunsen, Helmholz, who with their exact laboratory methods were the real leaders in science in mid-century, and stimulating technology and industry as never before. Another touch which reminds us how closely Stifter's ideals were associated with the past is Herr Drendorf's insistence on a kind of Grand Tour for his son as the final stage of his education. We think of such tours as belonging essentially to the aristocratic world of the eighteenth century, but merchant apprentices travelled too and as we have seen, Herr Drendorf's deepest interests had been awakened by foreign travel. Of course it is not considered necessary for Natalie to travel too, though the couple are engaged by this time, and their marriage has to be put off for no less than two years. Unlike Tolstoy's Natasha Rostov, Natalie takes this postponement without a murmur, but then, she never really comes to life at all. There will be no Marianne or Philine in Heinrich's life abroad. Sex is something that is never mentioned, so that Victorian English critics could not have found anything offensive in this novel, if they had known it, as they did in *Wilhelm Meister*. Marriage, at the age of twenty-five or so, marks the point at which Heinrich becomes fully adult and 'cultivated' ('Ausgebildet'), ready to take charge of a household of his own.

For Wilhelm, it will be remembered, it is the realization that he is a father – of an illegitimate son – that is said to be the beginning of wisdom, but not by any means the end of his 'Bildung'.

The discussion of the ideas about 'Bildung' expressed directly or indirectly in *Der Nachsommer* has thrown some light on Stifter's general philosophy and his relation to his times. There was no serious obstacle in the fact of his upbringing in a monastery school to his admiration for Weimar humanism, we saw, because his teachers were broad-minded Benedictines strongly influenced by the enlightenment. As Karl Viëtor says:

In the end a more positive view of the nature of man and of his role in the process of sanctification [than the Augustinian doctrine of grace] had prevailed and maintained itself in Catholic Christianity. Goethe was certainly inclined towards this [Pelagian] view, and the rigorous doctrine of orthodox Protestantism was clearly distasteful to him, but the belief in the essential and fundamental goodness of man was something he shared with all humanistic minds in the eighteenth century. That a man should think worthily of himself and feel reverence towards himself was the main principle of the new humanism. That did not make anyone into a disciple of Pelagius or a fellow-traveller of Catholicism, even if it is true that such views stand closer to the Catholic than to the Protestant tradition and practice.[14]

We are told that Stifter was a practising Catholic, one no doubt who regarded his religious duties as a matter of course, like his loyalty to the Emperor, and made no parade of either, but to judge by the way his characters behave in *Der Nachsommer*, this ideal world, the external practices of religion were not considered important by him, and his real faith was quite undogmatic. At any rate, although so many of the characters in the novel are fascinated by churches and by medieval religious art, we never hear of them attending a church service, except for the wedding of Heinrich and Natalie, priests play no part in their lives, silent grace before meals is mentioned but no other kind of prayer, and the nearest approach to the direct expression of religious feeling comes at such moments as when Heinrich contemplates the night sky at the Sternenhof on the day when he and Natalie have exchanged vows ('Die Entfaltung'), or when both, not yet acquainted, are moved to tears at a performance of *King Lear* ('Der Besuch'). The wedding service is described in two lines: 'At the church the parish priest of Rohrbach was waiting for us, we stepped in front of the altar and the wedding service was held.'

It is not surprising that people like these never speak of a future life or of any of the familiar Christian beliefs. The idea of redemption has no meaning in the absence of a sense of sin.

In the ideas of revelation, creation, providence and original sin in the church creed this doctrine [of Stifter's Benedictine teachers] saw the symbolic representation of purely rational ideals. Our duties towards God are a refinement of rational duties and man himself becomes the highest aim, the crown of being[...] Stifter is Catholic only so far as enlightened idealism allowed.[15]

Luise von Eichendorff, in spite of her deep admiration for Stifter's work, could not help remarking about *Der Nachsommer*:

There is a suggestion of heathen, anti-Christian feeling about it all, and in none of your earlier works did the contrast with those of my poor brother seem to me so marked. Yet both of you are champions of the good and beautiful, each praises God in his own way, and the songs of the nightingale and the lark, though different, both delight us equally.[16]

Instead of the hope of salvation, the inhabitants of the world of *Der Nachsommer* have before them the ideal of a truly civilized life on earth, a life fashioned to match their disciplined human desires. A spiritualized life of this kind, it seems to be conceded, is not natural but a triumph of culture, only possible in 'a few chosen circles' like those mentioned in the last paragraph of Schiller's *On the aesthetic education of man*. Stifter imagines a little enclave of harmony, untouched by the national and international, economic and social problems which beset the real world of his time. The leading figures in it have all come to despise the passions and the coarser pleasures of life, and to find lasting satisfaction only in personal relations inspired by unselfish love and a shared delight in all those forms of activity into which 'Geist' enters in some measure, so that they afford scope in varying degrees for intelligence, taste, knowledge and wisdom. Risach, thought of as a kind of Wilhelm von Humboldt, can indeed devote himself completely to the intellectual life only in old age, after many years spent in the capital in the service of the state, and Herr Drendorf only when he follows Risach into country retirement. Both have had to work like others for the freedom of their leisure hours, and only unceasing effort given to self-cultivation has opened up for them the cultural inheritance which is there for all. That both come from simple village homes is no doubt meant to suggest that the good life is not an aristocratic privilege, but they do belong to an intellectual aristocracy, and that only through their exceptional endowment and the favour of fortune. Stifter's *Der Nachsommer* is a swan-song of liberal individualism of the eighteenth century type. Stifter can still be for many a 'missionary of true culture', a 'priest of the beautiful', who continues 'to make the things of the mind attractive to a large public', yet this novel has for most of us now a strong suggestion of that 'dull gleam, that mysterious milky-way brightness', as of a distant celestial world, that Nietzsche, as we shall see, was to find in classical German literature. It is an indication of the continuing hold of that culture over him, for all his iconoclasm, and a reminder of the centrality of the idea of 'Bildung' in German thought for well over a century, that we find *Der Nachsommer* included by Nietzsche, one of its earliest admirers, along with only four other books, in what he calls 'The treasure of German prose':

If we leave aside Goethe's writings and especially *Goethe's Conversations with Eckermann*, the best German book there is, what is left of German prose literature that deserves to be read over and over again? Lichtenberg's *Aphorisms*, the first book of *Jung-Stilling's Life Story*, Adalbert Stifter's *Nachsommer* and Gottfried Keller's *Leute von Seldwyla* – and at present that is about all.[17]

146

FRIEDRICH THEODOR VISCHER:
AUCH EINER (1879)

Friedrich Theodor Vischer was a variant of a type well known to us from other more famous figures in German literature and scholarship, that of the clever Swabian boy from a Protestant background, who is selected through the *Landexamen* at fourteen for training as a potential minister of the church in Württemberg, but finds himself unable, in the end, to give full intellectual assent to its doctrines and turns to an academic or literary career. This is what would have happened to Schiller but for Karl Eugen's interference with the family's plans. Hölderlin, Hegel and Schelling were of course the outstanding *Stiftler* of this type a generation before Vischer; Mörike, who indeed became a *Pfarrer* in name but really devoted himself to poetry, was a few years senior to him and David Friedrich Strauss was his exact contemporary. The art historian Anton Springer, who knew Vischer, Strauss and several other Stiftler well during his half-year in Tübingen, praised them all for their intellectual honesty and sound scholarship, but saw in them all something of the valetudinarian. We can best see what he means by thinking of some rather similar earnest heretics in Victorian England, Carlyle, J. A. Froude, Matthew Arnold, Walter Pater – all great admirers of Goethe. What troubled them all was the feeling of homelessness in a world which, in Arnold's words, though

> So various, so beautiful so new
> Hath really neither joy, nor love, nor light,
> Nor certitude, nor peace, nor help for pain.

Nietzsche, who was fundamentally of the same kidney, had bitter and penetrating things to say of this personal culture inspired by secularized religious feeling in the volume of *Menschliches, Allzumenschliches* which appeared in the same year as *Auch Einer*, 1878. (See below, pp. 168ff.) What marked off Vischer from the other Swabians mentioned, except Schiller, whom he characteristically preferred as a man to Goethe, was that he was not so completely absorbed in the inward life, so oblivious of the world of more ordinary, normal men, as to be unconcerned about politics and the question of power.

Vischer, born in 1807 as the son of a minister who himself had gone through a *Klosterschule* and the Tübingen *Stift*, and who died in a typhus epidemic at the end of the Napoleonic wars, had four years at Blaubeuren and five at the *Stift*, the semi-monastic residential college for theological students at the University of Tübingen, with Strauss and several other very gifted class-mates. They were always writing *Knittelverse* to each other, and before leaving school Vischer had published in newspapers several imitations of modern folk ballads, about a miserly vicar who killed his illegitimate child, and similar horrors, which attracted much attention through their grim humour. He had really wanted to be a painter, it seems, and in spite of his gift of humour, experienced even at school fits of depression which resulted, as he thought later, from an inner conflict. Elements in this conflict were, beside early religious doubts and difficulties, his uncertainty about where his real talents lay, and probably that temperamental irritability about colds in the head, lost collar-studs and similar petty annoyances, about which we hear so much in *Auch Einer*. Here is Anton Springer's lively picture of him at the head of his *Stammtisch* in the inn *Neckartyrannei* when he was forty years old, and had been Professor of Aesthetics at Tübingen for three years:

The life and soul of our gatherings was Friedrich Vischer. He had just before this paid the penalty for an offence against university discipline, suspension from lecturing for a year. He felt encouraged by the new sympathy of the students following this, and invigorated by a period of quiet study. His success as teacher was greater than ever. He was still the same man in his loves and hates, but he struck a more cheerful note now in private intercourse. At our meetings Vischer regularly took the lead in the conversation, speaking himself more than anyone else and keeping us continually alert by witty sallies, spicy anecdotes and sharp satirical thrusts. Provided, that is, that he was in a good humour. Often a mere trifle was enough to put him off. If for instance the so-called chairman's requisites, the brass tool for stuffing and cleaning out pipes, or the jar full of spills, were not in their proper position, to the left of his hand, he would stay stuffy and huffy for a good quarter of an hour. He easily took a quite objective remark personally and then went for his opponent tooth and nail. To avoid unintentional offense, you had to get used in any case to his characteristically emphatic way of expressing himself and the lively fruits of his fancy.[1]

This description fits in well with what we read in *Auch Einer*, which is of course almost completely autobiographical, about the hero's behaviour amongst his regular evening companions at the inn, one of whom afterwards blames him for hogging the conversation, though what he had aimed at, we gather from remarks in his diary, was just to keep a civilized general conversation going. The interest of details like these for our present purpose is that here we have an intimate picture of a famous German professor in the golden age of the professor, and are reminded that he lived in a different atmosphere from that of an Oxford commonroom, and tended to be perhaps just a little authoritarian even at his most relaxed.

Vischer's break with theology came gradually, after he had passed both his theological examinations: the first, conducted by his university professors, brilliantly, for his point of view was not really so very different from theirs; the second, the *Dienstexamen*, two years later, after a year as *Vikar* in a small village and a further year as a kind of tutor at the Maulbronn *Klosterschule*, not so well, because the examiners were senior clergy, who wanted pedantic accuracy in details of doctrine. In the same year, 1832, he gained his doctorate in theology, and it was only now that he was able to emerge from the theological atmosphere on his *Magisterreise*, also part of the traditional training, which took him to the universities of Göttingen and Berlin in the winter term. He was still interested in nothing but metaphysics, the Hegelian system above all. He just missed the great man himself – Hegel had died in 1831 – but he heard Gans and others, and was much interested in Hotho's lectures on Goethe. The slow journey back to Tübingen in the early summer gave him further opportunities of broadening his mind, especially by visiting the art collections in Dresden and Vienna. He saw Prague too where, as in Vienna, he took a special liking to the place itself and its way of life, and in Vienna he first tasted fully the joys of the theatre, the comedies of Raimund and Nestroy, and classical tragedy at the Burg, with Sophie Schröder as Medea. His interests were shifting to the arts, and he chose the subject of 'The Sublime and the Comic' for his first piece of original work and for the disputation by which he qualified as a *Privatdozent* in 1835. Till then he made a living as coach at the Tübingen *Stift* in the congenial company of D. F. Strauss and other old friends. For two or three years now he had shared with them the Hegelian attitude to religion, according to which 'the ideas of religion represent in pictorial, symbolic form the same content as the concepts of philosophy'. Strauss with his passion for analysis had gone further, and was writing his *Life of Jesus*, bringing all the miracle stories of the New Testament under the concept of mythology. They all still held that a clergyman could with a good conscience present to his flock as literal truth what he himself understood only symbolically. They wanted, like Leibniz, Lessing, Herder and Schleiermacher, to be modern men, but not to give up what they felt to be the essential truth in Protestantism. That is why Vischer was moved so deeply by Faust's nostalgia for the beliefs of his youth in the monologue on Easter Eve. Many a modern assailed by doubt, he said in his first *Faust* lectures, will imagine that others are not tortured in this way. 'Will it not be welcome news for him to hear that German literature possesses a poem, in which these lonely sufferings of a mind in doubt form the main theme of the exposition?'

This passage shows us the spirit in which Vischer first approached the work of which he was to be one of the foremost nineteenth-century expositors, and it explains why he called a section of his early poems 'Faustian voices'. They seemed to him in his old age to express a kind of nihilism which he and others were to find again in Schopenhauer, of course much later, for although *Die Welt als Wille und Vorstellung* had been published in 1819, it had attracted no attention, and its vogue came, as we have seen, only after mid-century. This meaning of 'Faustian' was already current about 1830, as Hans Schwerte has shown, but the word was more commonly used by hostile critics of Goethe than by admirers. Vischer was by no means negligible as a creative writer. He was particularly good whenever his sense of humour was engaged, as in the youthful spoof ballads, in parts of his *Faust, der Tragödie dritter Teil*, in his comedy in Swabian dialect, *Nicht I.a.*, and in the novel *Auch Einer*. In 1835 he finally turned his back on a career as a minister and became one of the first academic interpreters of German literature, though literature was at first only part of the material, along with painting and sculpture, with which he illustrated lectures on what was styled 'Aesthetics' and was for several years dominated by Hegel's thought. Vischer gave most of his attention to working out a metaphysical basis for beauty and to making a catalogue of the aesthetic aspects of the natural world in rocks, plants and animals. He was never satisfied with this approach and finally, ten years after the first volume of his *Ästhetik*, brought out a very frank criticism of his own system. He gave up now the quest that Schiller had started, for the objective characteristics of beauty, having reached the conclusion that the beautiful is not 'an object' but 'a particular way of looking at things'. His views were of great importance for the German Realists of mid-century and for the development of the notion of 'empathy' (Einfühlung) by Theodor Lipps. Johannes Volkelt was only one of many scholars who paid tribute to the great value of his teaching for them. He was considered quite outstandingly good as a lecturer on literature in his successive posts in Tübingen, Zürich and Stuttgart, and drew large audiences everywhere. The introduction to aesthetics: *Das Schöne und die Kunst*, published from notes of his lectures in 1897, by his son, shows what he was like at his best. Fritz Schlawe in his excellent biography of Vischer (1959) says that his position in German intellectual life in his prime was often compared to that of Lessing a century earlier. He lectured and wrote well about Shakespeare, his favourite poet, as well as about the German classics, he was one of the early admirers of Hölderlin and Hebbel and Mörike, and he had a wide knowledge of art, cultivated in repeated journeys to Italy and one to Greece.

In his writings on art and literature, Vischer conveys to the reader a delicate sensibility, an infectious delight in the uniqueness of the artist or writer he is discussing – it is in this respect that his *Faust* criticism stands out in a wilderness of merely learned work – and his own creative work at its best is refreshingly individual. His weakness, as in his conversation, was to indulge too far his prejudices and personal quirks. He had shown this lack of judgment in his inaugural lecture in Tübingen in 1844, which must have created a record in leading to its author's suspension, so deeply had he offended not only the Pietists, but also the natural scientists, then still struggling for recognition. This was at the very beginning of the academic struggle between the arts and natural science. For Vischer then, the arts stood for *Geist* (spirit) and science for mere nature, the empirical, and he was all for *Geist*, like the Age of Goethe and also Hegel. Following the same tradition, he often gave the impression that for him there was

151

absolute value in humane culture, the heir to religion. In the inaugural lecture he gave offence quite early by praising even the 'arts' or accomplishments that figured then, as now, at the end of the lecture list – riding, fencing, gymnastics and dancing. He was opposed to the one-sidedly intellectual emphasis in education. He wanted scholars to walk erect, 'with chest out', and members of the senate to wear gowns and grow beards – to look more awe-inspiring. It is not surprising to find Eduard Engel writing of Vischer: 'In his external appearance as well as in his personality there was almost more of an old colonel than of a professor.' We have known a lot of professors since his time who have enjoyed wearing military uniform, but he was an exception in this respect then, as well as in the mildly democratic views which led to his being elected the representative of Reutlingen and sitting in the Frankfurt Paulskirche in 1848. He confesses in his memoirs that it was a very trying year:

I would have supported a republic if we had got so far, but what I had in mind as ultimate aim was a very stern and by no means sentimental and cosmopolitan kind of republic. Indeed of the two principles which were under discussion, that of national unity and power was much more important to me than that of personal freedom.

He wanted a union of Austria and Germany but also, as a Swabian, 'he was a strong opponent of the Prussian party in the Reichstag'. His political views come out, as we shall see, in his novel, and it throws some light on the movement away from Weimar cosmopolitanism and indifference to questions of power to note how a genuine liberal who, for most of his life, put 'Bildung' above everything and wanted all class distinctions to be abolished, could follow Fichte and Hegel in making a religion out of patriotism, and so in the end accept Bismarck as a necessary evil, and write with enthusiasm about the nation in arms, although certainly on the Swiss rather than the German model.

When Vischer, after giving many lectures on the history and theory of the novel, tried his hand at writing one in his later years – it was published when he was 71 years old – he experimented with a multiple approach in his search for a more consistent realism than German novelists had yet attempted. The narrator tells us about an odd character he meets on a journey, and about a number of episodes in this man's life, not as an omniscient story-teller, but as a chronicler communicating material as it comes into his hands, by stages. Most of it is supposed to be written by A.E., the hero, himself. There are repetitions and flashbacks, obscurities in one document which are only cleared up in another later, and difficulties caused by the use of phrases from the hero's private vocabulary, and all these obstacles seem to have been intended to intrigue an intelligent reader, though they will put off many. First we hear of the narrator's few encounters on an Italian holiday in 1865 with A.E. in person, then we read A.E.'s 'Pile-village story', sent to the narrator in manuscript. We catch another glimpse of A.E. through the narrator's eyes in 1870, when he first learns his acquaintance's name and address from the papers that fall from his pocket as he runs for a train. A year later the narrator tries to visit A.E., learns of his death and finds out what he can about him from his former friends. Finally he communicates to us the papers left to him by A.E., particularly a long diary, the entries in which are undated but clearly in chronological order.

Vischer's novel is in the tradition of the 'Bildungsroman', like *Wilhelm Meisters Lehrjahre* and *Der Nachsommer*, which he held to be still the natural type for his age. 'The novel looks for poetic vitality to the sphere into which it has withdrawn, owing to the growing aridity of public life: to small intimate groups, the family, private life, individuality, the inner life.' So Vischer had written about twenty years earlier in the sixth volume of his bulky *Ästhetik*. This seems to imply that public life would be a better or more natural source of interest for the novelist, if it were not, in Germany, so 'arid', a question-begging word, one might think. Was it really not interesting in itself, or were German writers, by long tradition, for some reason far less interested in it than their counter-parts in France, England and Russia? One comes back to Erich Auerbach's distinction in *Mimesis* between the two groups. Anyhow, Vischer had come to the conclusion in his aesthetics that 'the ultimate aim of the hero in a novel is always "Humanität" – a cultivated, humane outlook on life'. The centre of interest, that is, lies in the nature of man in general, in moral and philosophical ideas, rather than in the presentation and analysis of, for example, typical episodes in contemporary life. Until the beginnings of Naturalism, round about 1890, realism in German literature is usually confined, as Auerbach says, to historical, poetical or fantastic subjects. When it deals with the present it confines itself to circumscribed subjects, unpolitical or merely regional, or it adopts an ironical or idyllic tone, and shows us individuals or families, not social, economic and political complexes in their tragic development. Society appears as unchanging.[2] We have seen how well these remarks apply to Stifter. Vischer by 1878, we shall find, no longer keeps strictly to his theory. He admits quite a lot of comment, at least, on contemporary political events and opinions, but 'Bildung' as the modern substitute for religion is really his principal concern throughout. He expresses freely views which in his own personal experience had sometimes evoked strong criticism by masking what is largely autobiography as fiction, and further by inventing as narrator a character who is much given to comic exaggeration, and talks *ad nauseam* about his susceptibility to colds and 'die Tücke des Objekts', the apparent malice of things like banana-skins, the very old fixed ideas of Vischer himself.

A.E.'s diary, which takes up about two-thirds of the novel and more than any other section marks it out as a novel of ideas, reflects in general what had happened to Weimar idealism in an increasingly unfavourable environment, and in spite of its writer's disappointments and tragi-comical experiences, the attitude to life it suggests is still on the whole positive and optimistic. It is rooted in what A.E. calls his religion, the kind of belief still possible in the later nineteenth century for a fairly normal, clear-headed man – not one likely to be attracted certainly by Nietzsche's extremism, but one who at least tried to be strictly honest with himself. A.E. finds a psychological basis for religion in something like Schleiermacher's 'feeling of dependence':

Ask yourself every day: 'Am I the universe then?' In this way you can find your way to religion. Religion is the sacrifice of selfishness, religion is when you are shaken, crushed, softened through and through by the full force of the feeling: 'I am a mere nothing in the cosmic Whole unless I serve it.' Religion is therefore tragic joy in serving.[3]

As we shall see, this declaration has political overtones, which remind us of Fichte's conception of patriotism as religion. This notion is probably present to A.E.'s mind when he writes a little later:

No one can claim to be cultured unless he has religion! The only truly cultivating influence is religion; the most elegant of men remains a savage without it. But religion, you see, is different from what you imagine.[4]

It is revealing that the next entry runs:

The dog has something akin to religion inside him, by being a faithful servant. – It is a scandal that just because of his best quality, his name has become a term of abuse.[5]

Religion is different from what the pious think because the core of truth in Christianity has been obscured by unacceptable myths.

[Christianity] put a new soul into the world. It is the religion of warmheartedness. Its founder was a man with a free, benevolent, unclouded mind, and [he] wishes us to be loving, forgiving, good. None of the natural religions had that, it was something quite new.[6]

This is the old distinction made by Lessing and the Enlightenment between 'the religion of Christ' and 'the Christian religion'. A.E. continues:

Now this central belief soon lost its pristine simplicity, it was festooned with mythology. The founder himself believed in angels and devils, believed that he would come again as King Messiah and found the kingdom of heaven on earth. As soon as he was dead, the halo of myth expanded: miracles, resurrection, Christ becomes the son of God, his death a sacrificial death, following an old, bloodthirsty, horrifying idea of sacrifice, then Mary soon became a goddess.[7]

An objection not raised by the introverts of the age of Goethe, but highly characteristic of A.E., the ardent patriot, is that Christianity is from the beginning 'an unpolitical religion':

On top of that something very objectionable. The new world of love, the new religion, springing up in an enslaved people, knew nothing about the state and public life and didn't want to – still to-day and for all time an enormous defect in Christianity.[8]

A.E. fully realizes that for want of a religion the German masses are already in a very dangerous condition, yet they have no use for the 'pure religion' of intellectuals like himself:

The masses need and will always need a picture-book *to believe in*. However much harm the pigment may do, it is still a support. If religion goes, morality goes too. Religion with colour added better than none at all.[9]

155

The trouble is that a rapidly growing number of manual workers as well as middle-class people have become indifferent to religion of any kind. Meanwhile in the minds of the cultivated, the original 'despisers of religion' to whom Schleiermacher had made his appeal in the *Reden über Religion*, A.E. finds 'a very interesting chiaroscuro':

We have grown out of the Christian picture-world, and it has become for us a free imaginative creation like classical mythology. Yet not quite, no, we, even we, have not the same attitude to both. The former is linked for us with emotions, that have religious associations, without really being religion – a moving reminiscence of our childhood. Faust on Easter Day, – Christmas emotions, – and strongest of all: the attraction of the beauty of the Madonna ideal, of that heathen goddess whose picture moved and delighted the heart of the Middle Ages and cleansed it with a vision of all the innocence and moral goodness of true womanhood.[10]

Again one is reminded of the much smaller minority of agnostics in Victorian England, men like Matthew Arnold, A. H. Clough, T. H. Green, J. A. Symonds and Walter Pater who, in their nostalgia for faith, read Goethe with Carlyle's reverence for his enlightened spirituality, and often showed a tendency either towards ritualism or aestheticism. A.E. finds the position of the Protestant clergy even more ambiguous than his own, though he respects the intelligence and learning of his friend 'der Tetem' and admits that he has a useful role in the existing state of society:

With razor sharp logic he easily saw through the inconsistency of conceding to modern science its rights, within certain limits, and bidding it halt at those boundaries, or persuading oneself and others with fair phrases that one agreed both with science and with dogma. 'Besides,' he used to say, 'they are hypocrites really in any case, for they have to be always talking in church services and on their pastoral rounds about those very points of doctrine which they openly declare to be untenable. What good does the backdoor of symbolic meaning do them? False is false.'[11]

At times A.E. was much more caustic, called the clergy 'consecrated moral repairers' or wrote, no doubt with the *Kulturkampf* in mind:

In a proper state a clergyman would be simply a civil servant looking after popular education and traditional culture. He would lose all his magical nimbus; the nimbus always includes the notion of magic, and that is the root cause of the impossibility of peace between church and state.[12]

What then did A.E. himself believe? He was evidently what we should now call a secular humanist, like Gottfried Keller, in sympathy with the thought of L. Feuerbach and D. F. Strauss. He held firmly to Christian ethics but rejected their supernatural basis: 'Yes, if by faith we meant faith in the existence of a moral world order which we cannot strictly prove!' There are surviving traces of Hegelian thought, itself largely an elaboration of eighteenth-century convictions concerning the almost unlimited powers of 'Geist' – human intelligence, imagination, feeling and will at their highest pitch. But it is a revised form of Hegelianism, strongly influenced by contemporary science, by the Darwinian theory of evolution, no doubt, in particular, though Darwin is not mentioned by name. The result is something which, to a non-specialist, looks very like the Three-Layers-Theory in the metaphysics of the Neo-Hegelian Nicolai Hartmann, as it is advanced, for instance, in his *Problem des geistigen Seins*.[13] Man in his earliest stages, A.E. reflects, must have been very little better than one of the beasts:

Man must have fought with man furiously, like an animal, for a space to live in, for food, women, power. A struggle analogous with that through which long ago the types, the genera and species, came into existence. Through a series of dreadful experiences, lasting for an inconceivable time, this struggle must have led to the gradual emergence and establishment of legal, moral, political institutions, for instance until they realized that there must be private property, that the madness of the sexual instinct is only to be curbed by marriage. Thus a second world came into being within the world, a second nature above nature, the moral world. This is what I call, in my private philosophy, 'the second storey'. Now just as those natural types have become stable, after such long, hard processes, as if they had always been fixed, so it is too with the moral order. It rises above time from within time, it is an absolute, something true in itself (we can neglect the fact, which is a matter of indifference anyhow, that it came into being in time), consisting of eternal substances 'which hang up there, inalienable and indestructible, like the stars themselves'. They are evolving too of course, but this does not affect their essence. And the highest among these heights: the institutions, activities, which owe their existence to pity; and art and science.[14]

This belief is the source of the assertion which is made by A.E. repeatedly, like a refrain: 'The ethical is a matter of course.' His thoughts often return to the mystery of this emergence of 'Geist' from 'Natur', of the domain where 'the humane prevails against the

157

coarse, wild, angry, especially against the cruel, the bad', the realm which he must still think of as divine, with 'the dark foundation' (Jakob Böhme) always frighteningly close below.

A.E.'s humanism, in spite of the purely naturalistic theory on which it is finally based, is not of the proud type so common in his time, which deifies man as the absolute master of nature and omnicompetent director of his own affairs. It continues the tradition of Herder's kindly 'humanity', of an absorption in the inward which in A.E. himself becomes dynamic only by fits and starts, particularly at the sight of cruelty to an animal. There are two or three incidents during the narrator's early contacts with him which bring this out, and A.E. meets his death at the hands of a carter whom he has prevented from maltreating his horse. The diary stresses A.E.'s sense of dependence, but equally his capacity of losing all thought of self in the service of his ideals. Unlike Goethe, A.E. does not think of nature as a kindly mother. It is 'just as cruel as it is kind', and after his own experiences with the enchanting but merciless Goldrun in Norway, he invents a private mythology, according to which nature is the creation of a highly intelligent 'personal being' which is 'blind as well as wise, malicious as well as kind', in a word, 'a woman of genius'. Her allies, legions of evil spirits self-generated in the primeval slime, are still responsible for the 'malice of the object', by which they seek to deflect man from his higher purposes, for man was originally introduced to everything pertaining to mind and culture 'by a second, higher divinity, a male spirit of light'. This is fantastic nonsense connected with the comic *Leitmotiv* already mentioned, but behind it is not only A.E.'s memory of the humiliation suffered at the hands of Goldrun, but a mistrustful and rather bewildered attitude to women in general, and of course the scientific view of nature as 'red in tooth and claw'. It is characteristic that there are hardly any serene or idyllic pictures of landscape in the book. The most striking nature-picture is of a wild Alpine scene in a storm, when the narrator hears A.E., who reminds him here of a middle-aged Hölderlin, more virile than the poet and endowed with the humour he lacked, shouting against the wind to one whom he addresses as 'eternal God who dost not exist', a tirade full of contradictory and even cynical assertions.

This idealist in a world of science, whose antithetical view of 'nature' and 'mind' is symbolized by the two 'storeys' of his metaphysics, is much concerned too about the body-mind problem. He realizes that 'there is no mind where there is no vehicle for mind (brain)'. But he cannot imagine a vehicle for mind coming into existence 'if matter were only what we call matter'. He faces the thought of the ultimate destruction of all the world's hard won 'experience, knowledge, culture', when our planet, and even the solar system, come to an end, as it seems they must. He finds comfort in the idea, to be found in germ already in Herder, that:

These treasures have had their value in themselves. Anything that has value in itself is a source of pleasure, a blessing to us. Every man who rises to the level of the world of what is valuable in itself, in every minute while that happens, is eternal in the midst of time. How many men and for how long men thus participate in the eternal makes no difference. If on other stars there [are] beings similar to men, let them try to raise themselves into the timeless in this same way.[15]

This then is what A.E. considers the highest good for an intelligent being, to have the capacity, during his mortal life, 'to raise himself into the timeless'. He has thus a similar belief in the saving power of 'Bildung' to that expressed by Schiller in the poem 'Das Ideal und das Leben', to which we have found slightly varied parallels already, e.g. in Schleiermacher and Schopenhauer. An extension of life in time, or a second life beyond the grave, would bring no satisfaction if it did not itself include this possibility of escaping from time in the intellectual life – a thought in which Vischer refines on his predecessors. So A.E. addresses to an imaginary philistine these words:

From endless time, my friend, you will get nothing, not the slightest amusement. It will only yawn at you, and to belong to it is not better than eternal damnation.[16]

At this point A.E.'s diary abandons the mythical conception of the origin of 'the second storey', i.e. of civilization, our total stock of knowledge and values, and he reminds himself that we owe it to the unceasing efforts of countless generations of men:

The bread I eat to-day, the clothing that keeps me warm, the justice that protects me in association with many others – good men worked at these discoveries thousands and thousands of years ago.[17]

159

The continued existence of civilization depends on the prevention of any break in this continuity. If at any point in time there were no living men with minds, to keep civilization alive, there would, for instance, be no moral order in the universe, or our part of it; for nature in itself is neither good nor bad, but governed by physical laws:

> The moral world order is not outside you. It exists only through you. Believe in it, and you help – along with all good men – to make it. There the belief is the cause of what it believes. So it is with every ethical belief: what it believes, it makes.[18]

The secret of happiness, and happiness is possible and not to be despised, is work, creative work which adds no matter how little to the total stock of human culture. This is A.E.'s answer, as it would have been Schiller's, to Schopenhauerian pessimism:

> Strange: joy, he says, is only to be had in the contemplation of ideas, or in art. But he must have made his book himself, and that was work. Must he not have noticed then that work is enjoyable?[...] He is always prating about those evils against which it is surely worth while to summon up one's will. He knows nothing about pure pleasure in pure struggle.[19]

Human effort of this kind is what gives meaning not only to the life of the individual, but also to that of the world, to history. This agnostic wants us to speak of 'Nachsehung', not 'Vorsehung' (not providence but post-vidence), for it is man who must bring order into the material which nature blindly supplies:

> The whole of life, the whole of history is the utilization of chance. Chance is continually transformed into the realm of natural effect and of human thinking, willing and doing. Before, as it comes on the scene, it is blind; afterwards it becomes a mesh knotted by seeing eyes in the infinite web of activities. So really 'Nachsehung'.[20]

Among the departments of human life into which it is imperative to bring order A.E. includes political relations. Under the stimulus of events in Germany from the late 1840s on, he returns again and again to this topic. He is almost overwhelmed by the difficulties it presents, the conflicting claims of the ideals of freedom and order, his belief that many politicians act from low motives: 'If only the secret could be found of finding clean hands to administer the strict rules, the discipline which man requires!' His sympathies have always been liberal, but he fears in 1848 that the popular demand for a republic conceals anarchic tendencies. In that year, after his disastrous infatuation with Goldrun in Norway, he fights as a volunteer for the 'liberation' of Schleswig-Holstein and is wounded. Prussia's truce of Malmö with Denmark is a bitter disappointment. Later, in the early 1860s, he is elected to the Chamber of his small state, but bungles his first speech, after a fine beginning – the crucial moment comes when his voice through overstrain turns to falsetto, an example of the comic used by Vischer as early as 1838. A.E. loses his post as Chief of Police and retires into private life. In 1866 his sympathies are 'grossdeutsch' (i.e. in favour of a union of Germany and Austria) as always, and though he likes the Austrians much better than the Prussians, he has to admit that Prussian efficiency pays, much as he detests it:

Politics and private morality are indeed two different things; but the victory of a new political form built up on force, which is brought into action through a web of intrigue, must always have a demoralizing after-effect. The morality of the nation suffers a setback. It will be seen, when the new form comes into being – And yet – [21]

Similarly in 1871 he impulsively volunteers for service, but is soon disabled by an accidental fall. He rejoices at the victory of Sedan, but has fears for its moral effect:

When the day of Sedan came, he cried, visibly suppressing his soul's rejoicing: 'O dear, O dear! The Germans will not be able to stand so much happiness!' Finally he came out with this clear prophecy: 'We shall get what we want, but from making a habit of so much success we shall take a bad knock too. When the temple is built, see how quickly the crooks, money-changers and usurers will take up roomy quarters in it!'[22]

About a third of the novel is taken up by A.E.'s 'Pile-village story', which is of course meant as a further clue to its author's character. Besides being a parody of the then fashionable 'kulturgeschichtliche Novellen', short historical tales of past manners like W. H. Riehl's, or like Gustav Freytag's *Die Ahnen*, the work of academics with a gift for narrative, this story conveys the same central ideas about religion, culture, ethics and patriotism as the rest of the book. It was based on what Vischer had seen in Zürich in 1863 of the results of recent archaeological research into the history of Swiss lake dwellings, and the ideas come out particularly in the speeches made at a religious festival of the lake dwellers. The first speaker is a guest from Turik, Feridun Kallar. One thinks naturally of Gottfried Keller from Zürich, but this Kallar is an archaeologist himself, whose reflections about time and culture have been suggested by his own discoveries of still older settlements. He praises the benefits man derives from his attempts to plumb the depths of the timeless, and from the cultural achievements of his forefathers. 'Three things are our finest achievement: knowledge, activity and selfless love.' The arch-druid tries to counter these for him disturbingly liberal ideas with the accepted orthodoxy of the official religion, but a second stranger who is present, a young intellectual of those early days, attacks these dogmas vigorously, reminding his hearers of the 'Man-god' who succeeded the moon goddess they worship, and who stands for law, order, clarity or, in a word, for 'Humanität':

He is in us, he is justice, the courage which preserves peace, kindness, pity, knowledge, wisdom. He is those things. Wherever dumb instinctive animality is overcome, he is there. He also conquers time. We are clouds on the infinite sea of time, we are nothing, if we do not raise ourselves up into the rays of eternity.[23]

Arthur attacks the crudities of the old religion and urges the claims of patriotism as an essential part of religion. On the arch-druid's orders, Arthur is hurried off to prison, and he only escapes martyr-dom by the timely help of friends. The celebrations continue with songs of praise to the goddess Selinur for her powerful help against 'Pfnüffel', the perpetual colds with which the demon Gripo plagues them in their swamps. The other comic Leitmotiv of the whole novel, 'the malice of the object', is naturally also a prominent feature of the story.

Fritz Schlawe, in the most thorough and fair-minded study we have of Vischer's life and works, says that every detail in A.E.'s exper-iences and reflections can be matched in the author's own, and Ruth Heller has pointed to some of the most interesting of these corres-pondences.[24] *Auch Einer* is in spite of that a genuine novel, not an autobiography, it is a self-portrait which is an imaginative creation. It would be easy to show that by selection and by innumerable inventive touches Vischer has devised for himself a 'persona' in which he can still be recognized, but which sometimes caricatures and sometimes idealizes the man as his contemporaries knew him. There

162

are changes of accent and omissions in both portrait and setting which make this 'Dichtung' what it should be, more consistent than the literal 'Wahrheit'. This is just what makes the book so interesting as the reflection of a particular age, that the author has underlined for us the features he finds typical. A.E., the chief of police in a small provincial capital, whose real interests lie in philosophy, literature, art and travel, becomes a symbol of the educated middle class in the fifty years after Goethe's death. The gaps in his interests are as striking as their unusual range. His professional life is of little importance – he might just as well have been a bank clerk or a civil servant. But it is highly characteristic that he really lives for 'Bildung', and that his conception of 'Bildung' is what it is. It is typical too that he expresses no concern about the poor or the social movement, though he often pours scorn on the empty-headed aristocracy and the money-grubbing commercial class, who are particularly annoying to him when as 'culture philistines' – they crowd into his favourite Swiss or Italian holiday haunts and air their ignorant opinions. He would be an intolerable intellectual snob but for his sense of humour. The masses are for him a menace with their new claims, but his thoughts turn to disciplinary measures rather than to popular education. There is no romantic talk about the 'spirit of the folk' as a link with the divine, nor of nature either. In his religion, the surviving romantic features are the idea of man as 'citizen of two worlds' and that of self-sacrificial devotion to the state. Though Vischer was as a person very different from Nietzsche, much more robust and down to earth and altogether more commonplace, we shall find that they share a good deal, on the one hand in their devotion to culture as the meaning of life, and on the other in their unconscious acceptance of the prevailing views of the upper middle class in social and political matters. These two professors both feel a mixture of fear, contempt and indifference for the mass of the people and are filled with repulsion for democracy and socialism. They resent the intrusion of the half-educated commercial class into their preserves, want women to be kept in their traditional place and are lyrical in their praise of the military virtues and their exponents. Vischer is a nationalist, with some reservations, and Nietzsche a European, but what they both want is to be ruled by determined statesmen, who will make their country great.

FRIEDRICH NIETZSCHE: ALSO SPRACH
ZARATHUSTRA (1883-5)

It is clear from innumerable references in Nietzsche's works that the idea of 'Bildung' was one of his principal preoccupations at all stages of his life, though it finally grew, we shall suggest, into something that would have horrified most of the earlier writers we have considered, for it seems possible to understand the Superman and the Will to Power, the key ideas of Nietzsche's later writings, as the final development, of course in a highly individual mind and under the impact of many external forces, of the humanistic notion of 'Bildung' as self-improvement. Starting, at school, with 'classical education' in the Wolf–Schleiermacher–Humboldt tradition of the German universities after the foundation of the University of Berlin (1811), he accepts with enthusiasm in his first years at Basel Schopenhauer's version of the idea of 'Bildung', with its strong emphasis on the gulf between the masses and the man of intellect, especially the 'genius', and its almost total exclusion of humanitarian feeling and of political interests from the objects worthy of an intellectual's notice. Eager, like Fichte and Schelling before him, to communicate to his pupils not only his enthusiasm for his own subject but also his conception of the life worthy of an intellectual élite, the young professor lectures (1871-2) on 'The future of our educational institutions', and pours scorn on what passes for culture in the Germany of that day, so proud of its strength, its capitalistic expansion and its highly developed educational system, yet in his view completely lacking a national style. These unfinished lectures were only published posthumously, but the *Unzeitgemässe Betrachtungen* (Reflections out of season) of 1873-4 develop these ideas on lines which, in spite of Nietzsche's expressed indebtedness to Schopenhauer, begin to diverge markedly from his doctrine, so that the third essay, 'Schopenhauer as educator' (1874), tells us a great deal more about Nietzsche than about Schopenhauer. While continuing to ridicule the 'philistines of culture', the journalists, the pedants, the subservient civil servants turned out by German schools and universities, Nietzsche emphasizes more and more the positive aim of a genuine culture, which is, according to him, to produce great men, 'heroes', men not concerned with developing their precious personalities, while standing aside in contemplation of life, unmoved by its conflicts, but man as Schopenhauer is said here to conceive him, though the vision is really Nietzsche's own. Nietzsche has distinguished three types of man, the Rousseauist, revolting violently against the abuses of civilization in the name of nature, the man of Goethe's type, contemplative and conciliatory, rather too tame, and Schopenhauer-man, who says: 'A happy life is impossible; the highest to which a man can attain is a heroic one.'

He too wishes to know everything, but he wishes it in a different way from the man of Goethe's type, not to indulge a superior kind of effeminacy, in preserving his identity and enjoying the variety of things: he himself is the first sacrifice he makes. The heroic man despises thoughts of comfort or discomfort, of his virtues and vices, he rejects all this measuring of things by his measure; he has no hopes of himself and wishes in all things to see down to this hopeless basis. His strength lies in his power to forget himself; and if he thinks of himself at all, he measures back from his high goal to himself, and seems to see a paltry mound of slag behind and beneath him.[1]

The imagery of the last sentence is still reminiscent of Goethe's well-known letter to Lavater in September 1780 about raising the pyramid of his existence as high as possible into the air, and the one to Fritz Jacobi two years later about the 'slag' hammered out of his nature by his difficult life in Weimar. But the slag in Nietzsche's image, which may well refer back to Goethe's, suggests how negligible is the progress he has made in self-improvement, when he thinks of the sublimity of his ideal.

The next section of the essay (5) considers Schopenhauer as an educator in the light of his doctrine of the blind will to live which animates all creatures, and the escape from it which is open to some men through art: 'As long as a man clamours for life in the expectation of happiness, he has not raised his eyes above the horizon of an animal, except that he more consciously desires what a blind urge makes the animal seek'.[2] Much of human life is still led on this level, the basic natural plane, but men in society are held together by sharing one fundamental idea:

This idea is the fundamental notion of *culture*, in that this sets each of us one task only: to help on the creation of the philosopher, the artist and the saint in ourselves and outside, and so to share in the perfection of nature. For as nature needs the philosopher, so too it needs the artist, for a metaphysical purpose, namely for its own understanding of itself.[3]

Section 6 supports this interpretation by a quotation from Schopenhauer, about its being the sole task of humanity to produce great men, and expands the idea into an answer to the problem of the meaning of life. A young man should be taught to look upon himself 'as an unsuccessful work of nature, as it were, but at the same time as evidence of the highest and most wonderful intentions of this artist', a phrase which seems to echo the often quoted image from Plotinus about the statue hidden in the block of marble, but also ideas like Goethe's about the 'primeval plant'.[4] If a man thinks like this, he has acknowledged the claim of civilization, culture, upon him:

Everyone who ranges himself on its side declares by so doing: 'I see above me something higher and more humane than myself; help me, all of you, to reach it, as I will help everyone who makes the same discovery and suffers as I do from so doing: so that at last the man may again come into being who feels himself full and infinite in knowing and loving, in vision and capacity, and with all his wholeness keeps close to nature and is part of her, as judge and measure of things.'[5]

A passionately idealistic humanism, like love, Nietzsche goes on to say, is not to be taught: 'Only he who has given his heart to a great man receives in so doing his first initiation into culture', as he himself has done, we read between the lines, in his friendship with Wagner, the inspiration of his first published work, *Die Geburt der Tragödie* (The Birth of Tragedy). In the rest of the paragraph we again seem to see the idea of the Superman emerging from that of the 'Bildung' of the Age of Goethe, when Nietzsche speaks of Nature's struggle, first to advance as far as man, and then to go beyond him as he is now, so that for those whose eyes have been opened 'the men with whom we live seem like a field strewn with fragments of most precious unfinished statues, where everything cries out to us: "Come, help, complete us, put our pieces together, we long beyond measure to become whole."'

To reach the second stage of initiation into genuine 'Kultur', the aspirant must not only have these right ideas and feelings, but must proceed to action, namely to fight for culture and against customs, laws, conventions which hinder 'the creation of the genius', the goal of all his efforts. Some false tendencies which his German contemporaries pursue in the name of culture are denounced by Nietzsche in even stronger terms than in 'The future of our educational institutions'. He makes particular play with four types of selfishness masquerading as forms of high personal cultivation, 'Bildung'. There is the 'selfishness of the trader' which already, like the advertisements in our Colour Supplements, stimulated refined living for the sake of business and encouraged the notion that 'intelligence and money' or 'wealth and culture' belonged together by a kind of moral necessity, while those who quietly cultivated their intellectual interests without thought of gain were regarded as immoral cultural epicureans. There is the selfishness of the state, which sought to use universities and the whole educational system simply as a prop for existing institutions. Then there is the idea of culture as a beautiful form hiding ugly contents, a superficial elegance often borrowed from the French. 'To be cultivated now means not to let anyone see how wretched and depraved you are, how predatory in self-advancement, how insatiable in acquisition, how selfish and shameless in enjoyment.'[6] We shall find a very similar criticism of the Germany of the 'Gründerjahre', the boom years after 1871, in Theodor Fontane. Finally Nietzsche hits out at the selfishness of German scholarship and the doubtful features, listed under no fewer than thirteen headings, in the habits of the much-praised German scholar, who has always been on bad terms with 'the geniuses', men like Schopenhauer – and himself? In the two preceding *Unzeitgemässe Betrachtungen*, on 'David Strauss' and on 'Value and drawbacks of history', Nietzsche had already delivered a devastating attack on what he saw as the moribund condition of German humanistic scholarship and its irrelevance for genuine culture. The Germans were immensely well-informed, he had said, but very few had any feeling for style in art or literature. He saw their much-vaunted 'Bildung' as merely:

a sort of knowledge about culture, and a quite false and superficial knowledge at that. False and superficial because they tolerated the contradiction between life and knowledge, because they failed to see the characteristic feature of the personal culture of truly civilized peoples: that culture can only grow and blossom out of life, whereas with the Germans it is stuck on like a paper flower or poured over like an icing, and must therefore remain always deceptive and unfruitful. But the education of the young in Germany sets out from this false and unproductive conception of culture[...] Its result, taking a down-to-earth, empirical view of things, is the aesthetico-historical culture-philistine, who chatters on with shallow-rooted omniscience about state, church and art, the sensorium for a thousand kinds of second-hand feelings, the insatiable maw which does not know what genuine hunger and thirst are.[7]

Towards the end of 'Schopenhauer als Erzieher' Nietzsche says that Schopenhauer's own unorthodox education had been in many ways an ideal one for a modern philosopher. From his father he acquired independence and strength of character, and through his early travels he got to know men rather than books, and soon shed any national prejudices he might have. Nietzsche praises his cool attitude towards the state as well as towards the liberals of 1848, and shows himself to be just as little interested in current politics as Schopenhauer was, by calling it a mark of superior intelligence for anyone 'to take the state and his duties without making any fuss about them', and by declaring that 'all states are badly organized where any but statesmen need to bother their heads about politics'.

The criticism of contemporary 'Bildung' is continued with vigour in the volumes of aphorisms which Nietzsche published between the *Unzeitgemässe Betrachtungen* (1874) and *Also sprach Zarathustra* (1883–5), in the period which Nietzsche himself describes as a desert in his life, when his aim was 'the criticism of everything that is revered' and 'an attempt to reverse all valuations', a mercilessly cold re-examination of his positive beliefs and of the hero-worship which had marked his first five years at Basel. Under the influence largely of Voltaire and the French sceptics of the Enlightenment age, supplemented by contemporary 'positivism', Comte's anti-metaphysical philosophy of modern science, he tries to explain away psychologically not only religious feeling, but also the secularized forms in which, in his view, it had disguised itself in Germany. Here is an example of his technique from *Menschliches, Allzumenschliches* (Human, All-too-human):

Art acquires a soul. – Art raises its head where religions relax their grip. It takes over a number of feelings and moods created by religion, holds them to its heart and becomes itself more profound and full of soul, acquiring a quite new capacity for communicating exaltation and enthusiasm. The wealth of religious feelings, grown to a flood, breaks out repeatedly and tries to conquer new territory, but growing enlightenment has shaken the dogmas of religion and inspired deep distrust: so the feeling forced out of the religious sphere by enlightenment spills over into art, in isolated instances also into political life and even directly into scholarship. Wherever we see human efforts taking on a heightened, mysterious glow, we may suspect that ghostly terrors, the scent of incense and the shadow of the church have remained clinging to them.[8]

Like Goethe and others, Nietzsche still believed that it was for the general good if a man developed his own nature and followed his inner bent to the utmost, as he certainly did himself:

Making a whole person of oneself and keeping its highest good in view in everything one does – that takes one further than those stirrings of pity and actions undertaken for the good of others[...] Even now we wish to work for our fellow-men, but only so far as we find our own highest advantage in this work, neither more nor less. The only question is what one understands by one's advantage; it is just the immature, undeveloped, crude individual who will understand this most crudely.[9]

But his friendship with Wagner had taught him that there were great dangers in any genius cult, not least for the genius himself. For a time, such a cult might indeed be a salutary discipline for a young devotee, but not for his master:

It is at least doubtful whether the superstitious belief about genius, its privileges and special powers is of value to the genius himself if it takes root in him. In any case it is a dangerous sign if that thrill of wonder at himself comes over a man, whether it is the famous thrill of Caesar or, as here, the thrill of the genius, when the scent of sacrifice properly made only to a god penetrates to his consciousness and, overcoming his hesitations, he begins to consider himself something superhuman.[10]

The lines which follow are disturbingly prophetic; we can apply them in part to Nietzsche himself, and still more clearly to Hitler:

The gradual consequences are: the feeling of irresponsibility, of having exceptional rights, the belief that he confers a grace on those he allows to know him, mad rage at any attempt to compare him with others, or still worse, to rate him lower, or to point out faults in his work. Through ceasing to criticize himself, he loses at last one feather after another from his wings.[11]

In the second volume of *Menschliches, Allzumenschliches* the aphorisms most relevant to our inquiry are those in which Nietzsche criticizes the attitude of the German reading public of his time to their classical writers, and attempts an honest reappraisal of some of them. 'Blessed are those who have taste, even if it is only bad taste!' he cries (Aphorism 170). The trouble with his countrymen is, he thinks, that they no longer follow their own taste, as they had still done at the beginning of the century, for instance by flocking to performances of Kotzebue's very effective plays. They accept too readily what a small minority of highbrows, backed by the appeal to national pride, tell them they *ought* to enjoy, and so they become 'culture philistines'. In *Morgenröte* (The Dawn of Day), the most incisive so far of Nietzsche's critiques of accepted values, directed specifically against the moral prejudices of his time, aphorism 190 is devoted to reflections about 'the German culture that once was', the 'Bildung', that is, of the age of Goethe, when Germany first began to interest her neighbours. Now (in 1880) the Germans have shaken it off like a disease, 'and yet they did not manage to replace it by anything better than the political and nationalistic madness' of the age of Bismarck, which has made them for their neighbours more interesting still. Nietzsche now finds something false and pretentious in the moralizing idealism of Schiller, Wilhelm von Humboldt, Schleiermacher, Hegel, Schelling – he carefully excludes Goethe from the list, for he, like Schopenhauer, stood aside from these others and had his own ideas. This is how Nietzsche describes this 'Bildung':

It is a soft-hearted, good-natured, silver-gleaming idealism, with a weakness for noble poses and a noble tone of voice, a pretentious but harmless thing, inspired by the sincerest antipathy to 'cold' or 'dry' reality, to anatomy, to fulfilled passions, to any kind of philosophical abstemiousness or scepticism, but especially to the understanding of nature, unless it could be used for religious symbolism.[12]

What was it in such an emasculated and unrealistic view of life that appealed to foreigners? One thinks of Carlyle's intense admiration, or his disciple Sterling's description of the distinctive quality of the Germans as 'that they thought nobly of man'.[13] According to Nietzsche:

It was that dull gleam, that mysterious milky-way brightness, which shone around this culture. The foreigner said to himself: 'that is a very, very long way from us, beyond our seeing, hearing, understanding, enjoyment or appraisal. Yet it might be stars! Could the Germans in all secrecy have discovered a corner of the heavens and settled down there? We must try to get nearer to the Germans.'[14]

Of course the Germans were not really the first astronauts, Nietzsche concludes, and they recognize now themselves that they had merely had their heads in a cloud.

Another striking little essay – for these are now essays rather than aphorisms – is No. 207, 'Attitude of the Germans towards morality', where Nietzsche too picks out the habit of obedience as particularly characteristic of the Germans. This 'tendency to obedience' is idealized in their thought about morality, as revealed in maxims like: 'A man must have something that he can unconditionally obey.' Usually they hate to stand alone, or to improvise – 'That is why Germany uses up so many officials, so much ink.' But if he is ever forced to throw off his sluggishness 'he discovers his strength; then he becomes dangerous, angry, deep and daring, and brings to light the store of dormant energy he carries around, which no one before this (and not even he himself) had ever suspected'. We shall find Thomas Mann later saying something like this, about the Germans going berserk when they take to politics.

Even from these few quotations it is clear that although Nietzsche could still be described as a secular humanist and as fully conscious of his spiritual descent from the Enlightenment and from Goethe's Germany, his idea of 'Bildung' was becoming rather a consciousness of what separated him, and intellectually superior people like him, from the general mass, and made them indispensable as leaders, than a humanitarian sense of the oneness of mankind and the absurdity of intolerance and fanaticism. An awareness of their own intellectual distinction had of course entered into the ideas of culture entertained by many if not all of its German prophets. Many readers find it irritating in Herder and Goethe, and still more in Fichte and the Schlegels, and one unfortunate effect of Wilhelm von Humboldt's well-meaning efforts to spread 'classical culture' through his educational reforms had been to widen the gulf between the educated and the masses, as the products of higher and primary education respectively. This process had however scarcely begun when quite new opportunities began to present themselves to the German middle class, ways of raising their social standing and improving their standard of living through trade and industry, a development which quickly reduced the appeal of 'inwardness' and its values. In mid-century the German novel reader, Kohn-Bramstedt reminds us, was losing his former liking for introverted heroes like K. P. Moritz's *Anton Reiser*, and turning to authors like Freytag, Spielhagen, Auerbach and Keller, whose works 'reflect the new pride of the well-to-do middle class'.[15] Then after 1871 the traditionally liberal tendencies of this class adjusted themselves to 'the new prestige of the feudal stratum', as can be seen for instance from the pages of the family journal, the *Gartenlaube*. We shall see in Fontane's *Frau Jenny Treibel* how far this good observer thought a rich parvenu would go in devotion to the crown and flattery of the aristocracy. Sociological considerations are perhaps not quite irrelevant for the understanding of what Santayana called 'the higher snobbery' of Nietzsche.

In Frau Förster-Nietzsche's two books about her brother and in her introductions to his works she often seems to express naively the perfectly ordinary class feeling of the time, which Nietzsche's scornful paragraphs about 'Vornehmheit' (gentlemanly bearing) veil in beautiful phrases. In her introduction to *Morgenröte* for example we read:

All those movements which to-day aim at reducing or abolishing the privileges of the privileged classes were more and more violently rejected by my brother with every year that passed. In fact he considered it a reproach to the privileged that they did not insist more strictly on their rights, but shamefully renounced them almost without a struggle[...] He saw in the granting of universal suffrage not only an enormous political mistake, but above all a mistake in relation to the education of a nation.[16]

It is interesting to learn from the same source that Nietzsche always called the German officer corps 'our best German institution', because it stood for strict discipline in education and conduct. If we may believe Frau Förster-Nietzsche – and Karl Schlechta, it must be admitted, from his knowledge of her editorial methods would have us believe very little – her brother told her, on a walk in the autumn of 1885, about something he recalled from the time of his service as an ambulance man in 1870. It is a recollection which seems to throw some light on his imaginative glorification of hardness and the military virtues. His experiences with the wounded had been so heart-rending that for years he could not speak of them, but now, fifteen years later, he told her about how, one evening, 'his heart almost broken with pity', he had come to a small town and seen a cavalry regiment gallop through, 'like a shining thunder-cloud', followed by field artillery and infantry at the double, and he had felt then for the first time

that the strongest and highest will to life does not find expression in a wretched struggle for existence, but as the will to battle, the will to power and supremacy. I felt too how right it is that Wotan lays a hard heart in the breast of generals. How could they otherwise bear the immense responsibility of sending thousands to their death, in order to bring their nation and with it themselves to supreme power.[17]

Nietzsche continued to think of war in terms of glorious cavalry charges, and it is strange that one whose capacity for psychologically unmasking his contemporaries often anticipated Freudian discoveries should not have recognized in his own hysterical assertion of the virtue of hardness an over-compensation for the compassionate sensitiveness, which was in all probability his primary impulse. His reappraisal of all values in the direction of the heroically cruel may well, as Santayana suggests, have been due to the furious reaction of his imagination against reality. 'His talk about power, harshness and superb immorality was the hobby of a harmless young scholar and constitutional invalid. He did not crave in the least either wealth or empire. What he loved was solitude, nature, music, books[...] "Power" symbolizes the escape from mediocrity.'[18] It is tempting to think that for all his brilliant gifts of the intellect and imagination, Nietzsche's moral character somehow suffered an arrested development. Was it that much of the childish petulance natural enough in a clever boy, idolized after his father's early death by a whole household of women, and further encouraged perhaps by his outstanding academic successes, had survived in the grown man? Early recognition of his talent, reinforced by his friendship with Wagner, would make him peculiarly receptive to Schopenhauer's ideas about genius. So where Schleiermacher delights in discovering in himself and others ever new facets of humanity, giving the glory to God, Nietzsche emphasizes the rare emergence of the highest intelligence and cultivation, contrasts the fortunate few with the millions around them, and puts all his hope for the full realization of human possibilities on the deliberate breeding of improved types from promising existing stocks. The idea is already to be found in Schopenhauer (cf. above, p. 126) and in the age of Darwin it gained new plausibility. Though the process and its result are very vaguely conceived, the vision of the Superman is put into words with a great poet's skill in the handling of imagery, rhythm and sound, conveying Nietzsche's ecstatic joy in the child of his imagination with infectious lyrical force. The feeling at the bottom of it all is the desire to escape at least in imagination from the false and ugly world of the present, where in reality the supreme values are rapidly disintegrating and can only be re-established when the present nihilism has worked itself out, after being pushed to its logical limits.

The general drift of Nietzsche's later thought about how all values are to be re-defined is well suggested by the following passage from his unpublished writings – collected by his sister in the so-called *Der Wille zur Macht*:

There are no such things as mind [Geist], reason, thinking, consciousness, soul, will or truth: all are fictions, and unusable. It is not a question of 'subject and object', but of a particular type of animal, which only prospers given a certain relative *rightness*, and above all *regularity*, in its perceptions, so that it can capitalize experience...

The process of getting to know things [die Erkenntnis] works as a tool of power. So it is obvious that it grows with every increase in power...

The meaning of 'getting to know things': here, as with 'good' or 'beautiful', the concept is to be taken strictly and narrowly anthropocentrically and biologically. For a particular species to maintain itself and grow in power, it must, in its conception of reality, grasp so much that is calculable and constant, that a model [Schema] of its behaviour can be constructed on this basis. Survival value – not some abstract-theoretical need to avoid being deceived – stands as motive behind the development of the organs of information [Erkenntnis] ..., they develop in such a way that their observations are adequate for our survival. Putting it another way: the *measure* of our desire to get to know depends on the measure of the *will to power* of the species. A species grasps just enough reality *to become master of it, to take it into its service*.[19]

Nietzsche is here evidently feeling his way towards a replacement of the old philosophical and, as he would say, crypto-theological concepts by others based on biology, as he understands this science from what he has read about it in the age of Darwin. Man is a kind of animal, and his 'knowledge' is such information acquired from living as he finds useful for survival as a species. In Nietzsche's terminology, the desire to know is a function of the 'will to power' of the species, i.e. those with the strongest will to power learn most about the real world they inhabit, and vice-versa. Nietzsche would have liked Gilbert Ryle's phrase about 'the dogma of the ghost in the machine', but without admitting that his 'will to power' was equally a dogma, a reversal of Schopenhauer's 'will to live' idea, in that he did not find the will a tragic encumbrance, but saw in it the source of any hope he had of the eventual emergence of the Superman.

Nietzsche's thorough-going atheism and positivism did indeed involve a reversal of all the old values which made 'Bildung' now just meaningless for him, and not merely, as earlier, capable of being properly or wrongly interpreted. Speaking about 'A classical education' in *Morgenröte* (1880–1) he had deplored (aphorism 195) the waste of time at his school on classics. Together with mathematics and physics, some crumbs of knowledge about the Greeks and Romans and a lot of grammar had been forced down the pupils' throats, contrary to the first rule of education, to teach what the pupil really wants to know. They should have been shown how mathematics and the natural sciences have always been concerned with the thousands of practical problems encountered in daily life, 'at home, in the workshop, in the sky, in the landscape', and encouraged to continue this admirable work, instead of being taught that science was inferior to the humanities. Half a century before Hogben's *Mathematics for the Million* and *Science for the Citizen* Nietzsche was crying out for teaching on these lines, seeing science and mathematics as a response to social needs. But while constantly throwing doubt on the traditional notions of humane culture, Nietzsche continued for a long time, though not consistently, to express his belief in a man's power to change his own character. In *Morgenröte* again (aphorism 560) he declares that 'the immutability of character' is just a prejudice, and that we are free to cultivate like gardeners the potentialities that lie in our natures, 'the germs of anger, of pity, of reflection, of vanity' – an odd assortment! In many places, from *Die fröhliche Wissenschaft* (1882) to the last book he brought out himself, *Ecce homo* (1889) and the unpublished fragments, he reiterates the old maxim of Goethe and

175

Schleiermacher, 'Become the man you are!' In the first book mentioned, aphorism 270 reads: *What does your conscience say? –* 'Thou shalt become the one thou art.' *Ecce homo,* a kind of autobiography, has as its sub-title 'How one becomes, what one is'. From the late notes Jaspers quotes: 'Continue unceasingly to become the one you are – maker of your self! Thus you will retain the memory of your good moments and find the connection between them, the golden chain of your Self.'[20] But there are times when other trains of thought lead to aphorisms which are in plain contradiction to the belief in freedom in this sense. In his *Götzendämmerung* (Twilight of the idols) of 1888, for instance, Nietzsche has a paragraph on the 'Error of free will', in which he says: 'Men were thought of as "free" so that they could be judged and punished – so that they could become *guilty*: therefore every action had to be thought of as willed, the origin of every action as lying in consciousness.'[21] But 'we Immoralists' know that the idea of moral responsibility has been undermined by our belief in determinism, and look upon morality as contrary to nature.[22] To attack the passions, as the Church has done, is to attack life at the the roots. The passions are to be affirmed as a sign of life:

We are only fruitful at the price of being full of contradictions; we only stay young under the condition that the soul does not surrender, does not wish for peace...Nothing has become stranger to us than that goal of desire of earlier days, peace of the soul, the *Christian* goal; nothing makes us less envious than the cow morality and the greasy happiness of a good conscience. We have renounced the greatness of living if we have renounced struggle.[23]

It is a commonplace that good art often results from inner conflicts, but Nietzsche gives the idea expressed in the last lines quoted a far wider application. In one of the unclassified fragments he speaks about the impossibility of moral improvement:

We do not believe that a man becomes a different character, unless he is one already: i.e. unless, as often happens, he is a plurality of persons, at least of potential persons. In this case what you bring about is that another of his roles comes into the foreground.[24]

So once a criminal, always a criminal. The Church and the liberal humanists have overreached themselves in their efforts to raise man above the animal in himself, and in certain ways it is a mistaken effort, for: 'The strength and power of the senses, that is the essential in a sound and whole man. The splendid "animal" must be there to begin with – otherwise what sense is there in "humanizing"?'[25] Consistently with this, Nietzsche is pleased to see the military development of Europe in the 1880s, leading to more emphasis on the physical side of human nature: 'Pale-faced cringing (with mandarins in the lead, as Comte dreamed) is over. The barbarian in each of us is being affirmed, also the wild beast.'[26] This continues his famous 'blond beast' outburst in *Zur Genealogie der Moral* (1887), the affirmation of the 'Goth' and 'Vandal' in the Germans, acceptance of fear rather than disgust.[27] It is not the taming of the animal in man that we should be thinking of now, but the breeding of a higher type:

The domestication (the 'civilization') of man does not go very deep...*If* it goes deep, the immediate result is degeneracy (Type: the Christian). The 'wild' man (or in the language of morality, the *bad* man) is a return to nature – and, in a certain sense, his restoration, his *recovery* from the disease of 'civilization'...[28]

In innumerable passages like this, Nietzsche seems completely to neglect the social and intellectual inheritance of man, the fact accepted by the vast majority of modern historians and philosophers that human evolution now takes place almost entirely in the domain of thought, and of social action resulting from thought and foresight. Nietzsche relies instead on the breeding, by planned mating of good physical and mental types, of a still higher type of man, the Superman, born to be a master of his fellows:

The basic phenomenon: innumerable individuals sacrificed for the sake of a few – to make these possible. Life is not the adaptation of inner conditions to outer, but the will to power which, from within, subjects to itself more and more of the outer, and makes it part of itself.[29]

Nietzsche devotes scores of pages in the unclassified writings to descriptions of 'the great man' of the future. One example:

A great man, a man whom nature has built up and invented in the grand style. What is that? First, he has in all he does a long logic[...] Second, he is colder, harder, less given to second thoughts and free from fear of 'what people think'. If he cannot lead, he goes alone[...] Third, he does not want a 'sympathetic' heart, but servants, tools around him; in his intercourse with men, he is always intent on *making use* of them[...] He finds it in bad taste to become familiar[...] He prefers lying to telling the truth: it calls for more intelligence and will.[30]

How many, in our days, must have thought of Hitler on reading passages like this!

Surrounded as Nietzsche felt himself to be by nonentities, he is still full of hope that the future will produce these Machiavellian, infinitely resourceful men of steel, though he is far from explicit about what he expects them to do, except to assert their natural authority over the mass of men. Napoleon earns his full approval as a model, a master mind who could already conceive a united Europe.[31] Presumably Nietzsche thought of an area at least as big as Europe as the sphere of the Superman's activities. He speaks of himself and his fellow-Immoralists as 'We Europeans' from *Die fröhliche Wissenschaft* on (1882) and has no use for 'block-headed nationalism' now that the European nations have so many common interests. The economic unification of Europe 'is coming with necessity'.[32] If the Lords of the Earth are to have anyone to rule over, democracy must be allowed to continue, to keep the masses soft and docile:

I have found no reason yet to lose heart. Anyone who has kept his strong will and trained it, together with a farseeing mind, has more favorable chances than ever. For in this democratic Europe men's responsiveness to training has become very great. Men who learn easily and submit easily are the rule. The herd animal, even a very intelligent one, has been bred. Anyone who can command will find those who *must* obey: I am thinking, for instance, of Napoleon and Bismarck. The competition from strong and *stupid* wills, the greatest obstacle, is slight. Who cannot knock down these weak-willed 'objective' gentlemen, like Ranke or Renan![33]

There are indications that Nietzsche was not thinking yet of men of his own nation as the likely future Lords of the Earth. At any rate we find this jotting in his unclassified papers:

I am writing for a species of men which does not yet exist: for the 'Lords of the Earth'. In Plato's *Theages* we read: 'Every one of us would like to be lord of all men if he could, and best of all to be God.' *That* is the spirit we need. Englishmen, Americans and Russians...[34]

That Nietzsche offered heaven-sent pabulum for the S.S. or the Stahlhelm must by now be a thought that no one can repress, but before discussing the difficult and controversial question of Nietzsche's influence on his fellow-countrymen in their international relations and in their active and passive attitudes towards power, it may be helpful to remind ourselves by a few quotations of the form in which most of those who knew his work directly – far more would of course be acquainted with his ideas only in their more sensational aspect at second hand – first heard his message in *Also sprach Zarathustra*, the first part of which appeared in 1883 and the other three by 1885. However one may regard Nietzsche's teaching, this book is extremely impressive as a piece of sustained rhetoric in a great variety of poetic forms and moods. This gospel of Antichrist is by turns descriptive, lyrical, dramatic, satirical, prophetic. The imaginary modern prophet Zarathustra who voices Nietzsche's thought and feeling is clearly in many ways a counterpart to Christ, and many parallels to the New Testament suggest themselves, even in the form of the chapters and verses, modelled on Luther's Bible. Nietzsche might regard 'the theologians and everything that has the blood of theologians in its veins – our whole philosophy' as his opponents,[35] but he was inescapably one of the breed, and had all the passionate seriousness and 'arrogance', as he calls it, of a preacher of revealed truth. Though he is regarded as a German philosopher, little if any of his work is based on rational argument, and *Also sprach Zarathustra* more than any other of his writings depends for its effect not on reasoning, but on repeated and violent assertion and a direct appeal to the imagination.

Here then are a few striking passages concerned with ideas relevant to our theme, most of which are developed more fully in prose in the late writings briefly discussed above. After 'leaving his home and the lake of his home' at the age of thirty, and spending ten years in meditation in the mountains, Zarathustra returns to the plains and addresses the crowd gathered in the market-place of a town as follows:

I teach you the Superman. Man is something that must be surpassed. What have you done to surpass him?

Hitherto all creatures have created something beyond themselves: and you would be the ebb of this great tide and rather return to the beast than surpass man?

What is the ape for man? A source of laughter or painful shame. And that is what man must be for the Superman: a source of laughter or painful shame.

You have come all the way from worm to man, and much in you is still worm. Once you were apes, and man is even now more of an ape than any ape.

But whoever is the wisest among you, he too is only a clash and a cross of plant and of ghost. But do I bid you turn into ghosts or plants?

Behold, I teach you the Superman!

The Superman is the meaning of the earth. Let your will say: the Superman *shall be* the meaning of the earth!

I beseech you, my brethren, *remain faithful to the earth* and do not hearken to those who speak to you of supernatural hopes! Poisoners are they, whether they know it or not.

Despisers of life are they, moribund and poisoned themselves, and the earth is weary of them: so let them depart!

Time was when blasphemy about God was the greatest blasphemy, but God died, and with Him these blasphemers died too. To blaspheme the earth is now the most terrible thing, and to heed higher the bowels of the unknowable than the meaning of the earth.[36]

Zarathustra's heralding of the Superman is received by the crowd with indifference or ridicule, and he prophesies to them what will become of their society and of man if they continue on their present course:

When Zarathustra had spoken these words, he looked again at the people and was silent. 'There they stand, he said to his heart, there they laugh: they do not understand me, I am not the mouth for these ears.

Must one first destroy their ears, that they may learn to hear with their eyes? Must one rattle like drums and revivalists? Or do they heed only those who stammer?

They have something they are very proud of. What do they they call the thing that makes them proud? they call it culture, it marks them off from the goat-herds.

Thus they hate to hear used about them the word contempt. So their pride is what I will speak to.

Of what is most contemptible I will speak to them: and that is the *last man*.'

And thus spoke Zarathustra to the people:

The time has come for man to decide on his goal. It is time for man to plant the germ of his highest hope.

To-day his soil is still rich enough for that. But one day this soil will be poor and tame, and no high tree will ever grow out of it again.

Alas! The time is coming when man will no more shoot the arrow of his longing out beyond man, and the string of his bow will have forgotten its twang!

I say to you: you must have chaos within you, to give birth to a dancing star. I say to you: you still have chaos within you.

Alas! The time is coming, when man will give birth to no more stars. Alas! The time of the most contemptible of men is coming, who can no longer feel contempt for himself.

Behold! I show you the *last man*.

'What is love? What is creation? What is longing? What is star?' – so the last man asks, a-blinking.

The earth will have shrunk then, and on it the last man will hop around, who makes everything small. His race is inexterminable like the flea-beetle; the last man will live longest.

'We have invented happiness' – the last men say, a-blinking.

They have abandoned the regions where it was hard to live: for one needs warmth. One still loves one's neighbour and rubs up against him: for one needs warmth.

It is a sin for them to fall ill or to be mistrustful: one moves about with caution. A fool, who still stumbles over stones or men!

A little poison now and then: that gives pleasant dreams. And a big dose at last, for a pleasant death[...][37]

This is how Nietzsche sees the self-satisfied German middle class, with their pseudo-culture, their love of comfort, their moderation in all things, their disinclination for adventure and incapacity to follow an ideal. Their attenuated 'Bildung' is no longer a spur to endeavour but a social shibboleth. The only hope for man is to breed a better race. Zarathustra-Nietzsche continues in the first two parts of *Also sprach Zarathustra* to speak his mind on many topics frequently discussed in the author's other writings: Christian doctrines like the immortality of the soul, chastity, love of one's neighbour; or moral, social and political themes like friendship, marriage, war, the state; or his view of woman, the poet, the scholar or the philosopher. No logical order is apparent in the arrangement of the discourses, and they sometimes give way to prose poems like 'The song of night', 'The song of the dance', 'The song of the grave' which are purely personal.

Of the satirical chapters which abound in Part II, one of the most memorable is headed 'About the land of culture':

Too far within I flew into the future: and horror overcame me.

And when I looked around me, behold! Only time was left with me.

Then back I flew homewards – faster and faster: so I came to you, you of the present, and to the land of culture.

For the first time I brought an eye eager for you, and lively desire: with longing in my heart indeed I came.

And then what happened? Anxious as I was – I had to laugh!

Never did my eye see anything splashed over with so many colours!

I laughed and laughed, while my foot still trembled and my heart with it: 'This surely is the home of all colour-pots!' – I said.

Bedaubed with fifty colour patches on your face and limbs: so you sat there to my amazement, my contemporaries!

And with fifty glasses around you, flattering and repeating your play of colours!

Truly, you could never wear better masks, my contemporaries, than your own faces are! Who could ever – recognize you?

Scribbled all over with the symbols of the past, and these symbols painted over with new ones: In this way you have hidden yourselves well from all symbol-readers!

And even if one could try the heart and reins, how could one believe that you have any? You seem to be baked out of paint and pasted slips.

All times and peoples look out in motley array from your veils; all creeds and customs speak a motley message from your gestures.

If one took away from you veils and cloaks and colours and gestures, just about enough would be left for a decent scarecrow.[38]

So in a stream of opprobrious images the prophet returning to his native land expresses his contempt for German culture in the new Reich, when taste and style were at their lowest ebb, though information about the literature and art of the past had never been so widely diffused. It was the message that Nietzsche had begun to convey with his *Unzeitgemässe Betrachtungen*, but it comes over with a new intensity. The chapter ends with a picture of the lonely Nietzsche:

Strange sight and one for scorn are to me these men of the present, to whom my heart lately drove me; and I am driven from my father- and motherlands.

All that is left for me to love is my *children's land*, still undiscovered, in distant seas: for it I bid my sails now search and search.

Through my children I will make good my debt as child of my fathers: and through all the future make good *this* present.

Thus spoke Zarathustra.[39]

In the second half of *Also sprach Zarathustra* there is more variety, lyrical passages alternating with narrative and dialogue as Zarathustra moves about on land and sea and encounters new figures, each symbolic of some important aspect of life in contemporary Germany. Finally the prophet gains a not very reliable following of 'higher men'. At the very centre of the work, at the beginning of the third part, Nietzsche places the scene in which, with appropriately mysterious accompaniment, he proclaims what he held to be his profoundest belief, that in the Eternal Recurrence of all things, his substitute for the doctrine of immortality and the boldest expression of his affirmation of life as good (his 'Ja-sagen zum Leben'):

> Courage however is the best slayer, courage that attacks: it slays death itself, for it says: 'Was *that* life? All right! Let us have it again!'[40]

Some chapter headings are again intentional references to the Bible, for example: 'On the Mount of Olives', 'of old and new tables', 'The seven seals' and 'The last supper', although the parallelism in the content is not always clear. The central ideas, of 'immoralism', of contempt for Christianity and for the 'slave morality' behind liberal democracy and socialism, the appeal to basic instincts rather than to the intellect, the praise of adventure and living dangerously, of war as necessary and wholesome, and above all the concept of the Will to Power behind all life, and the vision of its final glorification in the emergence of a master-race of Supermen, all these are brought forward again and again in ever varying contexts.

There can be no doubt that Nietzsche was superbly gifted as a stylist. He had a mastery of expression in German which few have approached, reflecting a powerful intelligence, biting wit, poetic imagination, the keenest sense of what was relevant and effective at any moment for his purpose, great learning and a sensitive ear. Yet it is not surprising to hear from Karl Löwith that his influence has been strikingly small in England and America, 'where common sense and a rational scepticism do not allow the growth of any enthusiasm for such an extreme type of thinking'.[41] It is a very special type of thinking, proceeding from strongly felt intuitions or prejudices and an extraordinarily subtle psychological penetration into other people's thoughts. His great speciality is 'unmasking', finding hidden, and in his eyes discreditable unconscious processes behind propositions hitherto generally accepted. His great claim was of course to have unmasked Christian morality. A man who could do this, he said at the end of *Ecce Homo*, was 'a fate', 'He breaks the history of mankind in two. People live *before* him, people live *after* him' – that is, a new era begins with him, and he replaces Christ. This is the culmination (not long before his collapse in January 1889) of a tendency to megalomania which had been marked for some months, but which had been foreshadowed in the excessively self-confident tone of even his earliest writings, contrasting with his personal shyness. It may be looked upon as the harmless idiosyncrasy of a genius, though Jakob Burckhardt even in his Basel days felt that he would overreach himself, and it has to be admitted that other German geniuses in his time, above all the two he specially admired, Schopenhauer and Wagner, were not exactly modest either. What is particularly disturbing about Nietzsche is the irresponsibility of so many of his hundreds of references to national and international politics. As Löwith writes:

Nietzsche's writings have produced an intellectual climate in which certain things became possible, and it was no mere accident that they had a great appeal, as is evident from their appearance in mass editions, in the time of the Third Reich. It was no use for Nietzsche to declare that his 'Will to Power' was only meant to stimulate 'thinking', for the object of his thought was precisely the will to power, and he knew [as letters referred to by Löwith show] that as a principle the Germans would understand it very well. Anyone who speaks 'the language of world rulers' and knows himself, as Nietzsche did, to be a man of fate for Europe, cannot refrain from 'taking this fate into his hands' to prove he is what he says. The attempt to relieve Nietzsche of his historically effective guilt is therefore just as mistaken as the reverse attempt, to make him responsible for every misuse of his writings by others. Certainly Nietzsche would no more have recognized himself in Hitler than Rousseau in his admirer Robespierre, but that does not alter the fact that both prepared a revolution and opened paths to others which they themselves did not tread.[42]

It is probable, as Thomas Mann says,[43] that Nietzsche's dominant idea was that of culture, civilization, 'which is equated almost with life itself' and that, starting from Schopenhauer's thought that life is justified only as an aesthetic phenomenon, he came to see 'the goal of humanity in its highest specimens', but for one reader who can make any sense of what he himself presented as central, like the idea of eternal recurrence, there have always been thousands who took literally the *obiter dicta* in volumes 9 and 10 of the pocket edition of his works, published in 1906 under the direction of Nietzsche's sister. According to Karl Schlechta, the very well informed editor of the 3-volume edition of the works published in 1956, it is almost impossible to guess what Nietzsche himself would finally have made of the hundreds of aphorisms, scribbled by him on his walks, as they occurred to him, in well-used small note-books. It is quite certainly not what his sister produced with the help of her assistants from arbitrarily selected parts of the manuscripts, hurrying them on to get volumes together which *she* entitled 'The Will to Power'. Schlechta thinks that no systematic treatise would have emerged if Nietzsche had retained his sanity, that his genius was for aphorisms and not for logically unified works, and that in general this great mass of jottings offers no surprises to those who know Nietzsche's earlier work. It takes up five hundred pages as Schlechta prints it, in roughly chronological order, without headings or sub-divisions.

The large element of chance in the selection and presentation of Nietzsche's papers in the older editions adds to the difficulty of describing his influence, a difficulty already very great, as Jaspers says, because with all his originality he shared many basic assumptions with the educated middle class of his time, particularly the anti-democratic, authoritarian and anti-feminist ideas we have noted.[44] He added to them a new hardness and a militant atheism, and thus combined in himself attitudes not usually found in conjunction. Atheism normally went along with democratic and humanitarian sentiments such as he rejected, and the gospel of hardness and the military virtues with Christian orthodoxy and nationalism. He calls himself a European and ridicules nationalism, he criticizes contemporary German culture or lack of it in the strongest terms, yet much that he said could be used by patriotic propaganda in 1914, and still more, as we have seen, in the Third Reich. In 1914 there was a war edition 131–140,000 of *Also sprach Zarathustra* bound in field-gray, carried in their knapsacks, we are told, by thousands of young officers, which has a special four-page introduction of 'Nietzsche sayings for war and peace'. The first three (out of about a dozen) come from the so-called *Will to Power*. They praise 'robust ideals', 'hard discipline at the right time' etc., and others from earlier works and letters speak of the coming 'Classical age of war' (*Fröhliche Wissenschaft* 362), the strength and will to *inflict* great pain which 'belongs to greatness' (*Fröhliche Wissenschaft* 325), the indispensability of war to rejuvenate tiring peoples, 'German bravery' (from a letter of 1871) and so on. It is proof-positive that the notorious London bookshop advertisement about the 'Euro-Nietzschean War' was not complete nonsense.

After 1918, Nietzsche was probably more widely read in Germany than ever before. Few students can have escaped the impact of the small volumes of the popular edition, and Nietzschean ideas were passed on second-hand by innumerable writers and journalists, from Oswald Spengler with his pretentious *Downfall of the West* and Ernst Bertram with his mythopoeic study for highbrows downwards. A reliable history of Nietzsche's influence is probably still a long way off, but thoughtful people who lived through the period of the Weimar Republic and National Socialist Germany have described their own impressions. The philosopher Karl Löwith has been quoted. The sociologist Alfred Weber, the brother of Max Weber, wrote in the last year of the Second World War, and published in 1946, *Abschied von der bisherigen Geschichte*, a sketch of the general development of culture, or rather of thought about culture, from Homer to the end of the war, when power-blocks, he thought, were about to replace the free for all of numerous national states, great and small. A long chapter is devoted to an analysis of Nietzsche's share in the German catastrophe, in which Weber tries to be really honest about this dazzling figure, about whom so many in Germany had for a long time not dared to express their secret reservations.[45] It was no longer possible to be so cautious now that people saw what effects he had produced, and how 'the dictators of terror sent luxury editions of his works to each other as a comfort in their sufferings'. In some respects Nietzsche had at times been a healthy influence, Weber thought, e.g. when he told his countrymen after 1871 the bitter truth about their lack of real culture, when he praised a healthy body as the beginning of wisdom and thus encouraged, in Weber's view, the great development of sport and physical culture in Germany after 1900, and in the same period inspired notable intellectual and artistic movements. But the price paid for these benefits has been far too high, for much in Nietzsche's teaching gives undue importance to passing phases of thought, or reflects his own highly subjective fancies and phobias. His pseudo-scientific, positivistic approach to questions of value, his attempts to quantify all arguments as struggles for power – all that is very bad nineteenth-century stuff. The most disastrous consequences have flowed however from Nietzsche's twin obsessions, the fear of civilized 'domestication' and the fear of 'a revolt of the masses' and of democracy. One must be very ignorant of both the masses and 'the new middle layers', the main support of the National Socialists, to fear 'domestication', for Nietzsche's much-lauded Machiavellian 'virtues' have been only too much in evidence, along with brutal violence. The basis of Nietzsche's irrational fear of the masses was neither political nor sociological, but psychological. It was nourished by his hatred of mediocracy, his passion for intellectual distinction, for all that comes from solitary thought – combined with complete ignorance of the real masses and their problems. There is much more in Weber's second thoughts about Nietzsche, and many others later joined in the renunciation, in 1948 for instance Thomas Mann in a long essay on 'Nietzsche's philosophy in the light of recent history', one document in the history of the 'conversion of an unpolitical man' to be discussed later. Nietzsche had of course much influenced Mann's earlier thinking and became his acknowledged model for the hero of his *Doktor Faustus*. In the essay Mann found himself compelled to admit, in spite of his admiration for 'the most perfect aesthete in the history of thought' that 'If it is true that by their fruits ye shall know them, Nietzsche's case is lost.'

Of all these post-war second thoughts about Nietzsche expressed by his fellow-countrymen, the most convincing for the present writer are to be found in a short imaginary dialogue by that stalwart democrat and sound Anglist, the late Professor Levin L. Schücking. Three speakers are discussing the respective merits of classical German novels on the one hand, like *Wilhelm Meister* and *Der Nachsommer*, and great English novels like *Tom Jones* or the best of Dickens on the other, which are so much more readable because their characters are so lively and convincing. There is a lack of imagination in the Germans, one of the speakers says, which is as noticeable in real life as in fiction. They find it difficult, or rather they are unwilling, to put themselves completely in the position of others, and that is why one kind of humaneness is rather poorly developed in them. This is not the humanity associated with the idea of 'Bildung', which is concerned with raising the individual to the highest of which he is capable, but the humaneness which comes from respect for one's neighbour as a moral personality. The Germans confuse these two, as was shown when they put up posters in the First World War listing the German winners of Nobel prizes, as a rebuttal of the Allies' charge of inhumanity. This leads the speakers to the topic of true human dignity and the all too common German substitute for it, the bolstering-up of people's opinion of themselves by means of uniforms, orders and titles. Finally they come to Nietzsche, as a prophet of inhumanity, with his cult of hardness and the heroic.

In reality, some one says, this 'heroism' is more than anything else a reflection of the spirit of the Wilhelmine era, and Nietzsche's pompous banalities, coolly examined, reveal themselves as its most conventional opinions. Think of his arrogant words about the 'far-too-many', his contempt for 'plebeians', his respect for aristocratic 'distinction', his admiration of precisely the *Prussian* nobility, his lack of understanding for the moral value of manual work. That was the credo of every Prussian *Landrat* with his Junker spirit, from Tilsit to Cleve, who would tolerate no industry in the district he administered, contemptuously opposed any attempts at popular education and became lyrical about 'healthy uncouthness'. All these people, and their supporters in the higher bureaucracy and bourgeoisie, whose point of view resulted largely from Bismarck's defeat of the truly democratic Progressive Party, using the prestige of military success – all these people believed in war as a 'Stahlbad' [chalybeate spring, with suggestion of 'steeling'], scoffed at the idea of the emancipation of women, detested Socialism – just like Nietzsche. How characteristic is this philosopher's respect for everything military! Have we not known them, these university professors who, at Kaiser's Birthday celebrations, were proud to be able to march in the procession to the platform in reserve officer's uniform, instead of their doctor's gowns?

The speaker recalls finally the story (mentioned above, pp. 172ff.) of Nietzsche's having conceived the *Will to Power* at the sight of a cavalry regiment thundering by, and another sees in this episode Nietzsche's habit of making up for a deeply felt weakness in himself by a theoretical protestation of strength. Then the third speaker (a literary historian, the author himself) comes in with penetrating remarks about the aestheticism which reveals itself in Nietzsche's perverse equation of morality and power:

How closely related his doctrine of the Superman and his whole attitude to his time are for example to Gautier's complete rejection of contemporary morality and culture, Baudelaire's hatred of democracies and utilitarians, Flaubert's revulsion against the conception of human happiness which others formed as a matter of course. He shares with this school that itch to be perpetually challenging natural feeling in a showy way which is called 'épater le bourgeois'. If anyone once begins to see what Baudelaire calls 'Les fleurs du mal', their colours cannot of course be made too gaudy.

Finally a parallel is drawn with Swinburne's aesthetic ravings, his praise of Roman sadism for example in *Dolores*. But there is this difference:

In other countries playing with immorality was a literary game. Swinburne's most wonderful rhythms have never made anyone worse than he was, but only pleased the sense of harmony and enriched the imagination. In France the 1870 war already put an end to the *l'art pour l'art* obsession. But poor Germany has let herself be talked into taking this doctrine as a political gospel, and with war cries like 'Live dangerously!' borrowed from it, has thrown herself upon her neighbours...So in Nietzsche's philosophy the long vanished aesthetic movement, one might say, despatched a Parthian shaft into the heart of Europe.[46]

THEODOR FONTANE: FRAU

JENNY TREIBEL (1892)

Theodor Fontane has come to be regarded, rather late, as a European novelist, both in the extent of the recognition which has been accorded to him and in the now general appreciation of European as well as German qualities in his novels. He put new life into the traditional German 'Bildungsroman' by introducing features characteristic of the work of great French, English and Russian writers in the historical and social novel. He is above all the novelist of the new Germany after 1871, the Second Reich. He has drawn for us convincing pictures of a whole range of social types, from the landed and court aristocracy of Prussia, through the officer class and higher civil service, the Protestant clergy, doctors, teachers and the 'free professions' – writers, actors, musicians – to the commercial and industrial bourgeoisie, now growing rapidly in wealth and influence in a period of unprecedented economic expansion. The lower middle class serving the daily needs of the bourgeoisie in the towns, their servants, shopkeepers and craftsmen, and of the country nobility, their estate managers and agricultural workers, also play some part, but we see hardly anything in Fontane of the urban working class and of its already serious social problems. He prefers to draw people of some education, and it is a striking feature of the social criticism usually implied in his descriptions that it so often questions the real value of current educational methods and examinations, and even of the hallowed idea of 'Bildung', diluted and externalized as it now is.[1]

Intelligent and sensible characters in the novels are often made to express views similar to those we find in frequent references in Fontane's letters to the defects of the so-called educated classes. In his later years he repeatedly deplores, in the published letters to his wife and daughter, and particularly in those to his like-minded friend Friedländer, the changes which seem to him to have taken place in German society since what looks to him now like the golden age of the 1830s, when the humane values of Goethe's age were still recognizably dominant in the life and character of thousands of individual citizens, especially in the aristocracy and among professors and clergy. There are no people left like that, at the time of writing, though the country is of course far better off materially. 'They are all after the external', money and titles, but a true aristocracy of mind and heart is scarcer than ever, however much people indulge in self-congratulation.

Not just in Berlin, but in everything connected with Prussia you find the belief that we are something very special. But at the moment the very opposite is still true. In everything we are second-class, and sometimes even third or fourth. We have two things, elementary education and the army, in which we are probably number one, but not by so big a margin as we imagine.[2]

Again and again Fontane expresses privately opinions about Germany's lack of a genuine culture which remind us of Nietzsche, except that they are pitched in a much lower key. He finds especially among higher civil servants a lack of feeling for the finer things of life which makes them poor company, excellent as they are in many respects:

They know half a dozen odes of Horace, a bit of Homer and a bit of Ovid, and with this behind them they claim the right to look upon any modern efforts in this field (of literature) as twaddle. These superior people, who flood and penetrate our lives with their very limited views (and knowledge) about matters of taste, are one of the main causes that make the nations that are after all more civilized look down upon us – and hate us.[3]

Fontane blames above all a more than Chinese reliance on the examination system for most of these wrong ideas. 'A man passes three or seven examinations, and now he not only knows everything, but can do everything.' But abstract knowledge is no substitute for practical experience. 'Everyone thinks he is cut out for a really big job and he can't do the most elementary things.'[4] Moreover these well-attested products of the educational machine are so dull and uninteresting. 'When there was no education, everyone was interesting; the rapidly increasing woodenness of people dates from the introduction of examinations, and we are the most boring of countries because we are the country of examinations.'[5]

All this comes out in German writing, Fontane says elsewhere. Many kinds of people who have led interesting lives, 'ship's captains, rakes, clergymen', can write novels about them, but not professors.[6] In fact the general level of writing is low, that is, few German authors can make a subject interesting for the general reader: 'Our books, and this applies to scholarly works as well, are not as good as those of other civilized nations.'[7] Or more generally: 'I am coming to see more and more clearly that the merely "educated man", if he has nothing else, is really one of the dullest of God's creatures.'[8] This comes to very much the same as A. N. Whitehead's description, in his essay on *Education*, of the 'merely well-informed man' as 'the most useless bore on God's earth'. Fontane finds Berlin (in 1894) full of such bores. 'Education' (Bildung), he concludes, 'is something splendid; but what counts as education with us is something thoroughly second-rate and even downright silly.'[9] The main reason why Fontane has a weakness for the nobility of the Mark Brandenburg is that there are still original, four-square personalities among them, like Colonel Stechlin in his novel *Der Stechlin*. He admits that too many of them have very little education, and that they are as selfish as any other class. Especially in his last years he said very hard things about them to his intimates, though his *bête noire* remained a certain type of Protestant clergyman:

I am getting more and more disenchanted with my much beloved nobility, sad figures, offensively unpleasant egoists, incredibly narrow-minded, for dirty tricks only beaten by the fawning parsons (who always come out top).[10]

If Fontane in his later years, when he was writing his novels, called his rather ambivalent attitude towards the country nobility 'at best an unhappy love-affair', he never had any doubts about his dislike for the new bourgeoisie, the increasingly large and prosperous middle class of manufacturers and merchants of the second half of the nineteenth century, whose progress was spectacular in the 'Gründerjahre', the years immediately following the Franco-Prussian War, when Germany was a speculator's paradise. Fontane writes to his daughter:

I hate everything bourgeois as if I were a sworn social-democrat. 'He is a donkey, but his father has a corner-house' is a form of admiration in which I can no longer join. We rank ourselves now above the Chinese, but in one respect they are after all the most cultivated of peoples, in that knowledge is what they rate highest. With us one can almost say that it brings discredit.[11]

This money-worship was worst of course in large towns, and worst of all in Berlin. It was not confined to the business world:

The bourgeois, as I see him, is not really, or at least not exclusively, rooted in his money-bag. A lot of people, Privy Councillors, professors and clergymen among them, people who have no money-bag, or a very small one, have all the same a money-bag attitude, and see themselves therefore in the enviable, or perhaps not so enviable position of being able at any time to compete with a bourgeois of the first water. They all pretend 'to have ideals', they talk a lot of twaddle about 'the beautiful, the good and the true', and yet they only kneel to the golden calf, either by actually paying court to anyone with money and property, or by being consumed inwardly by longing for these things.[12]

It is an exactly similar impression of the triumph of commercialism, accompanied by lip-service to the old ideals, that we gain from Fontane's novels, where the same contrast as in the letters is drawn between the pretentious way of life of the rich and modish and the simple-hearted naturalness of many lower middle-class and provincial families. This contrast is the main point for instance of the story *Irrungen, Wirrungen*, in which an impoverished but extravagant young nobleman and officer, after a very happy affair with a charming young girl of the people, an affair into which both had entered with their eyes open, marries under social and financial pressure from his family a gay little empty-headed creature from his own class, whose money will solve many problems. As usual, Fontane makes his characters accept 'life with its seriousness and its claims', but Botho sees clearly that Lene, his first love, has far more natural ability, strength of character and spontaneity than anyone in his own circle. 'Everything she said had character and depth of feeling. Poor education [Bildung], how far you lag behind!', he says to himself. Another example, among many that could be mentioned, of the characters in Fontane who prefer a fortunate natural disposition to any amount of 'Bildung', is to be found in the conversation between two young officers in *Der Stechlin*, when Czako comments on the social success of some South German friends, 'not because of their culture, but because of their happy natural disposition', and adds 'and this natural disposition is surely true culture'. We see what this means from the picture Fontane draws of old Dubslav von Stechlin, one of these unaffected natural gentlemen whom Fontane admires.

The novel in which Fontane makes false pretensions to culture his main theme is *Frau Jenny Treibel*, where his bugbear, the rich bourgeois, is made to appear ridiculous and inconsistent, but still human, not like the incredible monsters in Heinrich Mann's satires. Fontane begins to build up the contrast between two typical Berlin families, the Treibels and the Schmidts, from the first chapter, where we see Jenny, middle-aged and no longer slim, driving up, with her lady companion beside her, to the Schmidts' newly painted but old-fashioned house in the Adlerstrasse in the heart of Berlin, near the Royal Mint. She is referred to as 'Kommerzienrätin', which means that her husband has been given the title of 'Commercial Councillor', as a prominent industrialist, but as she enters the house she is filled with memories of her early days. She sees herself making paper-bags for her father in the grocer's shop on the other side of this same street, already admired by their apprentice but conscious that she is not for the likes of him. The housekeeper admits her and takes her into the sitting room, where the portraits of Professor Schmidt's parents look down from the wall behind the sofa. Schmidt has the title of Professor as a senior master in a Gymnasium, and the author's short description of the portraits tell us indirectly that his parents had already been 'cultured people', the mother from a good country family and the father a civil servant with a decoration, the Red Eagle Order. Frau Treibel is made to tell us that he had the charming manners of someone from the old French colony in Berlin – Fontane's own background. Her mind is still full of old memories, and she begins to talk to Corinna about the time, forty years back, when she had already known this room, as a pretty young girl with chestnut-brown curls, who had had poems addressed to her by Corinna's father, then a student. She still had a little book of them, now handsomely rebound, and sentimentalizes over them sometimes in secret. We hear later that in the music with which her parties usually end, the obligato finale is always Jenny's rendering, in her reedy little voice, of one of these love-songs. 'O to be young!' she sighs. 'My dear Corinna, you have no idea what a treasure youth is, and how its pure feelings, still untroubled by any rough breath, are the best thing we have, and remain so.'

'Yes, youth is good', Corinna replies, laughing. 'But to be a 'Kommerzienrätin' is good too, and really still better. Give me a landau and a villa in a big garden! I am all for youth, but for youth with luxuries and nice parties.' We have now had a hint of the main foundations of the story. It would have been dull and unconvincing to present the bourgeois and the cultivated families as simple opposites in every respect – there must be inconsistencies on both sides which can be the germ of complications in their relationship. So Frau Jenny must be given her self-proclaimed love of poetry and music and be made to profess the warmest attachment to the relatively poor but cultivated Schmidts, while Corinna, though in most respects she is her father's daughter, is inclined to rebel against his austerity, and to wish for a little more excitement and luxury in her life. She is the only child of a father who, kind as he is, expects the attentions due to a German father whose wife has apparently died in the child's infancy. As one of the younger generation in the 1880s, in the new Germany of the Second Reich, she shares, naturally enough, some of the 'hankering after luxury which takes hold of everyone now-a-days', as she says later to her cousin Marcell. Of course it is immediately obvious that Frau Jenny is a complete hypocrite, that her love of poetry is superficial and sentimental, and that there is no limit to her desire for social position and all that money can buy. Corinna's father arrives home just in time to have a word with his old friend. Struck by the fashionable new word 'unentwegt' (a Swiss dialect word, perhaps from Keller, just taken up by journalists in the early 1880s) which she uses in taking her leave, he is reminded how little she has changed inwardly in forty years, and sums up her character in the following reflections:

She was fond of the sentimental in those days already, but always gave priority to flirtations and whipped cream. Now she has grown plump and almost cultured, or at least what people are accustomed to calling cultured, and Adolar Krola sings to her arias from Lohengrin and Tannhäuser – for those will be her favourite operas, I think.

Her mother, Frau Bürstenbinder, had proved quite right in her calculations when she took so much trouble to make a pretty little doll of her. 'Now the wee doll is a "Kommerzienrätin" and can afford anything, the ideal too, and even "unentwegt" [unswervingly]. A fine specimen of a bourgeoise.' We learn later that Herr Schmidt had really been in love with Jenny in his student days and considered himself engaged, but she had continued to look for someone with better prospects until Herr Treibel came along.

How deep Corinna's 'hankering after luxury' goes we only learn in the course of the action, which turns, as in family novels by the score, on the attractive young heroine's choice of a husband. The alternatives are, first, to accept her cousin Marcell, an only too obvious possibility, because they have known and liked each other since childhood, and he is favoured both by her father and Frau Schmolke, the housekeeper, a policeman's widow with a heart of gold, whose motherly advice Corinna respects. Marcell is a quiet, sensible young scholar of the genuine 'Schmidt' quality, a promising archaeologist, at present only a teacher of literature at a girls' high school, because in those days young men who aspired to a university career had to maintain themselves by hook or by crook after taking their doctorate, while waiting for the chance to become a 'Privatdozent' through the favour of some professor. The other alternative is Leopold Treibel, Jenny's rather sheepish younger son. He and Corinna are both twenty-five, but Leopold feels himself to be still treated like a child by his family and admires Corinna's independence – partly the result of her living alone with her original, unworldly father – as well as her interesting talk and her freshness of outlook. With a little encouragement he would be quite ready to fall in love with her, in the hope of escaping from what he knows his family to be planning for him. Corinna sees him as quiet and gentlemanly, and plays with the thought of marrying him simply for the 'luxury' he could offer her.

This conventional plot is merely the thread which links together Fontane's fascinating studies of the two families and their very different systems of values, against the background of Imperial Germany while the old Emperor, Wilhelm I, who died in 1888, is still on the throne. We are reminded of the time by little details now and then, the mention of Wagner's operas, for instance, or Schliemann's book on Mycenae (a little too early really, published in 1877), or the fact that the Treibels' villa, built soon after 1870, is sixteen years old. As usual, Fontane makes focal points out of particular social gatherings, here a dinner party and an excursion, which assemble the leading figures and give him opportunities for characterization through conversation. Not only the talk however, but all kinds of descriptive details too, help to introduce us to the Treibels at their dinner-party. There is first the villa, already mentioned by Corinna. It is in the Köpnicker Strasse, which ran eastwards, almost parallel with the Spree, from near the central island formed by Berlin's waterways. In the space between road and river there had originally been only a few factories, like Herr Treibel's dye-works, making Prussian blue, but in the years of expansion after 1871 the Treibels were no longer satisfied with their nice old house in the Alte Jakobstrasse, close to the town end of the Köpnicker Strasse, and moved out to the suburbs – like the merchant Herr Drendorf in *Der Nachsommer*, and thousands in real life in all big towns. They had not gone as far as to the fashionable Berlin West where Frau von Ziegenhals lives, for instance, one of the two ladies from court circles who honour the party, but just to the vacant plot between the road and the factory, from which, in spite of the big garden behind the villa, an offensive smell comes whenever the wind is in the north. Another drawback, in Jenny's view, is that there is no tradesman's entrance. A German villa is just a modern family house, as opposed to a flat, and here there must be several villas in a row, with insufficient space between them for a path to the back door. From later remarks we find that there are other houses on the opposite side of the street. The characteristic details in Fontane's descriptions often need a commentary like this to produce now the effect he intended.

In Herr Treibel's reflections before his guests arrive and his conversation at the dinner, he appears in a not unsympathetic light. To become a leading industrialist and gain a title he must have had energy and good judgment, and we learn now of his further ambitions, to enter the Reichstag, first for a remote constituency and then for one in Berlin, and so to make himself eligible for a General Consulate, perhaps, and a higher title – the *Kronenorden* is mentioned. The various 'orders' correspond of course roughly for Germany to our birthday honours, but they are bewildering in their variety at this time, because each of the greater German states – and many not so great – still had their own. Herr Treibel does not, like his wife, lay claim to high ideals, but there is nothing to suggest that he is not quite a decent fellow. He enjoys lively conversation over a good meal, with cigars and liqueurs and smoking-room stories afterwards, and though he has to keep doubtful political company to gain his ends, he at least expresses his dislike of Vogelsang's fanaticism in words which might have come from Fontane's letters: 'A reasonably sensible individual finds it really impossible to be fanatical.' Vogelsang, the comic turn of the party, is an army man, who must have been retired, by all appearances, for about thirty years, but turns up in uniform with sword and helmet, bearing himself with extraordinary stiffness and gravity. He is a political agent for the Conservatives, who is to help to put Treibel into a seat. The two old ladies of good family who are invited, one very fat and the other thin, with names that would have fitted their appearance better if they had exchanged them, are also caricatures, but their presence indicates Treibel's wish to keep in with the Conservatives and emphasizes his devotion to the monarch. In conversation with the expansive Frau von Ziegenhals, who cannot understand why, as a manufacturer, he is not a progressive, interested in local politics and the possibility of becoming mayor of the city, Treibel explains, after agreeing with her disparaging remarks about Lieutenant Vogelsang, that he expects his conservatism to be rewarded eventually with a higher title, and that it is anyhow more compatible than any other political label with his particular line of business, for the manufacture of Prussian blue for uniforms had of course enjoyed special royal favour since early in the preceding century: 'In Berlin Blue you have the Prussian, in symbolic form, so to speak to the nth.'

Frau Jenny as hostess had opened the conversation at table by asking Fräulein von Bomst, a former lady-in-waiting living in a grace and favour flat at Charlottenburg, about the young Princess Anisettchen, and having thus proclaimed her interest in the court and the royal family, she had soon turned the conversation to her pet subject, poetry. Not allowing herself to be deterred by Vogelsang's fierce rejection of one of her early favourites, the 1848 poet Herwegh, and in fact of poetry in general, with its 'outdated positions', she had countered his declaration that the world belongs to prose with an impassioned defence of poetry and the ideal:

All is vanity, and most of all, the things that everybody makes for so greedily, external possessions, capital, gold...I for my part am true to the ideal and will never renounce it. And I find the ideal in its purest form in the 'lied', especially in the lied that is sung. For music raises it to a still higher sphere. Am I right, dear Krola?

she asks, turning to her neighbour on the other side, an opera singer who had married a rich wife shortly before his retirement and was a little embarrassed by the question, but politely assured her that he had never known her wrong.

Meanwhile at the lower end of the table the other ambiguous figure in the story, Corinna, with a captive audience of three young gentlemen, is in splendid form, self-assured and well-informed on any subject that is broached. She makes a great fuss of the young Liverpool business man, Mr Nelson, who is returning a visit to Liverpool of the Treibels' elder son Otto, and being entertained by Otto's parents because it is their daughter-in-law Helene's ironing day – households then had huge stores of linen, it will be remembered, and washing-days might be a month or two apart. Corinna shows that she not only knows far more than Mr Nelson about his famous namesake and the Battle of the Nile, but that she can if necessary maintain the reputation of her sex in Germany for 'womanliness' by her invisible mending, a skill she has acquired at the handicrafts centre, the 'Lette-Verein'. As Marcell does not fail to point out to his cousin as they are walking home to the Adlerstrasse, she had really been displaying her cultivation and charm for the benefit of Leopold, who had listened to her spell-bound. Marcell cannot believe that she will really throw herself away on such a nonentity 'just to live in a villa and have a landau', but she seems unrepentant.

While the Treibels are giving their grand dinner party, Professor Schmidt is having his regular 'evening', a stag-party for a few colleagues from various schools in Berlin, not including his own, with its proud name, The Holy Ghost Gymnasium – more significant for German ideas of 'Bildung' if we translate 'heiliger Geist' as 'sacred intellect'. It is a kind of club, with only seven members, who call themselves 'The seven sages of Greece' and meet weekly in each others' homes. Usually someone reads a learned paper, to a rather inattentive audience, because every listener except Friedeberg, a mere art-master, thinks he could have treated the subject at least as well himself. This time there is no paper, but some very good talk, mostly by Schmidt himself who, besides a great fund of knowledge and wide interests, has a gift for humour with a bite in it that spares no one, not even himself. So here we listen to a group of people whose

'Bildung' cannot be doubted, for they are professionals at it, the guides of youth, and we learn a good deal about the culture of the age and problems arising from it. There is first some ironical talk about absent members, for no one really takes their meetings as seriously as all pretend, and theatre visits and the standing engagements which several of them had to play 'Skat', the popular card game, with a couple of friends, come first with them. Discussing one absent member's alleged difficulties with discipline, in school and with his wife, the retired headmaster Distelkamp, the senior member, says that the present generation of teachers isn't a patch on the last, when everyone could put the fear of God into his pupils. Schmidt thinks they were a lot of pompous boozers, and he is very critical of their scholarship after looking through old 'school programmes' containing their public lectures – on a subject like 'The horticulture of Paradise', for example, by a gardening enthusiast. What is in dispute is the old idea, going back to Wilhelm von Humboldt's day, that the Gymnasium master should be a productive scholar. According to Distelkamp, masters no longer believe in themselves and in what they are doing, so they have no authority. But Schmidt insists that many are better scholars than any of their predecessors, though they may not keep to the old traditions. With the new interest in archaeology, for instance, the study of the classics is changing its content. He produces in evidence Schliemann's recent report on his discoveries at Mycenae, without impressing Distelkamp, however, who cannot believe that a self-taught man is reliable in such researches. Their argument about the gold masks is interrupted by the late arrival of Friedeberg, and they are soon summoned by Frau Schmolke to the traditional meal of Oder crayfish, washed down by Trarbach wine. Everything is homely and informal, in contrast to the Treibels' party, and the sitting room where Frau Jenny had been received serves as dining room too, because there is no separate one in the flat.

Conversation goes on without a pause, and they are just discussing the value of characteristic details in history, from the literary point of view, when Corinna and Marcell arrive back from their dinner. Corinna soon goes to bed, but Marcell drinks a glass with his uncle's guests, and when they take their leave promptly at eleven o'clock he stays behind to ask his uncle's advice. He tells him about Corinna's behaviour at the party and about her declared intention to marry

Leopold if she gets the chance, but Schmidt comforts him by relating his own experiences with Jenny Bürstenbinder long ago, which have left him in no doubt about *her* character and about how she will react to any suggestion of a marriage between Leopold and Corinna:

> She is a dangerous person, and all the more dangerous because she doesn't fully realize it herself and honestly imagines that she has a feeling heart and above all a heart 'for higher things'. But she has only a heart for the ponderables, for everything that turns the scale and bears interest, and it will take a good half million to persuade her to let Leopold go, no matter where the half million comes from...The more of a court flavour there is about it, the better. They go in for liberal and sentimental talk the whole time, but all that is a farce. When they have to show their colours, then you'll hear: gold is trumps and nothing else.

In short, Jenny and her husband conform exactly to the bourgeois type described by Fontane in his autobiographical *Zwischen Zwanzig und Dreissig*. (See above, p. 193.)

For our present purpose, to find out what importance Fontane still attached to the old idea of 'Bildung' for life in his day, it is not necessary to discuss the rest of the novel in detail. The plot is worked out following a symmetrical ground-plan, the general nature of which is already clear. What looks like sheer hypocrisy on Jenny's part, the incompatibility between her enthusiasm for the 'Ideal', for poetry and music and 'culture' as the only things worth living for, and her even more evident craving for money, showy possessions and social esteem, for Schopenhauer's 'What a man is thought of' in every form, is rather more complicated, as Schmidt made clear in the passage just quoted. She is an unconscious hypocrite, who really thinks herself an idealist and can never resist the temptations of Mammon. In a series of situations, all resulting more or less directly from what happened at the dinner, the Treibels and the Schmidts reveal to us more fully the interacting motives by which we have already seen them to be governed, and though we know roughly what to expect, Fontane maintains our interest by repeated surprises.

First we see the Treibels at breakfast on the morning after the dinner, and learn that Helene, Otto's wife, would like to see her younger sister, another pretty Hamburg girl, married to Leopold, but that Jenny doesn't want any more of that clan, with their annoying wish to be taken for English, coming into her family, and that anyhow she has higher aims for Leopold, though she finds him unfortunately, like Otto, terribly sleepy and unenterprising. She half wishes he would fall passionately in love with someone, imagining him, in her romantic way, running off with a baroness, but Herr Treibel says he hasn't it in him to do that, and is more likely to be the victim of some poor young gentlewoman of advanced ideas, 'who of course might even be called Schmidt'. Even this perhaps accidental mention of the name does not make Jenny suspect what is coming, yet at this very moment Leopold's thoughts are all on Corinna, and he is nerving himself to propose to her as a first step, knowing well that there will be trouble at home. Trying hard to be a sportsman to please his mother, in spite of being turned down by the cavalry regiment in which he had wanted to do his year's service, he does an hour's quiet riding early every morning, along the Spree to Treptow for breakfast, taking the coffee that he likes and the glass of milk that Jenny insists on. To complete the exposition, we have already been shown Otto and Helene, also at breakfast and discussing Jenny's reluctance to invite Hildegard, the sister. We hear Helene nagging her husband in the 'terribly cultivated way' her father-in-law speaks of later, and asking: 'Who are the Treibels anyhow to be so stuck up?'

Nothing happens for a week, except that Vogelsang begins a disastrous campaign for Treibel in the provincial constituency. Then the second social event, the trip to Halensee, quickly leads to the climax of the story. The coffee-party at the Halensee restaurant is the idea of the young ladies who had sung at the dinner party, the Felgentreu sisters, and it reunites many who had been present, the Treibels, the Schmidts (Herr Schmidt too this time) and the singers, augmented by a male quartet, friends of Krola, whose voices later ring out through the Grunewald woods. It is interesting to see how naturally music, now not strictly 'Hausmusik' but at least partly professional, is still associated with social occasions. Schmidt and Jenny, Leopold and Corinna take the path on one side of the lake on the evening walk to Grunewald which follows the coffee-party, and the rest take the other, so that we have an old and a young pair of lovers (or former lovers) associated and contrasted, as in the garden scene in *Faust*, and Jenny is given one more opportunity to air her devotion to the ideal before her sincerity is finally put to the test. It is in her conversation with Schmidt on the topic which is always coming up, how to find a wife for Leopold. She rejects vehemently the notion that there is anything that can be called 'a matter of course' about his marrying Hildegard, and in her list of possible types for him, all of course more 'cultured' than Hildegard, there is a clear echo of Corinna's own mischievous suggestions to her in chapter I, with significant slight changes. Corinna had pictured the ideal daughter-in-law as a charming young person, perhaps an actress or painter, or a pastor's or professor's daughter, and this last sly stroke had raised just a flutter of alarm, quickly allayed by Corinna's innocent air. Now to Herr Schmidt Jenny mentions as desirable alternatives to Hildegard 'a baroness or the daughter of a Privy Councillor or Principal Court Preacher', that is a girl, if not from the nobility, her highest dream, at least from a family combining high culture with distinguished social position. But while she is saying this, the moment of decision has been reached by the younger couple, now well ahead on the path, and Leopold is brought to the point of proposing by Corinna's ingenious strategem of claiming prophetic powers and pretending to foresee a grand marriage taking place between him and Hildegard.

Infected temporarily by Corinna's self-confidence, the infatuated boy (for so we think of him, although he is twenty-five) faces his mother, as soon as they are home, with the truth, and she of course furiously refuses to contemplate such a marriage. Her husband, on the other hand, when he hears, is at first rather amused and pleased to find that Leopold is after all 'such a young devil'. As the kind and sensible person he is by nature, he is genuinely put out by her talk of 'ingratitude and scandal and disgrace', and warns her not to make herself ridiculous by her arrogance: 'We are not the Bismarcks or the Arnims or any other noble family from the Mark Brandenburg, we are the Treibels, prussiate of potash and green vitriol, and you are a former Miss Bürstenbinder from the Adlerstrasse'. But a little reflection in solitude brings him round to Jenny's way of thinking, as she had foreseen, because he was after all the product of three generations of manufacturers, growing richer all the time, and in spite of his personal intelligence and kindness, 'the bourgeois was deep in his blood, as in that of his sentimental wife'. Early next morning Jenny, now completely reconciled with Helene, writes the long-delayed invitation to Hildegard, who comes at once and is met at the station by Leopold. Before the invention of the telephone, post offices in Berlin were connected by a pneumatic dispatch system for conveying express letters along thin tubes, and after writing her letter to Hamburg, Jenny sends a note to Herr Schmidt by this 'tube post', saying she would like to see him. He receives her later that morning with his usual amused irony. She complains to him bitterly of a premeditated 'assault' on her son by Corinna, and soon the two female protagonists are brought face to face. It is almost a parody of the meeting of the queens in *Maria Stuart* and culminates in Corinna's rejection of Jenny's protests as arrogant and ridiculous, just what her husband had first said: 'For who are the Treibels? Prussian Blue manufacturers with a Councillor's title, and I, I am a Schmidt.' When her father comes back from seeing Jenny out, he embraces and kisses his daughter and says: 'Corinna, if I were not a professor, I would turn social-democrat', so disgusted is he, like Fontane himself, with these bourgeois.

Everything depends now on whether Leopold will break with his family or not, and the two ladies had expressed very different views to each other about the probabilities. Jenny proves right. Leopold reads *Werther* and writes pathetic little notes daily, but never dares to call, and after a week Corinna becomes disgusted with him and his family and confesses to Frau Schmolke how foolish she has been. Frau Schmolke, a most convincing creation, forms an effective contrast in these last chapters to both the bourgeois and the cultivated in the story. She is one of the people, the plain healthy stock on which these two so different blooms of civilization are both grafted. She has an instinctive warmth and unselfishness they both lack. Admirable as he is in so many ways, Schmidt needs a good deal of attention, is in fact rather selfish, as he himself admits, and Corinna, with her fashionable 'liking for the externals', is still more so. The person who comes out of it all most creditably is the patient and much tried Marcell, whose generous attitude Schmidt praises as typical of the spirit of classical education, and this passage is a final paean to 'Bildung'. Marcell hears through Schmidt of Corinna's change of mind, makes no reproaches and expects no abject apologies, because he understands his cousin from years of close friendship – the fact that they have always been as close as brother and sister is perhaps what first makes Corinna think of breaking out of their circle. When she shows her father Marcell's loving and understanding letter, he kisses and congratulates her and exclaims:

Now that is an example of the 'higher things' we speak about, the truly ideal, and not what my friend Jenny means. Believe me, the classical that they now make fun of, that is what liberates the spirit, is above any kind of meanness and anticipates Christianity, teaching us to forgive and forget, because no one is perfect. Yes, Corinna, there are classical sayings like texts from the Bible. We have for example the maxim: 'Become the man you are!' – something only a Greek could say.

Fontane then, though in personality and general background he had hardly anything in common with Nietzsche, confirms many of his negative criticisms of the age. The educated middle class seem to him less broad-minded and humane than in his youth, too proud of the examinations they have passed and of external honours, and too often blind to good art and literature. Those in trade and industry are not praised for their hard work and enterprise, like Gustav Freytag's heroes, but exposed as snobbish, ignorant materialists, good comic material perhaps, in their self-deception and inconsistency, and human in their loves and hates, but philistines through and through. Fontane finds true culture still in the institutions which had been designed by Wilhelm von Humboldt to perpetuate the ideals of his own élite, the *Gymnasien*. Friedrich Theodor Vischer, writing forty years before this novel appeared, had described the modern German culture based on classical studies as admirably humane, but inevitably esoteric, because these studies were for the few. Goethe's age, he wrote, had substituted for the old division between the people and the nobility a new one between the people and the educated, and the gap would never be closed without far-reaching political reforms. Of these there is no sign in Fontane, and the privileged of various types are all equally determined to maintain their status.

THOMAS MANN: DER
ZAUBERBERG (1924)

Erich Heller writes of *The Magic Mountain*: 'I have heard critics say that it is too talkative a book and, like other books by Thomas Mann, too ostentatiously knowledgeable for a work of the imagination. This criticism misses the very point of the work, for it is knowledge that is the subject matter of the novel, and the mind that comes to know is its protagonist.'[1] It would be equally true to say that in this novel, more obviously than in any other work of Thomas Mann's, though many of them show the same tendency, his principal theme is a typical modern man's search for 'Bildung', for the insight, the development of his innate faculties as well as the knowledge, which will make life seem meaningful even to-day. *The Magic Mountain*, more obviously than any other novel of this author, is in the tradition of the 'Bildungs-roman'. As we read it, we are interested more in the development of its hero's attitude to life in general than in the young man himself, for he is intentionally made passive and colourless, but unusually eager for daily new encounters with men, knowledge and ideas, so that by reflection on this experience he may learn in due time how someone constituted as he is may make the best of life. *Buddenbrooks*, *Tonio Kröger*, the Joseph novels and *Dr Faustus* all reveal an author who is almost intimidatingly cultivated, and who assumes in his readers a similarly wide range of interest in civilized values and ideas, but *The Magic Mountain* is more instructive than any of these other works as a reflection of contemporary attitudes, German and European, as Thomas Mann saw them, in the period immediately preceding the First World War. The novel appeared in 1924, but it had been begun, as a *Novelle*, in 1912.

In *The Magic Mountain*, by exploiting the advantages opened up to him by his choice of a place for the action, a large international sanatorium in the Swiss Alps, Thomas Mann is able to parade a great variety of individual and social types before the eyes of his open-minded and endlessly curious hero, without shifting him from one milieu to another in search of significant experience, as his predecessors in the Novel of Development had been in the habit of doing. This device provides the occasion for innumerable conversations between Hans Castorp and a whole series of colourful characters but, like the unity of place convention in classical drama, it confines the author within narrow limits in his invention of external happenings. It also makes necessary a patient and very self-centred hero. Clawdia Chauchat's remarks to Hans Castorp in their last conversation seem to suggest not only that he is to be taken as typically German, but that the passion for 'Bildung' of his fellow-countrymen has some dubious aspects for foreigners. She says:

It is well-known that you [Germans] live for the sake of experience – and not 'for the sake of life' [like her friend Mynheer Peeperkorn] Self-enrichment is what you are out for. C'est ca, you [yourself] do not seem to realize that that is revolting egoism, and that one day you [Germans] will be revealed as enemies of humanity.[2]

This is an idea to which we must revert at the end of our inquiry. It suggests a possibly catastrophic result for the world of the German pre-occupation with 'Bildung', if it remains self-regarding and 'uncommitted', causing the individual to neglect his social ties with his immediate environment and the wider world. The high-minded but disastrous indifference to politics which Thomas Mann was finally to condemn so strongly, after sharing it for over half of his life, is one aspect of this neglect.

To lend greater probability to Hans Castorp's openmindedness and thirst for experience, Thomas Mann makes him a Hamburger, a member of an old-established merchant family, who had lost both parents before he was seven and been brought up by a great-uncle, with all the comfort and attention due to a young patrician, certainly, but without a parent's love and guidance. At school too he had been vaguely aware of the lack of any firm convictions about the aim of life in his teachers, of their 'hollow silence' on such matters. As he grew up, he enjoyed as a matter of course the creature comforts of civilization expected by one of his class, and he accepted passively its one absolute principle, a quasi-religious respect for work, but even this was not with him an inner conviction and he easily found excuses, e.g. in his persistent anaemia, for not over-exerting himself in his studies, and for seeking exemption from military service. At the age of twenty-two, when he visits his consumptive cousin Joachim at the Berghof sanatorium, having been advised to take a holiday himself in good air after the unaccustomed strain of his engineering examinations, he still has a mind which is open and impressionable, whereas Joachim's is quite closed to anything not connected with the military career which is his single aim in life. He thinks it best not to have any personal opinions and simply to do one's service, to be in fact what Hans, adopting his friend Settembrini's interpretation of Joachim, calls a 'lanzknecht and purely formal existence' – a reminder that one function of Joachim in the novel is to represent the military outlook on life.[3]

But Hans Castorp's thinking too is less free than he sometimes imagines. He remains the Hamburg patrician he is by birth and education, who already as a child had felt so deep a sympathy with his conservative grandfather. 'Children and grandchildren look at people, in order to admire', the author comments, 'and they admire in order to learn, and to develop the hereditary potentialities which lie within them.'[4] Instinctively, at times of stress, he reverts to gestures and habits he had observed in his grandfather, especially his way of burying his chin in his cravat. An important consequence of his deeply rooted consciousness of his rank is that he remains entirely cut off from the life of three-quarters of his fellow-countrymen, the working and lower-middle class, and at the Berghof he meets hardly anyone except the comparatively well-to-do people who can afford its fees. Occasionally patients turn up whose behaviour arouses comment, like the affected Frau Stöhr, with her malapropisms and general stupidity, or Herr Magnus the brewer, a prosperous industrialist, content to see Germany made into one great barracks, as long as there is business efficiency and solid workmanship behind it, no matter if politeness be lacking.[5] But in general we have the merest glimpses of industrial and commercial life, always from above, and we hear nothing at all about the landowning and farming classes, and the agricultural workers under them, nor about the millions of factory hands. Whole aspects of the nation's life, like party politics or the social movement are similarly hardly touched upon. So the well-known dictum of Georg Lukács, that Thomas Mann gives us a picture of the 'total social reality of the time' by bringing together in one place a 'representative cross-section of its society', must be taken with more than a grain of salt.[6] Even *Wilhelm Meisters Lehrjahre* gives us a fuller picture of the German life of its time.

What Thomas Mann does give us is a vivid picture of the Berghof, its landscape setting, its staff, organization, daily and seasonal routine, and above all its international clientèle as distinct individuals, afflicted in differing degrees with the same disease, and generating together a psychological and intellectual atmosphere quite unlike that of the world outside. The habitual reactions and values of the Berghof patients are as far removed from those of the good citizen of Hamburg as those of the bohemian crowd of actors in the *Lehrjahre* had been from Wilhelm's boyhood world, and the effect of his transplantation on the hero is very similar in some respects. It makes them both begin to doubt some of the assumptions implied in the middle-class code, especially concerning work and 'respectable' behaviour. Hans soon learns from Joachim that living up at the Berghof one changes, for example, one's ideas about time. Three weeks are like a day, and the normal feeling for time is soon lost. One comes to accept idleness too without a trace of bad conscience. Before long Hans realizes, first through his early meeting with the Half-lungs Club, that sickness and death are also not taken seriously, as in the plains, but easily become 'a sort of spree'.[7] This self-protective mechanism of wretched creatures in dissolution is reinforced by the staff's way of handling the frequent casualties among the patients – their use of the safe interval while most patients are at meals for the administration of the last sacrament or the removal of coffins – and the doctor's angry reproaches to a young man who makes a fuss about dying.

Immediately after his encounter with the frivolous young pneumothorax patients, on his first morning walk with Joachim, Hans Castorp also meets Settembrini, the Italian humanist and arch-intellectual with an itch for pedagogy, and hears the first of many tirades against the insidious wiles of Hofrat Behrens, the doctor in charge of the sanatorium, a brilliant display of malicious criticism, 'the brightest weapon of reason against the powers of darkness and ugliness'. The frivolous patients and the shabby intellectual are equally remote from Hans Castorp's native bourgeois temper, and both serve as eye-openers for him, much as the actors and aristocrats had done for Wilhelm Meister. But the serious young engineer, though he soon comes to share the feeling prevailing at the Berghof of belonging to a group exempted by illness from taking thought for the future, and happily resigned to 'timelessness' and the suspension of responsibility, finds himself listening with ever growing interest to Settembrini's discourses and, not without occasional protests, lets the Italian make him the chief object of his pedagogic passion. It is Settembrini who first makes him aware of 'Geist', of all that the exercise of his inner freedom can mean for him, while confined by illness to the Berghof. It becomes his university, and his spirit blossoms here, as his intellectual interests are gradually aroused. Settembrini, the son of a scholar and poet, and himself a writer, is the spokesman of the Voltairian humanism of the Enlightenment, of mercilessly critical reason spiced with malice, detesting superstition, and therefore fiercely anti-clerical, but obstinately optimistic about human perfectibility.

Along with this new rational influence on his hero's 'Bildung', Thomas Mann introduces the irrational, 'Asiatic' attraction of the door-banging Clawdia Chauchat, with her contempt for convention, and also, for a time, the spectacle of Herr Albin's desperate jesting, as he plays ostentatiously with his knife and revolver, threatening at any moment, as one beyond recovery who can 'laugh at it all', to make his own quietus. Hans Castorp too has a vision of escaping from the 'pressure of honour', his respect for what people think about him, into the final freedom of nihilism. So the very correct and conventional upper middle-class Hamburger finds these two different forms of escape opened up to him in his early days at the Berghof, a one-sidedly rational and a one-sidedly irrational one, and for long he experiments with both. For the first time he realizes the inhumanity of his rich friends in Hamburg, seeing it, through Settembrini's eyes, as 'the natural cruelty of life', of 'nature' not yet humanized by 'culture'. But Settembrini mistrusts his rapid conversion, and ascribes these criticisms to the disturbing influence of the Berghof itself, where people 'easily get lost to life' and find a sort of new 'home'. He urges him to go back at once to Hamburg, to escape from this insidious atmosphere of irresponsibility. His place is with life, not death, and his romantic assumption that disease is allied with intelligence, with genius, and is more 'distinguished' than health, is a mere relic of medievalism. It is a perfectly natural, not an abnormal phenomenon, as Hans had been inclined to think, that a woman like Frau Stöhr can be both ill and stupid. Hans has come to the Berghof as one whom the shock of early bereavements, the death of his parents and grandfather in his early childhood, had made already 'vulnerable and sensitive[...] to the harsh and crude aspects of an unthinking worldly life, to its cynicism, we might say.'[8] Thomas Mann suggests further that the mysterious attraction which the boy Pribislav Hippe ('Hippe' means 'scythe' – the scythe of Freund Hein, the figure of death in German popular mythology) had exercised over him at school, when he was only thirteen, had been in some way associated in his mind with his reverence for death.[9] Mme Chauchat had immediately reminded him of this Slav boy with his high cheek-bones and Kirghiz eyes, and she came to be symbolic for him of all this irrational temptation to be 'half in love with easeful death', and to link the idea of love with that of disease, encouraged as such thoughts were by Dr Krokowski's lectures on this subject.

Thomas Mann had used a figure with many of the characteristics of Settembrini already in the *Betrachtungen eines Unpolitischen*, written during the First World War, but there this 'Zivilisationsliterat', as we shall see in the next chapter, had been presented as his own antipode, based on his brother Heinrich. Now Mann's hostility to this type of thinking has vanished, and Settembrini is evidently to be regarded as relatively justified. Joachim is made to apply to him a phrase very like that used, as we saw, by Carlyle's disciple John Sterling when trying to sum up the essential qualities of the Germans of Goethe's time. What Joachim says is that Settembrini 'thinks well of man in general'.[10] For Settembrini, the humanist has taken over the role of the priest, but his reasonable moralism, unlike that of classical Weimar, is inescapably political. Patriotism means for him radicalism, the hatred of tyranny of a follower of Mazzini, whereas for Hans and Joachim it means conservatism, as it had for Mann himself in the *Betrachtungen*. Literature is for Settembrini utterly committed to the fight for progress, helped by the beneficent influence of technical advance in uniting the peoples of the earth. He belongs to the 'League for the Organization of Progress' and is engaged on the volume concerned with literature for a collective work on *The Sociology of Suffering*. His way of speaking about progress as the 'natural tendency' of mankind, a belief which for him Darwinism only reinforces, suggests to us the ideas of the eighteenth-century Freemasons, even before we learn from Naphta that Settembrini belongs to the brotherhood. The leading Masonic aim, according to Lessing's *Ernst und Falk*, had been to overcome current prejudices about creeds, nations and classes. Similarly Settembrini holds it to be a matter of individual conscience to fight for social reform, pacifism, popular education and all such liberal causes. It is not in self-development that he sees 'Bildung', but in self-dedication to the political liberation of oppressed nationalities and the improvement of the conditions of life for all on earth.

The first effect on Hans Castorp's conversations, on the one hand with Settembrini and on the other with Dr Behrens, who arouses his curiosity about the human skin and bio-chemistry, is to start him off on an ambitious course of scientific reading, when he has provided himself through a bookseller in the village with text-books on human anatomy, physiology, psychology and all the sciences bearing on life. After these he turns to physics, to find out particularly about atoms and molecules and the infinitely small, before going on to morbid anatomy, infectious tumours etc. All this is very different from the book on *Ocean Steamships* which he had brought with him to read on the journey. It represents part of an educational programme comparable with those we have found, for example, in Goethe and Stifter. Hans is still learning from Settembrini too, at Christmas, for instance, about the historical importance of Christianity in the evolution of his kind of individualistic democracy, through its doctrine of the value of each individual soul, and the brotherhood and equality of all men as God's children. But the novelty has worn off this teacher's discourses, and Hans has begun to see the limitations of his abstract rationalism. The death of a patient well known to him reminds him that the love of freedom, the human attitude singled out by Settembrini in his praise of all that man can achieve by his own effort, is only one of the two basic tendencies of human thought. The other, it seems to Hans, is piety, the awareness of death in its solemn power, and of human weakness and fragility. The humanists have no monopoly of moral dignity, as one might think from Settembrini's harangues. The truth is more complex:

Everything is human[e]. The Spanish attitude, God-fearing, humbly solemn, observing strict limits, is a very estimable variety of humanity, it seems to me, and on the other hand one can cover up with the word 'human' any kind of slackness and slovenliness –

an observation with which Joachim, as a soldier, warmly agrees.[11] Hans feels too that there are other forms of morality besides Settembrini's 'practical tasks in life', 'Sunday fêtes for progress' and 'systematic elimination of suffering'. He finds it intolerable to live, as they do at the Berghof, with people suffering and dying in neighbouring rooms, while they themselves act as if it were no concern of theirs, and allow the management to maintain the pretence by spiriting coffins away at meal-times and so on. He persuades Joachim to join him in visiting the 'moribund' and taking them flowers. He does this not only from Christian pity, but also as a way of satisfying his need to take life and death seriously, in contrast to the many who stay on unnecessarily at the Berghof because they like its permissive atmosphere, but there is perhaps some irony here, because his own reason for staying is not always entirely above suspicion. Settembrini, hearing of these charitable works, pronounces him to be a 'worry-child of life', who himself needs to be cared for,[12] though the author tells us later that the new preoccupation of his hero arose out of a spirit of 'Bildung' opposed to that which inspired Settembrini as a teacher.[13] It seems very like what Goethe in the *Wanderjahre* had found to be specifically Christian, the 'reverence for what is below us', namely suffering, disease and everything repugnant to the living.

The other irrational influence, represented by Clawdia Chauchat, is allowed a climax, in which its nature is made more explicit than hitherto, before Clawdia disappears for a long time from the Berghof, just about half-way through the novel. The chapter 'Walpurgis night', with a title recalling the scene in *Faust, Part* i, of the witches' annual festival on the Brocken, from the text of which Settembrini quotes appropriate lines at intervals, describes the celebration of 'Fasching', Carnival, on Shrove Tuesday at the Berghof. As Clawdia passes by, in her new sleeveless gown of brown silk, Settembrini murmurs: 'Lilith is here', continuing, when Hans asks 'Who?' 'Adam's first wife. Look out for yourself!' 'This Lilith', he explains, 'became a phantom of the night, dangerous for young men through her beautiful hair.' He reproaches Hans for using the familiar 'Du' to him, even on this privileged night, because he is doing it 'only from the pleasure in licence'. But Hans goes on to justify himself at length, and to express in rather extravagant terms his gratitude to his mentor for the pedagogic interest he has taken, in the last seven months, in a 'worry-child of life'. Surprised at this outburst, Settembrini exclaims: 'That sounds like a farewell!' as indeed it proves, for Settembrini never again plays the prominent role he has had till now in Hans Castorp's education.

His protest about the use of 'Du' turns out to have been a hint in advance of the author's intention in making Hans use the same familiar form of address to Clawdia, against her wish too, in all their following conversation, which he initiates by asking her for a pencil, ostensibly for a parlour game that is being played. In reality he is consciously establishing a parallel between this love scene and his boyish infatuation with Pribislav Hippe in their school playground,[14] where the borrowing of a pencil had already served as an excuse for his approach. In the dream-like scene between Hans and Clawdia when, speaking French, which gives their encounter for him an air of irresponsibility, he forgets the German and bourgeois love of order which Clawdia half mocks in him, and as they watch the grotesque figures of the dancers in their fancy dress, urges her to accept his love, so long suppressed, there is a clear suggestion that he has reached another stage in his 'Bildung'. He is not the orderly Hamburger in this episode, but the adventurous son of the Hanse. That the love of adventure has its place in morality too is indicated in Clawdia's words about the conversations she has regularly in her rooms with a Russian friend. They talk about many things, even about morality:

Il nous semble qu'il faudrait chercher la morale non dans la vertu, c'est à dire dans la raison, la discipline, les bonnes moeurs, l'honnêteté – mais plutôt dans le contraire, je veux dire: dans le péché, en s'abandonnant au danger, à ce qui est nuisible, à ce qui nous consume. Il nous semble qu'il est plus moral de se perdre et même de se laisser dépérir que de se conserver. Les grands moralistes n'étaient point des vertueux, mais des aventuriers dans le mal, des vicieux, de grands pécheurs qui nous enseignent à nous incliner chrétiennement devant la misère.

Hans has been to some extent accustomed to dangerous thoughts like these by his reflections about Dr Krokowski's lectures. He claims now that it is his love for Clawdia which is the real source of his illness. It is a genuine passion worthy of these surroundings, 'de la folie, une chose insensée, défendue et une aventure dans le mal', and not simply 'une banalité agréable, bonne pour en faire de petites chansons paisibles dans les plaines'. His claim to a tragic passion hardly carries conviction, with Clawdia or with the reader. One feels it is one more 'experience' he is seeking. He concludes his strange suit with a page of poetico-physiological variations on the theme: 'Le corps, l'amour, la mort, ces trois ne font qu'un', thoughts about the mystery, the shame and the beauty of organic life, on its twin foundations of love and death. With ideas which remind us now of Novalis, now of Wagner, old Romantic doctrine reinterpreted in the light of Dr Krokowski's Freudian outpourings and the fruits of Hans Castorp's recent reading, he woos Clawdia 'd'une manière profonde, à l'alle-mande', to be rewarded by her reminder, as she leaves, to return the pencil. It is only later that we learn he did so, and received in return her X-ray photograph to carry in his pocket-book.

Still another phase of Hans Castorp's 'Bildung' opens in Book VI, after Clawdia's departure. His preoccupations are at first apparently more coolly intellectual than ever, the study of botany, astronomy and the early history of mankind, varied by private talks with Dr Krokowski about abnormal psychology. Soon the cousins find them-selves listening again to Settembrini, now living not at the Berghof, but in modest lodgings in the village. But Settembrini no longer has everything his own way intellectually. Hans hears him only in his passionate arguments with the Jesuit Naphta, an adversary carefully contrived by Thomas Mann to represent the intellectual revolt against reason in contemporary Europe. If reason is to be shown as vulnerable, it must be seen to be secretly motivated by self-interest, or class-interest, and this is what Naphta repeatedly suggests. At the same time he cannot honestly claim to be disinterested himself. His point of view must be seen by the reader as substantially explained by his origin and history, and the intellectual contest between him and Settembrini becomes the expression of a clash of interests and wills in the pre-1914 world. In the first argument Naphta begins with a Marxistic criticism of Settembrini's humanism, asserting that it is essentially bourgeois self-interest rationalised, the philosophy natural to a commercial and industrial middle class, utilitarian rather than

8-2

humane, and eager above all to justify the freedom of the individual to make his own fortune without interference from outside. True humanism, on the other hand, comes from the civilizing work of the Church and its moral discipline, and it can only be restored now in a hierarchic society, by the alliance of throne and altar – an ominous phrase for liberal ears! Naphta sees no genuine idealism in the liberalism praised by Settembrini, who looks forward to a future Europa dominated by the peace-loving nations. What is really coming, Naphta says, is a fierce conflict of rival capitalistic nations. A catastrophe is inevitable, it is the fate that Europe has brought upon itself. Settembrini insists on the idea of peaceful progress, human perfectibility through reason, but Naphta sees the nations as confused in their aims, and asserts that war might be a remedy for many current ills.[15] Listening to these arguments, Joachim, speaking of course as a soldier, but perhaps also as a more typical German than Hans, remains unshaken in his conviction that it is best for the private citizen to have no opinions, and simply to do his 'service' as ordered. Hans however is left with much food for solitary thought on the bench by the mountain torrent, where he spends hours trying to think things out about life and the world, or 'ruling' as he calls it.

When the cousins visit Naphta in his surprisingly well-furnished rooms over a tailor's shop, in the same house where Settembrini lives in a bare attic, the object which first arrests their attention is a fourteenth-century 'pietà', a crudely carved and painted statue of the mourning Virgin with the dead Christ across her knees. Naphta describes it as a Gothic work, in which everything expresses most forcibly suffering and the weakness of the flesh, yet in these repulsive features reveals spiritual beauty. What Settembrini criticizes, when he joins the party, is the admittedly intentional departure of the artist from truth to nature, and he proceeds to hold forth on the beauty of natural form, as the Ancients conceived it in classical art. To his surprise, Hans takes the other side, and the discussion continues between Settembrini and Naphta on the respective merits of form and naturalism in art, the latter being in Naphta's eyes a reflection of the degradation brought upon man by science. He believes its triumph to be a passing phase, which will be followed by a reaction lasting perhaps two or three hundred years, and culminating in a revival of scholasticism and of an earth-centred cosmogony, the medieval view of the world in all its glory. This sounds like Thomas Mann playing with Nietzsche's idea of the eternal recurrence. It can only happen, Settembrini replies, if we completely abandon our present conception of truth, and agree to accept as true what is good for us, which means, politically speaking, whatever the state requires. Naphta accepts this necessity, but with the important proviso that a distinction shall again be made as in the Middle Ages between a man's duty towards God and his duty towards the world. The state must acknowledge the Church as supreme. What exactly is meant by 'Church' comes out only gradually. Settembrini of course points out that what Naphta proposes will mean the end of individualism, of personality, human rights and freedom as now understood. Naphta retorts that they have almost gone already, and that what we need in their place is discipline from a new master, the deepest desire of the young at least being always to have someone to obey. The new authority can only be established by terror. He evades at first Settembrini's insistent questions about who is to impose this terror, asserting that men are ruled at present by money. Finally he prophesies that our present plutocratic system will be replaced by the dictatorship of the proletariat in the form of a Christian communism. That will go against the grain with intellectuals, but it will be carried through 'in the sign of the Cross', with the ultimate aim of winning universal recognition for the belief that all men are equal as God's children. The accompanying political ideal will be a classless society, in which the state will have withered away, the Marxist dream, instead of the liberal one of a capitalistic world republic.[16]

Naphta is evidently invented as a mouthpiece for various anti-liberal strains of thought current in Europe round about 1914, and still more ten years later, which can be effectively brought into contrast with the ideas of the liberal intelligentsia. Settembrini, for all his one-sidedness, is a much more credible character. It is only when Hans Castorp has had a full dose of his teaching and learnt from it what he needs that Naphta is brought in, in the second half of the book, to redress the balance and make Hans more critical. He finds now that there are philosophies totally opposed to Settembrini's agnosticism and liberal individualism, his belief in democratic institutions and self-determination for all peoples, his humanitarian opposition to class and national wars, and so on. There are some

217

obvious self-contradictions in Settembrini's doctrine, as the author evidently means us to see. He preaches pacifism, for instance, but would be ready at any time to fight in an Italian 'war of nationality and civilization' against Austria. He is altogether too didactic and too sure of himself for Hans Castorp's liking. For all his irony, he can never laugh at himself; we are told in fact that he never laughs at all. In this respect at least Naphta is more human, as he laughs heartily at some of Settembrini's ideas – but again, not at himself. In spite of Thomas Mann's ingenious story of his origins and upbringing, he remains a paper monster. He is supposed to associate piety with cruelty from his childhood memories of his father, the kosher butcher, so he defends the death penalty and confessional procedure – the attempt, in criminal cases, to extort a confession from the accused by hook or by crook. Like many famous Jews – one thinks first of Heine – he was by instinct a revolutionary, and at the same time something of an aristocrat, so when at the age of sixteen he was offered a Jesuit education, he readily took to it, especially as he soon came to think of the Catholic church too as both revolutionary – because it was unworldly and unmaterialistic – and also intellectually distinguished and elegant. His brilliant intelligence found satisfaction in the subtlety of his teachers, although their otherworldliness and Christian charity apparently left him unmoved. An orderly system of beliefs has become more important for him than morality, and he is enough of a Romantic to find the dignity of man in sickness rather than in health. Curiosity prompts him to look into the theory of communism, he finds in it the same systematic intellectualism, the same hardness and dogmatic 'certainty' as in Catholicism and he persuades himself that the two systems can be combined. What this means must be that he is fundamentally a nihilist, for the basic contradictions between them are surely irreconcilable. It is not surprising that Settembrini finds logic in Naphta only on the surface, and beneath it a hopeless confusion, an interpretation confirmed by Naphta's suicide.

By the time that Hans Castorp has been at the Berghof for a year, his attitude to the place has come to be very different from that of his cousin. Joachim by now has lost patience with the repeated postponements of his return to his unit, and insists on resuming his military career, against the advice of Dr Behrens. Hans, who is told he could safely leave, stays on, chiefly, as he admits to himself, in the hope that Clawdia will return. His relatives in Hamburg, hearing from Joachim of his unaccountable behaviour, send his uncle James to investigate matters, but uncle James himself nearly succumbs to the lure of the Berghof and beats a hasty retreat.

In the masterly chapter 'Snow' the author shows us his hero, after a narrow escape from death in a snowstorm, making up his mind on the ultimate questions. Thomas Mann explained his intentions in writing this chapter soon after the appearance of the novel, in a speech at Lübeck.[17] He admits here that as a typical Lübecker, he is more interested in towns than in the countryside, but says there is one element in nature which has always fascinated him, the sea. 'The sea is not a landscape, it is something that brings us face to face with eternity, with nothingness and death, a metaphysical dream, and to stand in the thin air of the regions of eternal snow is a very similar experience.' His attitude to nature in this form he sees 'as fear, as a feeling of strangeness, of an unseemly and wild adventure', and he points to the expression of this feeling in the 'Snow' chapter of *The Magic Mountain*:

Look at little Hans Castorp, as in his civilian breeches and on his *de luxe* skis he glides into the primeval stillness, the highly menacing and uncanny, the not even hostile, but sublimely and unrelatedly indifferent! He takes on the contest with it, as he naively does with the intellectual problems on heights his fate drives him to scale, but what is the feeling in his heart? Not a feeling for nature, if that implies any sense of belonging together. No, fear, awe if you like, religious dread, physical and metaphysical horror – and something else too: mockery, genuine irony facing the immensely stupid, a contemptuous shrug of the shoulders in front of gigantic powers, which in their blindness can indeed physically overwhelm him, but to which even in death he would offer human defiance.[18]

In the chapter itself, it is hard to find anything resembling the defiance expressed in that last sentence, which reminds one of Bertrand Russell's *The Free Man's Worship*. 'For the sake of kindness and love, man shall not allow death any control over his thoughts.' That is the sentence, emphasized by the use of letter-spacing, the German equivalent of putting a word or passage in italics, with which Hans Castorp's description of his dream ends, the dream in which, sheltering from the storm and half stupefied with fatigue, and from the effects of an unwise swig of port from his pocket flask, he had had a vision which invites symbolic interpretation. Its first part had been rather like the vision of all possible human delights conjured up for Faust by Mephistopheles after their first meeting. In an idyllic sunny landscape,

Men and women, children of the sun and sea, were everywhere moving about or resting, sensible, carefree, handsome young people, so pleasing to look upon – Hans Castorp's whole heart opened wide, painfully wide and lovingly at the sight of them.[19]

But wandering among these happy people, his attention is directed by one of them to a sort of temple, in the depths of which he sees horrible witches, eating the flesh of a child. Such horrors lie in the human past and are still part of life, we are given to understand.

The great soul, of which you are only a fragment, perhaps dreams at times through you, in your way, of things which she is always dreaming of in secret, – of her youth, her hopes, her happiness and peace...and her meal of blood.

After this experience Hans is able to put into words what he feels himself to have learnt from the interminable arguments of Settembrini and Naphta, from his experience with the living and the dying at the Berghof, and from his reading. As Thomas Mann says in the Lübeck speech, it is the old doctrine of the golden mean, seen now as the essence of the ethos of the German middle class. A few extracts from Hans Castorp's reflections may indicate their general drift, though the effect of the many echoes of his mentors' speeches will be lost:

Were they so polite and charming to each other, the sun people, with tacit reference to this very horror? That would be a subtle and very gallant inference for them to make! I will take sides with them in spirit and not with Naphta – nor with Settembrini either for that matter, they both talk nonsense. The one is full of lust and spitefulness, and the other can only blow his little trumpet of reason and imagines he will bring even madmen to their sober senses, all nonsense, surely. It is philistinism and mere ethics, irreligious, so much is certain[...] Man is the master of opposites, they exist through him, and therefore he ranks higher than they do. Higher than death, too high for it – that is the freedom of his head. Higher than life, too high for it – that is the piety in his heart[...] I will be good. I will allow death no control over my thoughts! For that is what charity and loving-kindness mean, and nothing else.[20]

Next summer Joachim is back again and the discussions with Settembrini and Naphta are resumed, the first topic being Freemasonry, interpreted by Naphta as a terroristic movement, but by Settembrini, himself a Mason, as still profoundly humanitarian, but no longer unpolitical, as in the age of Lessing, its aim being the perfection of humanity through a world league of Masons. To Hans privately Naphta reveals that Settembrini, being poor, has had difficulty in becoming a Mason at all, because the fees are high, most Masons being men of substance. "Bildung" and money, there you have the bourgeois! There you have the foundations of the liberal world-republic.' Freemasonry, in a word, is 'the bourgeois rabble formed into a club'.[21] In a later discussion with Naphta, Settembrini agrees that 'Bildung' is now a middle-class affair, but it is founded on the tradition of humane learning coming down from the classics. Literary genius is the noblest expression of the human spirit, and the man of letters, through his cultivation of the divine gift of language, is the modern saint. According to Naphta, this is sheer conservatism, clinging to a tradition which is not for all time, but simply the expression of the bourgeois-liberal epoch. German schools are already out of touch with reality and their pupils learn what is most valuable for them out of school through public lectures, exhibitions, the cinema and so on. Classical education is already despised by the masses as the ideology of the middle classes, and its days are numbered, a matter of decades at most. The final achievement of the liberal bourgeois has been pure nihilism, the destruction of all positive beliefs.[22] These discussions link up, it will be seen, with what we have found in Nietzsche and Fontane, who would presumably have sided with Naphta and Settembrini respectively.

The seventh and last chapter introduces a new figure, completely unlike any of the types of suffering, pleasure-loving or thinking humanity we have encountered at the Berghof so far. It is the Dutch coffee-planter Mynheer Peeperkorn, an outsize old man with a shock of white hair, eccentric in speech and habits, clearly used to command, but no intellectual. Settembrini finds him just a stupid old man, but for Hans Castorp he is strangely impressive. 'He could put us all in his pocket', he says, because Peeperkorn makes him realize that there is a mysterious, positive value in sheer personality. He is one of the men of passion spoken of by Clawdia in the passage already quoted (p. 207), who live for the sake of living, and not just to extend the range of their conscious experience. This 'self-forgetfulness' is something foreign to Hans Castorp's nature, but as a born 'culture-traveller' (an ironical description, of course, on the analogy of 'commercial traveller') he has the panoramic ability, to use a phrase early applied to Goethe, to appreciate and get to like even one so diametrically opposed to himself. He sees that Peeperkorn 'has a thing about being able to feel, a sort of *point d'honneur* about being fully alive', as he explains to Settembrini, who feels however that there is a good deal of self-dramatization about it, and that Hans is 'venerating a mask'. Peeperkorn is certainly full of mannerisms, some of them, as Mann admitted, copied from Gerhart Hauptmann, like perhaps his habit of raising his eyebrows, and thus furrowing his forehead horizontally, to make his small eyes look bigger. Anyhow, Hans and the planter take to each other, although they are rivals for Clawdia's love. She has felt pity, she explains to the sympathetic Hans, for Peeperkorn's 'anxiety about feeling', the sentiment that drives him to suicide after taking part in a final excursion to a splendid waterfall, symbolic of the dynamism which he worships and feels himself to have lost. After exposing his hero to torrents of words about life and its problems, Thomas Mann apparently felt it necessary to bring in this odd character to remind Hans, not without his usual irony, of what Goethe called 'the incommensurable', the inexplicable quality of life.

The remainder of the last chapter, after the death of Peeperkorn, shows us a Berghof overshadowed by the approach of the First World War, the state of Europe being reflected in that of the collection of sick Europeans at the sanatorium. Hans finds all around him the evidence of stagnating life – the section is headed 'The great stupor' – a stagnation which people try to forget in bursts of meaningless activity, in hobbies like photography, stamp-collecting, puzzle-solving, in learning Esperanto or merely playing patience. We are reminded of the political events leading up to the War by an occasional remark, e.g. by Settembrini's mention to Hans of the threat to Austria implied in current Russian diplomacy, a warning which Hans, though full of forebodings, is at the moment too deep in a game of patience to heed. Then for a time Hans is quite absorbed in the newly discovered delights of music, the Berghof having acquired a good gramophone, which Hans operates, often for hours alone. We hear much about his favourite records, all highly characteristic, 'Der Lindenbaum', for instance, with its Romantic association of love with death, 'Du fändest Ruhe dort' (you would find rest there). Even a craze for spiritualism develops from which Hans, still a 'culture-traveller', does not hold himself aloof, till he is shocked to the point of revulsion by the calling up of the spirit of Joachim, who had died soon after his second return to the army. Finally 'The great exasperation' sets in, a time of senseless impatience and quarrelsomeness among the Berghof patients, shared of course by Settembrini and Naphta, both now seriously ill, and no longer disposed to take each other's sallies with good humour. A reference to the *Titanic* disaster fixes the time as the spring of 1912. Naphta becomes more and more bitter in his ridicule of Settembrini's ideas:

The world republic, that would be happiness at last, surely! Progress? Alas, he was reminded of the famous sick man, always changing his position in the hope of relief. The unacknowledged but in secret quite general wish for war was an expression of this. It would come, this war, and that was good, although it would have different results from what those planning it promised themselves. Naphta despised the bourgeois safety-state...War, war! He had no objections, and the general lust for it seemed to him comparatively creditable.[23]

What finally drives Settembrini to exasperation is a harangue by Naphta, at coffee in a Kurhaus, on an excursion the pair make with Hans and two others in winter, a monologue on the problem of freedom, full of irony about the 'deeds' committed in its name. Indignant at the 'infamous' ambiguities which his pupil Hans is being compelled to hear, Settembrini calls on Naphta to stop, and a quarrel ensues which leads to a duel. Settembrini's justification of a final appeal to force in a private dispute is at the same time an explanation of the inevitability of war in the Europe of 1914:

The duel, my friend, is not just an institution like any other. It is the ultimate, the return to the primeval state of nature, only slightly moderated by certain conventions of a chivalrous kind, which are very superficial. The essential about the situation remains the absolutely primitive corporeal conflict, and it is every man's business, however far from the natural his life may be, to keep himself prepared for this situation.

At the duel Settembrini fires into the air and Naphta shoots himself.

Not very long after the duel, while Settembrini is still alive, the War breaks out, and this at last drives Hans Castorp, after seven years at the Berghof, back to the plains. Our last glimpse of him is in battle, and it is left an open question whether he will survive, for the novel, we learn at the end, has been 'A hermetic story', told for its own sake, not for his. 'Hermetic' refers back to Naphta's description of the initiation ceremony of the Freemasons in chapter VI, where Hans had been told that the neophyte 'must be eager for knowledge and fearless', that the grave was the chief symbol of the initiation, and that the way of purification led the young man eager for the wonders of life through the fear of death and the realm of decay, clearly a parallel to Hans Castorp's quest for 'Bildung' at the Berghof.[24] Now at the end of the long process Hans is called 'an uncomplicated young man', well fitted for his role because of an adventurous strain in his character inherited from his Hanseatic forbears. In the Lübeck speech Thomas Mann gives us a good brief reminder of his new novel's main theme, when he speaks of his hero's 'Hanseatic nature',

which proves itself not after the manner of his forefathers in superior piracy, but in a quieter and more intellectual way: in his enjoyment of adventures of the heart and mind, which carry this ordinary young man off to the realm of the cosmic and metaphysical, and make him truly the hero of a story which undertakes, in a strange and almost parodistic manner, to renew the old German Wilhelm-Meister-type 'Bildungsroman', this product of our great middle-class epoch.[25]

The traditional Bildungsroman, as the product of a stable society, had usually shown how the initially callow but openminded and lively hero had after varied experiences and innumerable discussions with people of all kinds found his feet in the world. Like most novels for the general reader, it ended happily and with the implication that with the lessons he had learnt, the hero was ready for whatever the future might bring. *The Magic Mountain* can be said 'almost to parody' this kind of novel in that the hero comes to terms, in the course of it, not so much with life as with death, or at least with death as the ever-present shadow of life. Already as a boy Hans feels a certain fascination for the phenomenon of death, and in seven years at the Berghof he lives surrounded by the suffering and the dying and, though he feels the lure of the irresponsible and learns through his two mentors how far along the road to nihilism the modern world has moved, he retains his generous humanity even when faced with the worst. A return to a happy life 'in the plains' was however an artistically impossible ending to his search, one ruled out anyhow by the explosive state of the world. It seems fitting that Mann should break away from the old pattern, and leave his hero facing with fortitude the hideous results of Europe's return to 'the ultimate, the primeval state of nature'. His long and complex mental development as an individual has brought him round to acknowledging the claims on him of the society into which he was born, though no doubt also 'with genuine irony facing the immensely stupid'.

THE CONVERSION OF AN
UNPOLITICAL MAN

It is a fortunate accident for the understanding of German thought about the relationship between culture and politics, as it developed under the pressure of events between the later years of the Wilhelmine Reich and the foundation of the Federal Republic, that Thomas Mann, a supremely articulate, conscientious and intelligent witness of these events, felt himself impelled to speak his mind about them, not only symbolically in his novels and stories, but directly in essays and speeches on current affairs. Studying these writings, particularly the *Betrachtungen eines Unpolitischen* and the two volumes of *Reden und Aufsätze* (1965), one is led to the conclusion that Thomas Mann has few if any rivals as the representative of the best German thought and feeling, the enduring German conscience, in the most disturbed and tragic half-century of German history.

It is well known that Mann's political views underwent what looks like a complete reversal, though he often disputed this interpretation, seeing his whole life's effort as directed towards a fuller humane life for all. His example may at least show how it was possible for a patriotic German conservative to grow into a supporter of the Weimar Republic, an impassioned opponent of Hitler and, in his last years, a convinced democrat who, as an American citizen, deliberately lived in Switzerland and declared himself to belong to no party but that of 'humanity'.

At the beginning of the First World War Thomas Mann was thirty-nine years old and was quickly rejected for military service, but in the general unrest and suspense he found himself unable to continue the creative writing he had planned and begun before the war – the *Zauberberg* was the chief item – until he had cleared up his ideas about the rights and wrongs of the war and particularly about the question singled out by Allied propaganda, the attitude on both sides to freedom and democracy. After writing in the first year of the war his historical sketch *Friedrich und die große Koalition* and two patriotic articles, he spent more than two years on a series of essays on the war-aims question which he published in 1918 as a book of over 600 pages, *Betrachtungen eines Unpolitischen*. It is a tedious, rambling book which shows little of the psychological penetration, witty irony and shapeliness of his novels and stories, but one can well believe that some inner compulsion made him go on and on, endlessly re-handling the same basic themes, the contrast between the literary artist and the man of letters, between German 'Kultur' and Western civilization, between middle-class stability in a hierarchic society and modern notions about progress and democracy. His intentions, as he remembered them a generation later, are put succinctly in a letter to Hermann Hesse (8 February 1947): 'The pacifism of the political journalists, Expressionists, Activists of that time got on my nerves as much as the self-satisfied moralism of Allied propaganda, half Jacobin, half Puritan, and I defended in reply to it an unpolitical and anti-political Germanity, Protestant and Romantic in essense, which I felt to be the basis of my existence.'

These abstractions however do not explain the bitter personal tone of the book, which is due to differences, only partly political, between Thomas Mann and his elder brother Heinrich. Both had been bent on writing from an early age, Thomas no doubt at first in imitation of his four years older brother and following the same models, but determined in his dour way to do better and before long succeeding. They spent most of 1896–8 happily together in Italy, supported from home, but the novels they both began then, *Buddenbrooks* and *Im Schlaraffenland*, had already shown their different preoccupations, and the differences had grown greater with time. Heinrich was always too slapdash and crude for Thomas's taste, and Thomas too little concerned with social and political problems for Heinrich's. There were differences in their friends and way of life too, especially after Thomas had married (in 1905) into a wealthy and cultivated Jewish family. His respectability and artistic asceticism were as distasteful no doubt to Heinrich as much about Heinrich was to him, his bohemianism, his theatrical friends and mistresses, and his provocative studies of bourgeois life like *Professor Unrat*, the novel of the film *The Blue Angel*, one of Marlene Dietrich's early triumphs. In the first year of the war Heinrich was annoyed by his brother's patriotic article 'Gedanken im Kriege' and responded by veiled criticism of him in his essay 'Zola' late in 1915 in *Die weißen Blätter*, where he masks himself as Zola and paints a lurid picture of Germany under Wilhelm II, calling it France under Louis Bonaparte. Thomas, as his note-books show, rejected his brother's activism, his idea that literary men and politicians should combine against reaction.[1] The man of intellect, according to Thomas, would only make a fool of himself by attempting direct action. He should be content to influence thought. He particularly resented what he took to be barbed references to his own writing, in which he was accused of toadying to the establishment and of misplaced ambition. For six years the brothers would have nothing to do with each other, and they were not fully reconciled for some years after 1922, when Thomas toned down and abbreviated the *Betrachtungen* in a new edition.

The opponent whom Thomas Mann criticizes throughout the *Betrachtungen* under the name of 'der Zivilisationsliterat' is therefore in the main his brother. A letter to Ernst Bertram (25 November 1916) speaks explicitly of the need he has long felt of symbolizing and personifying the differences of outlook, which are the curse of Germany, in his brother and himself. 'There is no German solidarity and final unity', so that Germany is not really a nation. His own natural stance was unpolitical, an attitude of intellectual freedom, but as he said later, he was 'a man of balance' and instinctively leaned to the left if the boat heeled over to the right, so he sounds perhaps more chauvinistic than he really was.[2] Anyhow, he quite deliberately expresses his full approval of the system of government of pre-war Germany, for instance in this passage at the end of the introduction:

I proclaim my deep conviction that the German people will never take to political democracy, for the simple reason that it cannot take to politics at all; and I feel that the much abused 'authoritarian state' is the form of government suited to it, best for it and at bottom what it desires.[3]

The typical middle-class German like himself is indifferent to politics, Mann says, because he is so much more interested in the things of the mind, and this devotion to culture is good because it tends to make him humane.[4] There are other ways of explaining the German indifference to politics, as we shall see in discussing Troeltsch, and the cultivated are by no means always humane – Vercors was to illustrate this point unforgettably in *Le silence de la mer*.

But the history of 'Bildung' makes the assumption a natural one for a German, as earlier chapters have shown. Mann's 'teachers' Schopenhauer, Nietzsche and Wagner are all brought in to prove that 'the political element is missing in the German idea of "Bildung".'[5] Mann quotes Nietzsche's third *Unzeitgemäße Betrachtung*: 'All states are badly organized where anyone but members of the government needs to be bothered with politics, and they deserve to come to a bad end through these shoals of politicians.' When Mann speaks of the middle-class man, the 'Bürger', he is thinking, he tells us, of those who had come through the age of Goethe, which had 'atomized the Bürger into a human being', as Turgeniev puts it, that is, made him into a 'Romantic individualist', a person in his own right, not just one of his prince's subjects among many, a 'philistine'. Things have changed in the Bismarck era, he has to admit, and some would say that the typical 'Bürger' has become a capitalistic-imperialistic 'Bourgeois' (he is thinking of Sombart's *Der Bourgeois*), a mineowner perhaps, ready to sacrifice thousands of lives for his own enrichment.[6] Mann's only reply to this fatal objection to his thesis is to say that he himself is not such a Bourgeois, but the product, like Hans Castorp, of a north-west German city democracy, patriarchal and conservative, never much concerned, he admits, about social and political questions but devoted, with the sense of duty and diligence of a good 'Bürger' – like his Tonio Kröger or Gustav Aschenbach – to his art. His present home is in Munich, which has some claim to be a city of the arts, though it certainly has its coarser elements too. But Mann has a good word for the modern business man in other cities too, regarding him as a 'Leistungsethiker', a firm believer in the traditional middle-class gospel of work – we saw the type in Hans Castorp's home town in the Protestant north – and associating him with his hero Nietzsche, 'the most thoroughgoing and fanatical ascetic among thinkers'.[7] It was this same spirit of 'Durchhalten', of choosing the hard way and holding on to the end, that he had found in Germany in 1914 and celebrated in his book on Frederick the Great.

It had long been predictable that Heinrich would not share his brother's patriotic enthusiasm. In the letter of 17 February 1904 in which Thomas tells him about meeting Katja Pringsheim, his future wife, he already speaks about Heinrich's move towards 'Liberalism' and doubts whether he himself will ever follow. 'To begin with, I understand little about "freedom "'. For me it is a purely moral and spiritual concept, the equivalent of "honesty". (Some critics call it "coldheartedness" in me.) But political freedom does not interest me at all.' He can only understand Russian literature which, he agrees, is tremendous, as having resulted from enormous pressure. 'What *does* "freedom" mean? The very fact that so much blood has been shed for the idea makes it for me something strangely *un*free, something quite medieval[...] But I suppose I don't know anything about these things.'[8] Thirty years later, during the campaign against Hitler, it might have embarrassed Mann to be reminded of this passage, but as it stands it is quite understandable in a man of culture and an artist who had come to maturity in the 'Nineties'. At the end of 1913, enquiring about Heinrich's progress with *Der Untertan*, his best social-critical novel (published 1918), Thomas, very depressed at the time through family worries and overwork, speaks of his 'incapacity to find his bearings intellectually and politically' as his brother has contrived to do.[9] He speaks too of 'a growing sympathy with death, which is part of my make up: it was the problem of decadence which always absorbed me, and that is probably what prevents me from being interested in progress'. *Buddenbrooks* of course, though it was the story of several generations of a German merchant family in the nineteenth century, had hardly mentioned the social consequences of the Industrial Revolution, the growth of a working class, the problems of its life and the beginnings of socialism. The changing manners of successive generations had been brilliantly suggested, but the theme had been an idea from Schopenhauer, their weakening hold on life as they became gradually more sensitive to ideas and art and music. As Mann says in his 'Lebensabriss' (1930), to explain how he shared, at the outbreak of the1914 war, the 'solemn feeling of German intellectuals that they were in the hands of fate, a belief that contained so much that was true and false, right and wrong', he was 'disposed by native endowment and education rather towards the moral and metaphysical than towards the political and social'.[10]

This marked intellectualism, combined with what must have seemed even to him later a strange blindness to social and political realities, lies behind Mann's often repeated praise of German devotion to 'Bildung' in the *Betrachtungen*, and his equally warm approval of his country's capacity for obedience.[11] What seems important to the German people, he writes, is 'Bildung' and the morality which stems from it. 'Playing politics makes people coarse, vulgar and stupid. Envy, insolence and rapacity are the lessons it teaches. Only the cultivation of the mind makes men free. Institutions matter little, convictions are all-important. Become better yourself! and everything will be better.' Freedom of the mind will only survive as long as order is maintained by some powerful central authority, preferably a strong monarchy which leaves religion, art and scholarship free. 'I want objectivity, order and decency. If that is philistine, a philistine I will be.'[12] Sayings like these could be paralleled, as we have seen, in Goethe and Wilhelm von Humboldt, whose conception of culture was also aristocratic, based on a status society of graded ranks. But Thomas Mann finds support for his views also in more dubious quarters. He would like to see his country adopting the organic political philosophy of the Romantic Adam Müller, whom he cannot praise too highly, but he sees a further movement towards the radical-democratic as inevitable.[13] That is why he is 'unpolitical'. 'From the very fact that mind, philosophy, superior thought have obviously no further part to play in politics, it follows that intellectual life must be kept separate from that of politics, leaving this to pursue its own fated course while itself rising above any such fatality to serene independence.'

Another laudable capacity which Mann finds particularly well developed in the Germans, alongside that for 'Bildung', is that for self-subordination without loss of dignity. 'Pride, honour and delight in obedience seems to-day to be a German idiosyncrasy and a source of international bafflement.'[14] He thinks of a cadet saluting an officer hardly older than himself, with delighted alacrity and a sort of humour, as if it were all a romantic game. 'Only someone who is nothing at all has an interest in emphasizing human equality.' This is a very flattering way of describing a German characteristic which seems to have been almost proverbial for centuries. The eminent jurist Friedrich Karl von Moser wrote in 1758: 'Every nation has its own principal motive. In Germany, it is obedience, in England, freedom, in Holland, trade, in France, the honour of the King.'[15] Herder in the *Humanitätsbriefe* spoke of the Pope who already referred to Germany as 'terra obedientiae', and Goethe, to Eckermann in 1828, contrasted the effect which 'the blessing of personal freedom, the consciousness of the English name' had, even on children, with the habitual attitude of apprehension which he saw when he looked through his window at German children playing in the snow. Mann's praise of cheerful obedience sounds like an over-explanation when one remembers Bergson's comment on the attitude towards authority in the early 'closed communities' in which he thinks man may first have acquired the social instincts which became the basis of moral obligation, an attitude of unquestioning obedience from habit. 'Une subordination habituelle', he says, 'finit par sembler naturelle, et elle se cherche à elle-même une explication.'[16]

In putting forward these views, Thomas Mann frequently appeals for support to the great tradition of German humanism coming down from Goethe and his contemporaries, and continued in Schopenhauer and Nietzsche, by each in his own, at first sight perhaps rather surprising way. 'Bildung', he writes, 'is a specifically German idea; it comes from Goethe, it got from him the connection with the plastic arts, the sense of freedom, civilized outlook and worship of life in which Turgeniev used the word, and through Goethe this idea was elevated into an educational principle as in no other nation'.[17] It makes people impatient with idle talk, for instance about politics, and it must be admitted 'that "quiet" culture, which Goethe contrasts with the French way, that is, with politics, encourages a quietistic attitude and that the profoundly unpolitical, anti-radical and anti-revolutionary nature of the Germans hangs together with the primacy which they have given to the idea of "Bildung".' It has also been said however, for example by Gustav Freytag, and Thomas Mann agrees with him, that Germany's cultivation of scholarship, literature and art first for a long time purely for their own sake, contributed towards the growth of political nationalism, because 'their pure flame tempered the gentle disposition of the Germans with its glow, and steeled it gradually for a great political struggle'.[18] Thomas Mann uses this as an argument for holding that his brother's activistic democracy is unnecessary and quotes Goethe's words to Luden in 1813, to the effect that though he had been able to forget the 'political wretchedness' of Germany through art and scholarship, the comfort they gave was a poor substitute for the consciousness of belonging to 'a great, strong, respected and formidable (yes, he used the brutal word "formidable") people'. Does it not look, Mann adds, as if Goethe had regarded Germany's great period of culture as one of preparation, and that he was consciously working for the future 'day of glory' when Germany would be unified and would rule?[19] So although every German intellectual feels a very strong temptation to revert to the old condition of non-participation in politics, of watching with an ironical smile from the side-lines, he doubts if any will fail to respect and defend Germany's great struggle for power and influence, even though it may be admitted that Bismarck, 'the man of power', was in many ways, when one thinks of the old Germany, a disaster. Anyhow, he finds it quite natural that the 'world power of the mind' ('Weitvolk des Geistes'), grown to mighty physical strength, had taken a deep draught at the spring of ambition. It aspired to become a world power, and if God so willed, *the* world power of reality, if necessary (and clearly it would be necessary) by means of a violent break-through. Had not Spain, France, England all had their hour of world power and glory? When the war broke out, Germany fervently believed that her hour had struck, the hour of trial and of greatness.

In spite of his admiration for Adam Müller's 'organic' political theory and in spite of his full acceptance of German war aims, as he saw them, and of such acts of war as the invasion of Belgium, the sinking of the 'Lusitania' and unrestricted submarine warfare, Thomas Mann has strong reserves about the powers that should be exercised by the state. He does not like too much organization and resists any 'enslavement of the individual by the state', though the 'ethical socialism, generally called State Socialism' is acceptable, as opposed to 'Marxist socialism with its rights of man'. He is with Lagarde (*Deutsche Schriften*, 1878) against Hegel with his state-idolatry.[20] He quotes with approval Lagarde's statement that the state should stand in the same relation to the nation as the 'Hausfrau' does to the master of the house, when she relieves him of all externals so that he can get on with 'the really essential things' – a nice illustration of the paternalism which is so deep-seated in the German social tradition! What Lagarde wanted was rule by technical experts, including men who had learnt the business of administration in local government, but excluding professional parliamentarians, so that there should be no opportunity for 'everyone to join in journalistic chatter about everything'. It is not surprising that his views were to be frequently brought up later by apologists for totalitarian rule, with its total rejection of 'talking shops'.

Thomas Mann's views during the First World War about the basic political assumptions of his countrymen are not entirely representative because they are those of a professional writer, always very much concerned about the interests of his profession in particular, as is clear for instance immediately after his discussion of Lagarde's ideas, when he makes a special plea for consideration for the 'aristocratic and individual', the 'uniquely gifted mind', i.e. for literature and art, in the years of economic strain which he foresees as inevitable after the war.[21] It is interesting therefore to compare Mann's reply to Western propaganda with that made about the same time by an equally distinguished German intellectual with an entirely different background, the theologian, historian and sociologist Ernst Troeltsch, in a lecture given in Vienna in October, 1915 and printed in the *Neue Rundschau* of January, 1916.

In this lecture Troeltsch acknowledged that the ideal of political freedom had originated in the West and that when, in the eighteenth century, it spread to Germany, it exercised a considerable influence there, though it was quickly adapted to German institutions and traditions. He admitted certain real differences in outlook between Germany and the West, some of them not entirely to Germany's credit. Germany was in truth less advanced than the West, for instance, in that certain medieval forms of society (he was thinking of the semi-feudal Prussian Junker) had lingered on there too long in the modern industrial world. The differences were partly due to the necessity of restricting the application of Western ideas of freedom in a continental state in an exposed position, because of its need of a strong central authority. [Bismarck made the same point forcefully when, in his Reichstag speech defending the army estimates on 6 February 1888, he said that Germany, being exposed to attack on at least three flanks, felt herself compelled to remain united and strong: 'The pike in the European carp-pond prevent us from becoming carp.'] But the chief cause of the differences between Germany and the West was that she had developed a different idea of freedom in general, and therefore different forms of political freedom from those prevailing in the West.

234

The British notion of freedom, Troeltsch explained, had resulted from the merging of feudal traditions with the stubborn individualism of the Puritans and Dissenters in the age of the English Revolution of 1688. The country gentry, in alliance with the merchant class, developed the sense of independence and personal initiative as the main features of British freedom, and provided it with a parliamentary basis. Further contributions came from the experience of a nation of pioneers in their colonial enterprises, from the free expansion of British commerce in the early capitalistic age, from memories of many past achievements and from the secure international position won by this 'Herrenvolk' and ascribed by it to just the qualities mentioned. The monarchy, the high aristocracy and the established church were regarded as national institutions, not as hindrances to freedom. They had largely adapted themselves to the nation's needs and exercised a useful social function. Only in the nineteenth century had French democratic ideas broken into this system and attained some influence.

This analysis is apposite to our study of the German unpolitical man because it reminds us of the many features in our national history to which there was in 1914 no parallel in German experience, so that as the sociologist Troeltsch saw the questions in dispute in war propaganda, it was quite unreasonable to look for the Englishman's idea of political and personal freedom among his own countrymen, when their institutions and the history behind them were so different. Troeltsch went on to describe in some detail British, French and American ideas of personal and political freedom as products of history, before defending the German idea of freedom on historical and philosophical grounds. The German idea had been influenced on the theoretical side by Locke and Rousseau, he thought, and on the practical side by the British constitution and the events of the French Revolution. But fundamental modifications of these borrowed ideas had been effected in German institutions by Stein, Scharnhorst and Boyen, and in German political theory by Kant, Fichte, Hegel and others.

'Freedom,' Troeltsch writes,

in the sense of sharing in the determination of state policy, is not for us the creation of the will of the government by counting heads, nor the control exercised over an agent by his client, but free, conscious, dutiful devotion to the whole entity constituted by the state, the nation and their history. As the expression and essence of the whole community, this totality must be freely willed and continually recreated in its own activity. Thus princes and officials regard themselves as the first servants of the state and the citizen feels himself to be a member of the state organism. All are organs of one sovereign whole, and in dutiful devotion unceasingly create it. This freedom consists of duties rather than rights, or at least of rights which are at the same time duties. The individuals do not compose the whole, but they identify themselves with it. Freedom is not equality, but the service of the individual in his due place and function. In this lies the dignity and the active influence of the individual, but also the cause of his being restrained and confined to a particular function. All the political gains resulting from national unification – equality before the law, parliamentary assemblies, universal military service, are adapted to express this spirit. It is the 'mysticism of the state' which in our great thinkers and historians has felt itself to have affinities with Plato[...] and which finds expression in varying degrees in all the great German creations of the century.

Troeltsch's interpretation of the German conception of freedom and attitude to the state is clearly a much subtler and more elaborate explanation of the relationship of the individual to authority which Thomas Mann calls 'obedience', and it has the same counterpart in Troeltsch as in Thomas Mann, the idea of 'Bildung'. In the same lecture in Vienna, Troeltsch pointed to the close analogy between the idea of the state as a super-individual entity, and that of the church, as community and as institution. Free surrender of oneself as a matter of duty and conscience to the state resembled the self-surrender of the faithful to the church, and had in fact developed out of it. In the same way the inward-looking habit of mind, the stress on personal religion, characteristic of Lutheranism and even of German Catholicism, had been secularized, he said, into the pursuit of personal culture, the 'self-perfectionism', to translate the expressive Russian term, of Goethe and his age. 'Bildung' was the necessary complement to the German attitude to the state, just as personal religion had been to self-subordination to the church. Conditions in the little despotic states of the old Germany had turned men in upon themselves, causing them to seek in what Schiller calls 'Das Ideal', the realm of ideas and imagination, a compensation for the shortcomings of 'Das Leben', the ugly realities around them. This was the kind of personal independence still most highly valued by the best Germans,

Troeltsch claimed, the attitude to life of the Greek philosophers and poets, as the Germans of Winckelmann's age had come to see them. Troeltsch did not therefore believe that in pre-war Germany Potsdam had displaced Weimar, to speak in the familiar symbols. They were both, he believed, active forces still, and must remain so, if the German attitude to the state was not to become rigid and lifeless, or personal culture sentimental, over-intellectual and politically indifferent, 'unpolitical'.

After Germany's defeat Troeltsch, like Thomas Mann, revised some of the views he had put forward early in the war. The result is to be seen in a lecture packed with thought, *Naturrecht und Humanität in der Weltpolitik*, given in Berlin in 1922 and published in the following year, just after the author's death. Thomas Mann's review of it will be mentioned later, but as a parallel to his development, some leading ideas from the lecture about the differences between the German system of ideas in politics, history and ethics and that of western Europe and America, as Troeltsch saw them in 1922, may best be discussed at this point. The second lecture is devoted to a fuller exposition of the modifications of the received European tradition in political theory brought about by the German writers and thinkers of what Troeltsch calls the Romantic Counter-revolution, beginning with Herder and culminating in Hegel, and much concerned with what we now call Historicism, and with 'organic' notions about a group-mind. The new ideal was 'half aesthetic and half religious, but instinct throughout with a spirit of antibourgeois idealism', which rejected the natural-law theory of society and the idea of the natural rights of man, the theory which culminated, according to Ernest Barker, in the American Declaration of Independence in 1776 and the French Revolution of 1789.[22] The German Romantic theory emphasizes not 'social atoms on a footing of equality with one another' and 'universal laws of nature', but personalities and their unique realization of the capacities of Mind (Geist). Not only single individuals but groups and nations are thought of as unique personalities, 'all struggling together and all developing thereby their highest spiritual powers'. Instead of the old idea of Progress, on the basis of reason, well-being, liberty and purposive organization, directed towards the unity of mankind, the theory puts forward that of Development. Development takes place in a world in which different and complementary cultures contend with each other in a sort of race, in which first one people and then another by great effort goes into the lead, enjoys hegemony for a time and then hands on the torch to the next. The general resemblance between this conception and Thomas Mann's ideas in the *Betrachtungen* is clear. After the war Troeltsch advocated a return in many respects from this 'heroic' theory of history, familiar to us from Carlyle's *Heroes and Hero Worship*, to something nearer to the common European tradition, which had in fact been elaborated most fully by German professors in the seventeenth and eighteenth centuries, down to Kant. He wanted the specialists to show more 'active vigour and practical sense' and to think more about cooperation than rivalry with other nations, in order to shape a better future. They must pay special attention, he thought, to the Rights of Man, and to the working out of an ordered system of relations between states. These were liberal ideas, but in home affairs Troeltsch was not yet prepared to accept German Socialism, any more than Thomas Mann at this time. He also emphatically rejected the fashionable cynicism of Spengler's *Untergang des Abendlands*.

Since the Second World War, one of the most interesting attempts to explain the very slow progress of liberal ways of thinking in Germany before her defeat in 1945, and the apparently successful beginnings of democracy in the Bundesrepublik, has been made by Ralf Dahrendorf, drawing on his experience not only in Germany, but in England and the United States. Dahrendorf has repeatedly put forward the view that what may be called the feudalism, in the widest sense, of eighteenth-century Germany did not disappear while the new industrialism of the following century was transforming the country. It survived in the unshakably paternalistic and authoritarian habits of thought and feeling predominant among the Protestant civil servants of all grades, the soldiers, diplomats and landed aristocracy who remained devoted to the old Prussian tradition of the state, and it spread to captains of industry. The Weimar Republic had very little success with its half-hearted attempts to dislodge this 'establishment', and it was only the fanatical determination of the National Socialists, in their pursuit of totalitarianism, to destroy the power of the aristocracy, the higher bureaucracy and rival older élites of every kind which, paradoxically, cleared the ground for a modern

238

democracy in the end. Even the men of the resistance of 1944 would have wanted to restore the old authoritarianism, Dahrendorf says, and Peter Hoffmann, perhaps the best historian of the movement, agrees that they were 'revisionists'. Instead of pairing 'Bildung' with this spirit of obedience, as Thomas Mann does, Dahrendorf speaks of 'non-participation', the cultivation of the private rather than the public virtues, as the dominant attitude in German society, praised in literature and practised in politics, and he finds the same kind of submissive attitude to authority in the family, in education, in the Church, in industrial relations and in the law. There is always the feeling that some father figure may be relied upon to produce the best possible solution of any conflict of opinion or interests, whereas in countries which really believe in solving problems by rational discussion, such differences are accepted as inevitable, bound to crop up again when circumstances change, and therefore best regulated by tentative measures, subject to later revision. We have had ample evidence in our texts of authoritarianism and the cultivation of the private virtues, and Dahrendorf's sociological ideas are a valuable supplement to Troeltsch on the German conception of freedom and Thomas Mann on 'culture' and 'obedience'.[23]

The first public sign of a marked change in Thomas Mann's political opinions came on 15 October 1922, nearly four years after the end of the war, when he made a long speech in Berlin at a big meeting arranged to celebrate the sixtieth birthday of Gerhard Hauptmann, who had already come to be regarded as the Goethe of the new Weimar Republic and played up nobly. The speech was printed, under the title 'Von deutscher Republik', in the November *Neue Rundschau*, a Hauptmann number.[24] As Mann expected, this pronouncement came as a surprise even to many good friends, most of whom thought of him after the *Betrachtungen*, as did the general public, as an unrepentant conservative. He took care to try the speech out before an invited group, which included Heinrich, on 6 October, and he had already written to some friends about it, to Arthur Schnitzler, for instance, a month before this. Even in December he was still writing, for example to Ida Boy-Edd, to explain his motives for the step. From the selection of his letters published by Erika Mann (Volume I, covering 1889 to 1936, appeared in 1962), it seems that while maintaining all along his belief in the value of German culture, in particular of Weimar humanism, for a tragically divided world – the message of the 'Schnee' chapter in *Der Zauberberg* – he had long been undecided about his narrower political allegiance after the German revolution, the imposed peace and the setting up, after long discussions in the Constituent Assembly, of the Weimar Republic. While correcting the proofs of the *Betrachtungen* he expressed his fears, in a letter to Philip Witkop of 23 May 1918, some four months before the end of the war, that 'the whole of Europe might have to go through the Bolshevik phase' and yet, he added, 'the belief in "freedom" is also impossible for mankind to-day. What belief is left?' Here of course he ascribes his own views to the whole of mankind. On 2 April 1934, a year after leaving Germany, he was to write to René Schickele, discussing the feeling in the country in early Nazi days, that things were bad and there was much dissatisfaction, 'but the German people is good at putting up with things, and as it has no liking for freedom, but feels itself neglected under it, it will seem to itself in better shape under the harsh discipline of the new constitution, and still be "happier" than under the Republic.' His own conversion to 'freedom', i.e. a belief in democratic government, had by then long been complete, but it had taken him over a decade completely to overcome his deep distaste for politics.

In the last year of the war he was still, as we saw, outspokenly unpolitical and anti-democratic. On 19 June 1918 for instance he wrote to Fritz Endres: 'The conversion of the German people to politics! Yes, yes. If only it would not result in democracy, in democracy as a "constitution" in every sense, political and spiritual, in the stooping of Germany to democracy, and among other things, to its bowing the knee to that wretched *Real-Politik* which Wilson has summed up in the phrase: "Opinion of the world is the mistress of the world".' This was written when the Treaty of Brest-Litovsk had already shown what kind of a peace the High Command would impose on the West if victorious. We have no comment by Thomas Mann on this, on the hurried concessions to parliamentary democracy when Prince Max of Baden was made Chancellor on 3 October 1918, or on the proclamation of a republic, first in Bavaria, where Mann lived (7 November) and then in Prussia (9 November) and the Kaiser's flight to Holland. The Manns lived through the anxious days of Kurt Eisner's idealistic but incompetent government, followed after his assassination (21 February 1919) by six weeks of chaos and then by a short-lived Soviet republic. Eisner had been a 'literat', a journalist and writer, and the Soviet government included amongst its leaders the Expressionist poet Ernst Toller. It was suppressed after three weeks by the roving Free Corps of ex-soldiers, and in the middle of this period, on 21 April 1919, the Manns' youngest son Michael was born at their house in Munich, to the sound of heavy gun fire and after an anxious wait for the doctor, held up by the closing of a bridge. All the families around were plundered and harassed by the 'Reds', but the Manns escaped, owing to Toller.

In his *Doktor Faustus*, Thomas Mann makes Serenus Zeitblom, the narrator of the story, responsible for the following impression of a political meeting in Munich at the time of the Soviet republic in the spring of 1919. It has every appearance of being a bit of autobiography:

The word 'painful' is not too strong if I try to characterize the impression made on me, as a a purely passive observer, by the meetings in Munich hotel rooms of certain 'Councils of Intellectual Workers' etc. which came into existence at that time. If I were a novelist, I could perhaps describe a meeting of this kind, a meeting at which some man of letters, a dimple-cheeked sybarite not without charm, might give the address on the subject of 'Revolution and the love of man' and start a free, diffuse and confused discussion, kept going by the most unlikely types, such as only came to light for a moment on such occasions, clowns, maniacs, ghosts, trouble-makers and esoteric philosophers – I could give a vivid description, I say, of such a helpless and futile council-meeting from my agonizing memories. There would be speeches for and against the love of man, for and against the officers, for and against the people. A little girl would recite a poem; a soldier in field-grey might be prevented with difficulty from going on reading from a manuscript that began by addressing the audience as 'Dear citizens and citizens' wives!' and would no doubt have taken up the whole night; an evil specimen criticized all previous speakers mercilessly, without honouring the meeting with any positive opinions of his own – and so forth. The behaviour of the audience, which delighted in rude interjections, was turbulent, childish and coarse, the chairmanship incompetent, the atmosphere terrible and the result less than nil.[25]

At about the same time in 1919, if we may believe *Mein Kampf*, Hitler, as 'education officer' of a Munich regiment, attended a meeting of the 'Deutsche Arbeiterpartei' at which Gottfried Feder

spoke – 'These associations sprang up everywhere, only to disappear
ingloriously after a short time', he says – and having taken part in the
discussion, Hitler was invited to the next committee meeting, in 'Das
alte Rosenbad', a low-class inn:

> I went through the dimly lit main dining-room, which was empty, found the
> door to a side-room and had the 'session' before my eyes. In the half-light of
> a broken gas-lamp four young fellows were sitting at a table, among them the
> author of the little pamphlet, who immediately greeted me cordially and
> welcomed me as a new member of the 'German Workers' Party'[...] The
> minutes of the last meeting were read and passed. Then it was the turn of the
> Treasurer – the association had in its possession in all seven marks and fifty
> pfennigs – this report too was accepted and minuted.

Then the correspondence, half a dozen letters, was read and there was
a long discussion about the answers to some of the letters. 'Terrible,
terrible. It was a pettifogging society of the worst description. So
this was the club they wanted me to join?' However, he did, and it
became the National Socialist Party.[26]

At the end of March Mann wrote to Ponten that there was much
that seemed to him humane and good in communism. It aimed at
abolishing the state and ridding the world of the poison of politics, a
goal which no one could object to, though proletarian culture was
something to be avoided at all costs. When Kurt Martens asked him
that summer for a word of comfort and advice for the people, to be
published in his *Münchener Neueste Nachrichten*, Mann had to
refuse, as he felt this was not the time and he had nothing helpful yet
to say. But to Gustav Blume a week later (5 July 1919), in a long letter
in reply to evidently friendly comments from a stranger on the
Betrachtungen, he says that now that the great German tradition from
Luther to Nietzsche and Bismarck, which he had been defending in
his book, is regarded by many even in Germany as dead and
dishonoured, the only thing to do is to try to adopt a contemplative,
fatalistic attitude, read Spengler and look upon their defeat as the
inevitable final stage of an ageing civilization. Life may be quite
tolerable under Anglo-Saxon dominance and the old Germany will be
remembered, even if only with Romantic nostalgia. Six months later
Mann gives strong approval to Count Keyserling's plan for a School
of Wisdom at Darmstadt, saying in a letter of 18 January 1920 that
nothing is more important than to provide German conservatism with

solid intellectual foundations. He even writes an open letter to the
Count which ends with a vision of a future Germany devoted to
culture, like German music transformed into reality, a model for the
nations.[27] The little volume of two idylls, *Herr und Hund* and *Gesang
vom Kindchen*, which came out printed on war-time paper in the
summer of 1919, conveys the spirit of those years in Mann's life when
he was living quietly in Munich as a good family man, coping as well
as he could with the dangers and problems of the day and gradually
finding his way back to creative writing. There are bitter lines in the
last canto of the *Gesang*, about the 'questionable victory' and the still
more questionable peace which was coming, and Mann is far from
rising to the level of his obvious model, *Hermann und Dorothea*, in
reformulating the great commonplaces, but the baptism scene does
bring us near to the man and the writer in those unhappy days when
'die sorgende Wirtin' can only provide for her guests at the baptis-
mal supper as well 'Wie die Blokade es zuließ der kalt gebietenden
Angeln'.* It is the baptism of the youngest daughter, Elisabeth, on 23
October 1918, which is described. In Mann's letter to Bertram (2
February 1922), the letter in which he tells one of the godfathers at the
baptism ceremony about his reconciliation with Heinrich, and his
approaching Goethe-week lecture in Frankfurt-am-Main, he says that
he has had no time to be sentimental in the years since the war, when
he has had to fight for existence while physically under-nourished
himself. The thought which entirely absorbs him at the moment, he
says, is that of a new, personal fulfilment of the ideal of 'Humanität',
of Weimar humanism, as opposed to abstract Rousseauistic humani-
tarianism – the sort castigated in the *Betrachtungen*. This is what he is
going to talk about at Frankfurt, in the presence of President Ebert,
before the performance of *The Magic Flute*. Hauptmann is to speak
before *Egmont*. It was part of his essay on 'Goethe und Tolstoi' that
he read on 1 March 1922.

In 'Von deutscher Republik' and more forcibly in the preface to the
text published in the *Neue Rundschau*, Mann repudiates the suggestion that what he is saying is incompatible with the message of the
Betrachtungen. 'This message of encouragement for the Republic
exactly continues the line of thought of the *Betrachtungen* and applies
it to present conditions, and the conviction behind it is as before,

---

* 'As the blockade of the Angles allowed, in their cold regulations.'

without retraction, the same belief in the humane German tradition.'
Like E. M. Forster, Mann does not really call for more than 'Two
Cheers for Democracy'. He hopes that this demonstration of support by a notorious 'Bürger' will do the Republic some good, but he is
careful to 'define it first', as he said in the letter to Ida Boy-Edd later,
'and how! Almost as the opposite of what to-day exists! But just for
that reason: the attempt to breathe something like an idea, a soul, a
spirit into this miserable state without citizens, seemed to me not a
bad thing to do.'[28] What he has in mind is the kind of reformed state
which he thinks the young Germans of 1914 had set out to fight for.
He obviously wishes to persuade people to give up thinking, as almost
all Germans naturally did, that this form of government is simply the
result of military defeat, and to win over its chief opponents, the
young and the middle-class, for what is generally called democracy,
though he prefers to call it 'Humanität', to persuade them to transfer
their patriotism to this Germany, in spite of its new name. At the same
time he dissociates himself from the militant young conservatives of
the 'Frei-korps', with what he calls their 'sentimental obscurantism,
which organizes terror and brings disgrace on their country through
hideous and insane murders', and he pays a warm tribute to their
latest victim, Walther Rathenau, the late Foreign Minister. One of his
chief motives for coming forward in this courageous and public-
spirited way seems to have been his disgust at the behaviour of the
Free Corps, who formed, of course, the nucleus of the National
Socialist movement. *His* conservatism must be humane and cultivated, in the tradition of Goethe and Nietzsche, as he understands him.
There is surely room for something more truly German than the
'imperial gala opera' provided for them by 'that talent' (the Kaiser).
'That was amusing, but it was an embarrassment.' They had hoped
their neighbours in Europe did not hold *them* responsible – though
they did – and had turned back to culture. But now there is at last the
possibility of a unified culture, of a political form which really
expresses the whole national life. In any case, as he had already
reminded them, this was no time for dreams of a restored monarchy.
'The Republic is a fate, and one towards which "amor fati" is the only
proper attitude. That is not too solemn a word for the matter, for the
fate in question is no trifle. So-called freedom is no joke or relaxation...Its other name is responsibility, a word which reminds us

that freedom is a heavy burden – especially for the brains of the country.' Mann went on to remind his audience of what a Russian writer had recently told them about the social responsibility which had long rested on the shoulders of writers in Russia, tacitly admitting that German literature had been too little concerned about social questions. The rest of this over-long address, which Mann himself later, in 'Kultur und Sozialismus' (1928)[29] was to contrast unfavourably with the *Betrachtungen* as a piece of writing, is mostly taken up with long quotations from Novalis, brought in, as it were, to make his case respectable, by showing that already in Romantic times Novalis had seen the necessity of combining novelty with conservatism in national affairs. He had proposed bringing in the church, as in the Middle Ages, to reconcile and guide the divided laity, and Mann finds a modern substitute for the church in humanism, 'Humanität', which he has learnt through Walt Whitman, recently translated by Hans Reisiger, to equate with democracy. A comparison of these two writers, the original germ of this lecture, leads Mann to the theme, familiar from the *Zauberberg* and earlier works, of the 'sympathy with death', or the past, which developes into a strengthened resolve to serve life.

The much shorter speech 'Geist und Wesen der deutschen Republik', which Mann was invited by a group of republican students in Munich to give at a meeting held in memory of Walther Rathenau in June 1923, is clearer and more eloquent than 'Von deutscher Republik'. It is not the main speech of the meeting, the tribute to Rathenau, but a very appropriate introduction, in which Mann tries dispassionately to explain what, as it seems to him, the new form of government means, or can be made to mean, for his country. Given goodwill, he is convinced that it can serve the most desirable national purposes, his ideal being the fulfilment of German 'Menschlichkeit', the good life as their best traditions conceive it, which will only come through 'the unity of state and culture' – the phrase familiar from the earlier speech. Mann starts from the German idea of 'Bildung', describing it in the fine passage already quoted in the Introduction (p. vii). It is of course the German middle class that he has chiefly in mind, as he speaks to these students, and what he rightly stresses is something which he has only recently become aware of himself, namely that this in many ways so admirable ideal of personal culture is incomplete while it continues to neglect the political dimension. The failure hitherto of the educated German to take an active interest in the political element in social life, that, he sees now, is the root cause of middle-class opposition to the idea of a republic, that is, of self-government. 'When we are asked to pass from inwardness to objective reality, to politics, to what the nations of Europe call "freedom", it seems to us a warping of our nature, indeed the destruction of our nationhood.'[30] Admitting that that is their natural reaction as Germans, Mann continues, 'is it German to maintain that our national character cannot and should not be improved?' For him the answer is no, and what is particularly needed to complete the German make-up is a sense for the objective, for politics and 'freedom'. Isn't this perhaps what Hölderlin may have meant when in *Hyperion* he calls his countrymen lacking in harmonious development, 'not whole men, but fragments and patchwork'? Does he not mean that true humanity includes inner and outer, the personal and the objective, conscience and action, and that the Germans, as 'Bürger' and men, broke off the process of development prematurely, before it included a political sense?

Appealing, as usual, to the authority of the German classics, Mann interprets Goethe's *Wilhelm Meister, the* 'Bildungsroman', as a poetic prevision of Germany's progress, in due time, from inwardness to concern for objective goals, the political sphere, republicanism, and not just as a monument of personal culture and pietistic autobiography. From being occupied at first exclusively with his own development, Wilhelm comes to be interested, in the *Wanderjahre*, in education generally, for his son's sake, and finally in the sphere of social relations and the role of the state, 'undoubtedly the highest stage of the human'. Give the present-day German time enough, and he will go through the same stages and come to see that all-round culture, to be complete, must include a sense of political responsibility. The conditions of life resulting from the war and the peace are far from being favourable to this advance at present. People abroad can have no conception of the humiliating hardships the great majority have to endure at this time (the height of the inflation), 'they do not know that German mothers must wrap their babies in newspapers for lack of linen' – commandeered by the French. For all this the new regime receives the blame. External political pressure (the occupa-

246

tion of the Ruhr) encourages political pessimism, the philosophy of brutality (of the Free Corps). An ominous paragraph follows about alarming movements of ideas in the post-war world outside, which puts concisely the message Hans Castorp hears from Naphta. A widespread feeling of depression like the mood that followed the Napoleonic wars has given rise to inhumane action – Bolshevism in Russia, Fascism in Italy, Horthy's regency in Hungary and certain shady movements in France are instanced. (Mann does not mention of course that Hitler had led a demonstration in Munich in January. The putsch led by Ludendorff and him was to come in November.) Democracy, individualism, liberalism, personal freedom are already meaningless and obsolete ideas to many in these movements, and are being replaced by their opposites, individualism by group loyalty, freedom by iron discipline and terror. They all crave for the absolute, and obscurantism is the inevitable result. But he does not believe that in the country of Goethe, Hölderlin and Nietzsche, who were not liberals indeed, but good humanists, the exploitation of anti-liberal ideas can succeed. 'The republican youth of Germany', he concludes, 'understands that "Humanität" is the idea of the future, the idea to which Europe will struggle through, with which it will inspire itself and for which it must live – if it does not wish to die.'

With these two pronouncements Thomas Mann had defined the political attitude which he was to maintain for the rest of his life. His reference to obscurantism was the first of the long series of outspoken attacks which he was to make on National Socialism, and it came as we have seen in the very year of the attempted 'putsch' by Ludendorff and Hitler in Munich, so ten years before Hitler came to power (in January 1933) and Mann's exile began. Now that the editors of successive collected editions have brought together as many as possible of Mann's occasional speeches and essays, one is amazed at the quality and quantity of the great novelist's output of writing about current affairs, produced when he was at the height of his creative powers and probably always gave his best hours to his art. The author of *Buddenbrooks* and *Der Zauberberg* was on any showing one of the leading European novelists of his day and he had already more than once been considered for the Nobel prize for literature before it was awarded to him in 1929. It was inevitable that he should frequently be asked for his opinion on current questions, and he was

247

conscientious about his representative duties as a leader in art and thought. Conscience as well as regard for his own good name compelled him to write about the dangers he saw coming and occasionally to reply to one of the innumerable attacks that were levelled at him after 1922, not only by the gutter press, and increasingly as the National Socialist movement grew. In what follows, only a few of Mann's essays and speeches can be briefly discussed, always with the aim of following the development of his thought about the need for a new attitude to politics on the part of the educated German.

Mann did not speak about politics at any length in the 1920s after the two pieces discussed, but one or two reviews and short articles, as well as the debates in *Der Zauberberg* and remarks in letters, show that he remained consistently liberal, if not yet quite ready for socialism. A review published on Christmas Day, 1923, of the lecture on *Naturrecht und Humanität in der Weltpolitik* by Ernst Troeltsch discussed above, says that Troeltsch was not content simply to analyse the differences he saw between German 'political-historical-moral' thought and that of the West and America, bringing out the contrast between the ideas of the German-Romantic counter-revolution and the older Western political philosophy based on natural law. Troeltsch also warmly advocated Germany's return to the main line of development, proving that he too had changed his ideas since the end of the war, and in the same direction as Thomas Mann. Many Germans, the reviewer says, even some 'who had long dwelt in the Magic mountain of Romantic aestheticism and studied it deeply', had lately been thinking, though less precisely, along similar lines, and certain confessions (his own, of course) had been badly received and treated as the talk of a base renegade. Although he understood this backward-looking conservatism, he was determined not to be diverted from his friendly attitude to the demands of life, and pointed to the example of Switzerland, and German parts of Austria, where there had been no such divergence of political thought. He hinted that Germany should not close its mind to the idea of the League of Nations, which was in the same natural-law tradition.[31] Stresemann was to take Germany in of course in 1926.

In 1924, asked for a comment on the fifth anniversary of the proclamation of the Weimar Constitution, Mann says that it is of course not perfect, but it is a manifestation of a will and capacity to live which are admirable and astonishing, when one remembers the circumstances in which it was created. He speaks of the German people's unparalleled resilience, not only in recent history. Though it always resists the idea of change, it acts as if it accepted the motto chosen for it by its greatest poet: 'Stirb und Werde'. He follows this up by quoting very appositely a page from the drama *Empedokles* by Hölderlin, whose post-war vogue was at its height, interpreting it as a vision of a truly democratic society.[32] There are several references even in the selection of letters edited by Erika Mann to the reception of Thomas Mann's apparent swing towards liberalism by German opinion as reflected in the press. They were mainly hostile and frequently inaccurate, but he seldom had time or any wish to reply. One witty and spirited retort however, published in *Die literarische Welt*, is reprinted in *Reden und Aufsätze*[33] and the response to this in other periodicals is discussed in a letter to its editor on 2 March 1928.[34] The offending article had been a quite inaccurate and apparently almost libellous comment in the *Berliner Nachtausgabe* on a conversation between Mann and a young Frenchman in Munich, printed in a Paris newspaper. Mann had been working for years for a good understanding between France and Germany, he had had a splendid reception in Paris in 1926 (fully described in his *Pariser Rechenschaft*)[35] and several leading French writers had visited Berlin. The nationalist press in Germany had reacted in what seemed to Mann its usual stupid way. 'Nationalism', Mann had explained to his French interlocutor, 'is with us inevitably and disastrously stricken with lack of talent, it does not count intellectually, it cannot write or exercise any fascination in a higher sense, it is pure barbarism. A curse, a metaphysical interdict hangs over it, it is the unforgivable sin against the Holy Ghost, and a writer who succumbs to it degenerates without hope of recovery.' France, on the other hand, had really distinguished nationalist writers like Barrès.

Although Mann claimed, as we have seen, that the ideas expressed in 'Von deutscher Republik' were not inconsistent with those of the 'Unpolitical Man', he repeatedly repudiated the views of the German nationalists after the war, as we see for instance from his letter to Arthur Hübscher of 27 June 1928, after Hübscher had criticized his emendations of the *Betrachtungen* in the second edition. He insists in this letter that he has no liking for politics and belongs to no party. He only wants to defend what is reasonable and humane, and therefore in his sense 'German'. 'There are some kinds of narrow-mindedness and malice which my intelligence and character cannot stand. I openly admit that I want to have nothing to do with people (like some Munich professors!) who after the murder of Rathenau said: "Bravo, that's one out of the way!", and that I find the Munich middle-class press dreadful.' He has no golden message for the young and has never tried to be a leader. 'All that men like me could hope to do would be to set an example to confused young people – and that only through modesty, caution and good will.'[36]

In 'Kultur und Sozialismus' Thomas Mann brings up to date the reflections on the ideas behind German politics which he had begun in the *Betrachtungen*. The essay was published in *Preussische Jahrbücher* in April, 1928. He still claims to be consistent with his former self, but he admits now that he had left out of consideration in his book the fighting war in all its sordid reality, with all the material side of its origins, conduct and aims. It was possible for the war of ideas to obscure the ugly realities for him because of his unpolitical idealism as a middle-class German with an insufficiently examined conception of culture. At the end of the war, he believes, it was harder for the Germans to bear the shock of the collapse of their system of ideas, their 'Kultur', than the facts of military defeat and political collapse. Those who held on to their traditional idea of culture could not help looking upon the democratic republic as something foreign to their country's real nature. The Germans have difficulties in adapting themselves to their new form of government because all the psychological preconditions are lacking. The great Germans recognized abroad, Luther, Goethe, Schopenhauer, Nietzsche, George, were not democrats, and it was they who created the German idea of 'Kultur', with the capital 'K' which aroused so much feeling abroad in the war. 'Kultur' is etymologically the same word as 'Kultus' with its religious connotation (cf. 'Kultus-minister') and Germans have long felt a quasi-religious, almost mystical respect for culture (he is evidently thinking of both self-development – 'Bildung' – and of objective culture, the arts and sciences – 'Kultur'). The German attitude towards the serious theatre, so different from that of the West, is a striking example. Ideally the theatre has come to be a sort of

250

temple in Germany, to which you go for the good of your soul, as to a good concert or art-collection, whereas in the West the aim of amusement predominates, perhaps rising to social satire. Mann thinks only of the dramatists who have gradually evoked this response, and one misses some consideration of the social and even political background, the patronage of petty princes and later of towns, and behind that the division of the old Germany into a multitude of small states with few temptations towards power politics, and prestige reasons for favouring the arts. Instead we have some vague and unconvincing sociological theory about the 'Gemeinschaften' or communities making up a 'Volk' supporting a 'Kultur', and on the other hand the 'Gesellschaft' or society in a 'Nation' with a mere 'Zivilisation'. 'The concept of the nation is historically bound up with democracy, whereas the word "Volk" corresponds to the really German, that is culturally-conservative, unpolitical way of thinking, opposed to any atomic form of society.'

'German socialism', Mann continues, 'the invention of a Jewish social theorist educated in Western Europe, has always been felt by devotees of German culture to be a foreign element, at variance with our folk tradition, and simply anathema for them: justifiably, insofar as it leads to the undermining of the cultural idea of folk and community by that of the social class. This disintegration has in fact already proceeded so far that to talk about folk and community to-day seems pure romanticism.'[37] In spite of being based on the study of economic facts and not on idealistic metaphysics, socialism has a stronger appeal for intelligent people at present than conservatism with all its romantic aura, being so much better attuned to the requirements of everyday life. The social-democratic policy about legislation, the rationalization of government and administration, and the international organization of Europe is much more sensible than that of its opponents. To illustrate the barrenness of conservatism, Mann points to Stefan George's complete lack of interest in social themes and problems, maintaining as he does Nietzsche's similarly patrician attitude, and he ends with an appeal to the educated middle class to support not of course communism, with its fanatical idea of a proletarian dictatorship, but moderate German socialism.

Mann repeated some of these views about socialism in his 'Deutsche Ansprache – Ein Appell an die Vernunft', a speech made on

17 October 1930 in the Beethovensaal in Berlin, apparently on his own initiative, so that he has to apologize at the beginning for seeming to assume the role of a second Fichte, and addressing the German nation. He had come to Berlin to give a reading from his works on the following day, but in view of the result of the general election a month earlier, in which the National Socialists had gained 18% of the votes, after a year or two of economic depression and a succession of political crises, he felt it would be fiddling while Rome burned if he did not, as a public figure, make some effort to warn the country about the seriousness of the situation and to 'appeal to reason' even at the eleventh hour. The election of 14 September has shown, he says, that the country is being carried away by the shrill catchwords of fanaticism. He briefly reviews events since the war, condemning the Versailles Treaty as intended to hold the Germans permanently down, but resulting in the present chaos. The Weimar Constitution has defects, but no one has concrete proposals for overcoming them. The phenomenal success of National Socialism is due to public discontent with the political and economic situation, combined with the widespread feeling that an epoch is ending, the era dating from the French Revolution with its liberal principles based on the power of reason – freedom, justice, education, progress. There are many signs now of a revolt against reason, of a tendency to invoke instead the dynamism of passion, of ecstasy, the dark unconscious powers of the mind. The half-educated have a barbarous craze for words like 'rassisch, völkisch, bündisch, heldisch' and the dangerous political romanticism they express. The old decencies are 'bourgeois', dictatorship by force prevails in Finland, Russia, Italy, and in Germany fanaticism is preached as a gospel of salvation. The leaders in this movement pretend to the outside world to have renounced force in the settlement of foreign disputes, and their frenzied patriotism is vented in hatred of their political opponents and the pursuit of a totalitarian state. Only the Catholics have an ideology that is secure against them. The bogy of communism gives them their hold over the middle class, but he insists that social democracy is something quite different, repeats the phrases used about it in 'Kultur und Sozialismus' and ends with warm praise for Stresemann's achievement of a peaceful revision of Versailles. It was a brave effort, made in spite of noisy interruptions and disorder in the hall caused by National Socialists

and Conservative extremists, but things had gone too far to be much affected by Thomas Mann's thinking aloud before an audience of intellectuals. The lecture did not of course pass unnoticed by the nationalist popular press, and it was greeted with howls of derision and abuse. Thomas Mann wrote a long article early in 1931, 'Die Wiedergeburt der Anständigkeit', suggested by a revival he had just seen of Ibsen's *Pillars of Society*, in which he contrasts the idealism of Ibsen's day with the temper of his own time. He discusses in particular the effect of the fashionable preoccupation with the irrational when its slogans filter down to the half-educated, and he attacks with bitter irony the 'childish conceit' of a Hamburg reviewer of the 'Deutsche Ansprache'.

Thomas Mann had maintained in 1923, in 'Geist und Wesen der deutschen Republik', that to be truly humane, Germans needed to develop the political interests and capacities which they had hitherto neglected, in their exclusive pursuit of Kultur. He often comes back to this idea as his central new insight, that the political is not opposed to humane culture, but a part of it. In 'Kultur und Sozialismus' (1928), as we saw, he went on from a detached liberalism to a moderate socialism, repelled as he was after the war by the backward-looking and narrowly nationalistic parties of the right, with their fringe of irresponsible and violent young, whose excesses were soon matched and outdone by the new party of National Socialists with their fanatical racism, and the terror-tactics they developed, ostensibly to protect the country from Communism. Thomas Mann's 'Rede vor Arbeitern in Wien' of 22 October 1932 marked for him the beginning of a new epoch in his life and thought, he declared in his opening words, being his first speech as a middle-class writer to an audience of working-men and socialists. What he said was very much the same as he had written in 'Kultur und Sozialismus' four years earlier, but we find here for the first time an unambiguous plea for compassionate socialism and the express repudiation of the normal indifference of the educated in Germany to social questions, as something beneath their consideration. The second half of the speech repeats the substance of his attack in 'Deutsche Ansprache' on the National Socialists and their 'philosophy'.

An address which was to have been read for Mann at a meeting of a Socialist society in Berlin (the 'Sozialistischer Kulturbund') on 19 February 1933 is 'Bekenntnis zum Socialismus', an open declaration of his belief in socialism. The meeting never took place, because Hitler became Chancellor on 30 January, but the text of the proposed address was published in the society's periodical. It is a renewed and more explicit expression of support of the Republic, arising out of his conviction that thinking people of middle-class origin should side now with the workers and Social Democracy. His main argument is contained in the following paragraph:

As a man of this kind I feel deeply how dishonest and life-repressing it is to look down scornfully on the political and social sphere and to consider it of secondary importance compared with the world of the inward, metaphysics, religion and so forth. This way of comparing the respective values of the inward, personal world and the life of society, contrasting metaphysics and socialism, for instance, and representing the latter as lacking in piety and sanctity, as a merely materialistic desire for happiness in a termite society, is not admissible to-day. It is not admissible, in a world as anti-divine and bereft of reason as ours, to represent man's metaphysical, inward and religious activities as inherently superior to his will to improve the world. The political and social is one aspect of the humane. The interest and passion for humanity, self-dedication to the problem of man, sympathy with his lot, this interest and this passion are concerned with both aspects, that of the personal and inward and also that of the external arrangement of human life in society.[38]

Mann appeals this time to Nietzsche as his authority from the great German past, quoting from *Also sprach Zarathustra* (Die Reden Zarathustras, Von der schenkenden Tugend, 2) the passage about remaining faithful to the earth, and bringing fugitive virtue back to the earth, to give it a meaning, a human meaning. 'That is the materialism of the spirit, a religious man turning towards the earth,' Mann adds, and socialism is just this refusal to bury one's head in the sand, and the resolve to tackle the problems of collective life, to humanize it. It is in this sense that Mann is a socialist. He is a democrat because of the fundamentally humane ideas, like that of freedom, on which democracy is based. It is natural that some of the young should have reacted against these abstract ideas in favour of the native traditions of their own 'Volk', but their romantic notions are being manipulated by the Right for its own ends. The heroic age of nationalism was the nineteenth century, when it was still in Germany a revolutionary idea for which men went to prison, but now it belongs to the past. 'Every man of feeling and understanding and every respectable politician knows that the peoples of Europe can no longer live and prosper in isolation, but that they all depend on each other and form a community destined to march together, a community which should be recognised and made into a reality.' The European idea, it will be seen, was something quite familiar to Thomas Mann long before the Second World War, and in the middle of the war, in one of the fifty-five wireless talks he addressed to Germany through the BBC, the one for August, 1941, he assured his listeners that the world would need Germany, and Germany would need the world, when the war was over. 'Germany will never have been happier – and it knows this at heart even now – than as a member of a world at peace and unified in freedom, and depoliticized through the curbing of national autocracy. Germany is just made for such a world, for if ever "Machtpolitik" was a curse and distorting unnatural pose for a people, it was that for the fundamentally unpolitical Germans.'[39]

It was Hitler's rise to power which finally brought about in Thomas Mann what he called 'Die Politisierung des Geistes', the final conversion of the Unpolitical Man. Looking back at the end of the war he wrote to Hermann Hesse on 8 April 1945:

We have all, under severe pressure, experienced a kind of simplification of our ideas. We have seen evil in all its horror, and in doing so – it is a shame-faced confession – we have discovered our love of the good. If *Geist* [spirit, mind] is the principle, the power that wills the good, the anxious attentiveness to changes in the image of truth, 'divine care' in a word, which strives for an approach to what is right, enjoined, behoving, here below, then it is political, whether it likes that title or not. Nothing living, I think, can get round the political to-day. A refusal is also a political decision, one in favour of the wrong cause.

Heinrich Mann had been deprived of his German citizenship before his brother and had led the 'Popular Front' of émigrés in Paris, but from 1936 Thomas Mann became the intellectual leader of the German intellectuals in exile. He wrote in 1937 the preface to the first number of *Maß und Wert*, their periodical published in Stockholm, and to the first numbers of the following two volumes. All were manifestos, and they had been preceded by his solemn warning against the dangers in store from Hitlerism for Europe in 'Achtung, Europa!' in 1935. From 1938 till the end of the war he lived in America and made a number of political speeches there, as well as writing the radio addresses already mentioned. At the same time he was finishing the long *Joseph* novel and writing *Doktor Faustus*, in which Serenus Zeitblom, the narrator, describes incidentally the conditions of life and the atmosphere around him as he writes. From chapter xxxiii on it is a picture of Germany since 1918 that is presented to us in this way, at first from Mann's own memories and after 1933 from the reports of others. Serenus is obviously the mouthpiece of Thomas Mann, and he undergoes the same development in his political views as we have followed in his creator.

'Achtung, Europa!' is the text of a message from Thomas Mann which was read in French at the meeting at Nice in April 1935 of the 'Comité de la Coopération Intellectuelle'. National Socialism is not mentioned by name, because it was not until the following year that Thomas Mann lost his German citizenship, following his open letter of 3 February 1936 to Eduard Korrodi in the *Neue Züricher Zeitung*, in which he expressed his conviction that nothing good could result from the present German regime, for Germany or the world. The address is an indictment of those responsible for the moral and intellectual debasement of 'the masses' which is in progress in many countries. 'The decisive point is that they [the new young] know nothing about "Bildung" in its higher and deeper sense, about self-improvement, individual responsibility and exertion, and make things easy for themselves instead in the collective.'[40] They like marching and singing songs which are a mixture of debased folksongs and leading articles. 'These young people enjoy for its own sake the feeling of abandoning care and seriousness and losing themselves in a mass movement, with hardly a thought for where they are going.' Their leaders do not try to raise the masses by education, but only to rule them by working on their instincts, by propaganda. The cultivated nations look on bewildered, but Mann warns them that their tolerance in present circumstances may lead to war and the end of civilization.

Mann's immediate personal reaction to the news from Germany after he had left it on a lecture tour to Holland, Belgium and France in February 1933 is fully documented in the printed pages from his diary of 1933 and 1934, 'Leiden an Deutschland'.[41] Anger and scorn inspire comments and descriptions full of bitter satire when the Führer speaks to the nation, for instance, on 'Kultur', but there are also pages of reflections on the nature and history of politics, where the germs of later speeches and articles are to be found. In a couple of pages written apparently late in 1934, for instance, we find Mann acknowledging more clearly than before how much Germany has to learn from other countries in the by no means despicable art of politics:

Politics as the "art of the possible" is indeed a sphere resembling that of art in that, like art, it mediates creatively between mind and life, idea and reality, the desirable and the necessary, conscience and action, freedom and necessity, morality and power. It includes harsh, necessary, amoral elements[...] and one remembers in this connection the statesman who, at the height of his successes, when he had succeeded in uniting his country and making of it a great power, declared that he did not know whether he could still count himself among the decent people.[42]

If it completely forgets its ideal side and reduces itself to brute force and deception, it easily degenerates into a devilish and criminal activity, incapable, for all its terror and destruction, of lasting effects.

Nations which have politics in their blood have an instinctive capacity for reconciling, at least as they see things, their political actions with their conscience. They will the means, but never quite lose sight of human decency and morality as ends. Germany on the other hand shows its political incapacity by its clumsy misunderstanding of these niceties. 'Though by no means evil by nature, but gifted in the direction of the spiritual and ideal, it considers politics to be entirely a matter of murder, lies, deception and violence, something completely and one-sidedly filthy, and as soon as it thinks the moment has come for it to give itself over to politics, it practises the art according to a corresponding philosophy. The French say: "If a German wants to be ingratiating, he jumps out of the window." That is also what happens when he wants to play politics. He thinks he must behave in such a way to frighten people out of their senses[...] The variety of things that "raison d'état" has to cover and explain, for a German turned "political", goes beyond saying.' But in reality, 'politics is a function of human society, the totality of the human mind includes an interest in it, and just as man does not belong exclusively to the realm of nature, so politics is not wholly concerned with evil. But the German thinks that it is, and it is therefore no wonder that politics distorts, poisons and ruins him.' The danger to the world that results from the existence at the heart of Europe of a power with such a beast-of-prey philosophy of politics is obvious. In his declaration in the *Betrachtungen* that politics is a dirty business, Thomas Mann had had domestic politics mainly in view, and here the whole emphasis is on foreign affairs, international politics, but there is evidence all the same that his point of view has changed from that of the typical German, as he described it now after the rise of the Nazis, to the more enlightened conception ascribed here to nations with a native flair for politics.[43]

This idea of the uncultivated one-sidedness of the unpolitical German is strongly stressed in Mann's editorial introduction to his new periodical *Maß und Wert* in 1937, where the diary entry we have quoted is repeated almost word for word. After discussing the current misconception of politics in Germany, he says again:

Totality – there is only one, humane totality, the totality of the humane, of which the social and political is a segment and component part. The German 'Bürger' did not know that. He thought he could, for the sake of his inwardness and culture, negate politics, 'steal away from under it', as Richard Wagner said, and many of Germany's calamities have resulted from his mistaken notion that it was possible to be an unpolitical cultivated man.[44]

What is happening now is that the German has gone from one extreme to the other and has 'totalized politics, the state', which is far worse, for to force the whole of life into a political strait-jacket is a crime, with criminal consequences. The new periodical is dedicated to the service of freedom and 'Humanität' but not of 'Humanität' just in the classical sense, which neglects one aspect of the humane, but of a new, perfected conception of humanism still in the making.

After 1938, when Thomas Mann settled in the United States, similar ideas about the relationship between culture and politics are still the burden of his principal speeches, often made to Americans of German origin. In his 'Rede auf dem deutschen Tag in New York' in 1938, for example, he repeats that it is a mistake to think of culture and politics as necessarily opposed to each other, and to look down on the one from the heights of the other. He sums up his message in the sentence: 'It was a mistaken belief of the German "Bürger" that it was possible to be an unpolitical man of cultivation.' The results of that error are now plain to all, Germany's lack of political instincts, the over-compensating worship of the state and of power, and the inhumanity which results from this.[45] In 'Das Problem der Freiheit' he comes back next year to the question of the tensions between democracy, based on the idea of freedom, and socialism, based on that of equality. He recalls Goethe's and Heine's attitude to the problem and declares again that a purely individualistic and intellectual 'Humanität' constitutes a danger for 'Kultur' which, properly understood, means the totality of the humane, including the social elements. To make politics absolute, on the other hand, as dictatorships and Bolshevism do, means the end of freedom, which depends on the maintenance of a just and reasonable, a 'humane' balance between the claims of the individual and the social.

Even so private an occasion as the dinner in honour of Heinrich Mann on his seventieth birthday – he had only recently escaped to America from occupied France – evoked a speech from his brother which revolved round the now familiar antithesis of culture and politics. It is one of a whole series of speeches which these literary brothers addressed to each other on birthdays. As Hermann Kesten wrote about this occasion:

When we celebrated Heinrich Mann's seventieth birthday it was just like old times: Thomas Mann pulled out a manuscript and congratulated from it. Then his brother pulled out his bit of paper and expressed his thanks, also from the typed page, while we sat at dessert, a score of men and women, and listened to German literature in its home circle. Feuchtwanger, Werfel, Mehring, the Reinhardts and some film people were amongst those present.[46]

In his speech Thomas Mann succeeds in giving a new turn to the now familiar thought about political institutions forming an essential part of a civilization, and about the fatal flaw in the habitual way of thinking of the cultivated classes in Germany, that it was too little concerned with the practical problems of social and political life. He quotes with strong approval some sentences from an unnamed English critic who, while deeply admiring German culture, is always depressed to find German poets and philosophers being led by their thought in the end 'to the edge of an abyss – an abyss from which they could not withdraw, but must fall into headlong, – an abyss of intellect no longer controlled by any awareness of the sensuous realities of life.' Nietzsche seems to Mann a tragic example, and he contrasts his 'intoxicating doctrine of the anti-humane' with occasional letters, like the one about the disastrously early death of the Emperor Frederick III, Queen Victoria's son-in-law, 'the last hope for German freedom', letters which reveal, he thinks, the real man behind 'the romantic poem that was his work'. The 'realities of life' are inescapable to-day, and he is convinced that an epoch is beginning when the arts will simply have to distinguish again, on religious and moral grounds, between good and evil. Heinrich, he says, had been one of the first moral critics of his age, in books like his *Untertan, Professor Unrat* and *Die kleine Stadt*. He praises too his untiring campaign against Hitlerism, and at the darkest moment in the war, expresses his own confidence that as a victory for Hitler would result in a world completely given over to evil, a negation of all humane aspirations, there will come a revolt against this nihilism as of the elements themselves, and 'iron facts' will crumble away before decent human feeling. He repeated this eloquent passage in that month's broadcast to Germany.

At the end of the German war Thomas Mann gave a lecture in English on 'Germany and the Germans' in the Library of Congress (29 May 1945), in which he attempted finally a brief sketch of the German national character on a historical basis.[47] There is no question here of attacking the 'bad' Germany in the name of the 'good'. He insists that there is only one Germany, and that what he says is the result of his own experience as a German, a piece of self-criticism. Germans are much given to self-criticism, he says, being highly introspective by nature, and it is this inward-looking habit of thought, the source of the German passion for 'Bildung' and also of German ineptness in practical politics, which is again his real subject. He neither excuses nor accuses, but tries to understand, as a citizen of provincial Lübeck who has become a cosmopolitan American. Lübeck, he recalls, had something quite medieval about it, not only in its appearance but in the suggestion of irrational depths he found in its spiritual atmosphere. It is the author of *Doktor Faustus* who is speaking, putting into plain English some of the ideas he was to convey symbolically in his coming novel, in which a modern

260

Faustus, modelled on Nietzsche, in part suffers the lot of Germany herself. He wants to convey in his lecture, he says, that the German mind has made a secret compact with the demonic. How had this come about? Partly, he suggests, through the Reformation. Martin Luther (the counterpart of Faust in the popular imagination) was superlatively German, Mann thinks, in his introspectiveness combined with a mystical musicality, for example. He does not like him, for his anti-Europeanism, and for the combination he finds in him of choleric robustness and coarseness, lyrical tenderness and crass superstition, but he acknowledges his greatness and his enormous influence on German history. 'He was a freedom-hero – but in the German style, for he understood nothing about freedom', about political freedom, that is, siding as he did with the princes in the Peasants' Revolt, unlike Tilman Riemenschneider, one of Mann's heroes. 'Luther's anti-political devotion to the rulers, the product of German-musical inwardness and unworldliness, has not only stamped itself in the course of the centuries on the subservient attitude of the Germans to their princes and all official authority. It has not only created, or at least favoured, the German dualism of boldest speculation and political immaturity. It is also representative in a monumental and defiant way of the typically German falling-apart of the desire for nationhood and the ideal of political freedom. For the Reformation, like the rising against Napoleon later, was a nationalistic freedom movement.'[48] The passage which follows these words was broadcast by Mann to Germany as part of his address on 2 April 1945. It is to the effect that political freedom in Germany has always meant freedom from foreign domination, the freedom to be German and nothing else, nothing more, whereas in democratic countries it means the freedom of the individual, a moral freedom. German freedom had really meant militant slavishness, and the Nazis had hoped to extend it to the whole world.

The trouble is that the Germans have never had a real revolution like the French, whose idea of a nation was born in their revolution and includes the ideals of civic freedom and European unity. It was greeted as a liberalizing idea, even abroad, whereas German patriotism, even in the days of Jahn and Maßmann during the 'Wars of Liberation', had a crude and boorish way with it which antagonized Goethe, for example, as the very antithesis of the super-national culture which was his ideal. The failure of the Germans to achieve civic freedom in any of their attempts at revolution, in 1848 or 1918 for example, had given them a strange idea of politics. The passage already quoted from the preface to *Maß und Wert* (p. 258) is repeated here, about the Germans going berserk when they take to politics, instead of practising it as the art of the possible, with due regard for moral values.

Why is it, Mann asks himself, that in German history evil so often results from good? There is surely something demonic about it. Take the capacity for 'Innerlichkeit' which has so long been a German characteristic, the delicacy and depth of feeling, the unworldly absent-mindedness which went along with love of nature and a deep seriousness of thought and conscience in so many Germans and lies behind the achievements in metaphysics, in music and in the inimitable German 'Lied'. This quality inspired the Reformation, a mighty emancipation, yet how much evil followed after, the division of Europe, the Thirty Years' War and all the devastation and suffering it brought about! The great Romantic movement was another expression of 'Innerlichkeit', and its positive achievements are undeniable, in literature and literary theory, in folk-lore, linguistics and history, and in many other fields. Enthusiasm and vitality marked all its efforts, the wish to pierce beyond useful knowledge to the irrational sources of life. It was music revolting against literature, mysticism against clarity, a willingness to face the dark sides of experience and history, putting power higher than intellectualism and rejecting all rhetorical attempts to whitewash reality. 'Here is the link between Romanticism and that realism and machiavellism which achieved in Bismarck, the only political genius Germany has produced, its victories over Europe.' His German unification was not at all democratic, his Reich was a pure power state aiming at European hegemony, a dangerous mixture of vigorous efficiency and dreams of past greatness, Romanticism endowed with every technical skill. 'Nothing great in literature and art came out of Germany now, that had once been the teacher of the world. It was only strong. But in this strength and beneath all the organized efficiency the Romantic germ of sickness and death was still at work. It was nourished by historical misfortune, the sufferings and humiliations of a lost war. And German Romanticism, descended to a pitiful mass level, the level of

262

a Hitler, erupted into hysterical barbarism, into a drunken fit and convulsion of conceit and crime, which is now reaching its dreadful end in national catastrophe, a physical and psychical collapse without parallel.'[49]

The melancholy story of German 'Innerlichkeit' shows, Mann concludes, that there are not two Germanies, a bad and a good, but only one, whose best gifts turned through some devil's art to evil. The bad Germany is the good one gone wrong, the good one in misfortune, in guilt and collapse. It is not for him to throw stones, for he too is a German. Can we dare to hope that after this catastrophe some better form will be found for Germany than a national state, that the first tentative steps will be taken towards a world in which the national individualism of the nineteenth century will be softened and perhaps finally disappear, giving the mass of the good in Germany more favourable conditions to grow in?

CONCLUSION

We have been chiefly concerned in this book with the tension in a number of German writers between inward-looking and outward-looking thought, the kind of question with which we are perhaps most familiar in our own thinking about school and university education, the eternal problem about the relative importance of developing the individual capacities of the pupil and of preparing him for a useful role in society. Our few studies do not justify any general conclusions about the exact relation between the tradition of inwardness and habitual German attitudes to political and social activity, but they do perhaps offer a few impressions of national character in the making.

The efflorescence of German literature and philosophy in the later eighteenth century, looked at in the context of European history, appears as a delayed Renaissance. The kind of individual perfection aimed at by the theory of classical 'Bildung' was, as we have seen, a harmony of developed capacities – an aesthetic ideal, the like of which John Passmore, in his comprehensive study of *The Perfectibility of Man*, finds for the first time in Pierre Charron's *Traité de la Sagesse* (1601). 'The perfect man is a work of art, the harmonious realization of an educator's ideal; education, not God, is the source of grace. This was a typically Renaissance attitude to the human being and human perfection, carried over by Charron into the early seventeenth century and made central by Shaftesbury.'[1] Shaftesbury's extreme importance in the shaping of German ideas about culture was emphasized in my *Culture and Society in Classical Weimar*. The present work has shown that the classical idea of 'Bildung' inherited from Weimar met with obstacles of many kinds in the nineteenth century. It was progressively externalized and watered down, if not completely distorted, as by Nietzsche. It seems indeed doubtful whether such an ideal in its pure form can survive in an industrial and politically conscious society.

For a final comment it is perhaps appropriate to turn to Eduard

Spranger, the philosopher who wrote the two standard works on Wilhelm von Humboldt, on his philosophy of 'Humanität' and on his administrative reform of Prussian education. Writing shortly before the First World War to his friend Georg Kerschensteiner, the reformer of the continuation school in Germany, he said:

Our time has to advance beyond the individualistic temper which has so far made us great. The time has come when only the individual incorporated in a super-individual organization receives from his age all that it can give him[...] The fine free development of the personality is no longer the final goal in our civilization of to-day, but the personality which receives its finest values from the social totality, and gives its own back in return.[2]

Later he tries to describe a new ideal of life, to replace that of Humboldt, which he has given up with regret:

Our way and our time have changed. We too, certainly, are seeking a humane ideal of life, a life worthy of a man for all members of society. But it is no longer this humanism of a purely aesthetic type, but a way of life to be worked out on the basis of a true sense of reality[...] in which productive effort of every kind will be a source of satisfaction. A fully human existence can result from this too, not for self-enjoyment à la Tegel, however, [Tegel was of course Humboldt's family estate] but for work with a will in the spirit of the *Wanderjahre*, in which I find all the types of men of our new age prefigured[...] What we are looking for is the content of a humane ideal for our time. For 'Humanität' is really only a formal concept, which every age fills out with its own living substance.[3]

NOTES

Chapter 1

1 Some titles: E. Spranger, *W. v. Humboldt und die Humanitätsidee*, Berlin, 1909; E. Spranger, *W. v. Humboldt und die Reform des Bildungswesens*, Berlin, 1910; F. Schnabel, *Deutsche Geschichte im neunzehnten Jahrhundert*, vol. I, section 4, 4th ed. Freiburg i.B., 1948; W. v. Humboldt, *Schriften zur Anthropologie und Bildungslehre*, ed. A. Flitner, Düsseldorf and München, 1956; E. L. Stahl, *Die religiöse und die humanitätsphilosophische Bildungsidee und die Entstehung des deutschen Bildungsromans im 18. Jahrhundert*, Bern, 1934; R. Leroux, *G. de Humboldt; la formation de sa pensée jusqu'à 1794*, Paris, 1932; R. Leroux, *L'anthropologie comparée de G. de Humboldt*, Paris, 1958; W. v. Humboldt, *The Limits of State Action*, edited with an introduction and notes by J. W. Burrow, Cambridge, 1969.

2 *Gesammelte Schriften*, Prussian Academy Edition, ed. A. Leitzmann, vol. XV, Berlin, 1918, p. 455.

3 Spranger, *Humanitätsidee*, p. 16.

4 *Briefe an eine Freundin* (cited hereafter as *Freundin*), ed. Leitzmann, Berlin, 1909, vol. I, p. 50.

5 R. Haym, *W. v. Humboldt*, Berlin, 1856, p. 626.

6 *Wilhelm und Karoline von Humboldt in ihren Briefen* (cited hereafter as *W. und K.*), ed. Anna v. Sydow, 7 vols., Berlin, 1906–16, vol. I, p. 39.

7 *Aus dem Nachlass Varnhagens von Ense*, vol. I, Leipzig, 1867, p. 24.

8 *Ibid.* p. 54.

9 *Ibid.* p. 115.

10 *W. und K.*, I, p. 3.

11 *W. und K.*, gekürzte Volksausgabe in einem Bande, 2nd ed., Berlin, 1935, p. 2. (The letter is not in the original seven-volume edition.)

12 *Aus dem Nachlass Varnhagens von Ense*, I, p. 105.

13 *Ibid.* p. 113.

14 *Gesammelte Schriften*, XIV, p. 69.

15 *W. und K.*, I, p. 35.

16 *W. und K.*, I, p. 281.

17 *W. und K.*, II, p. 5.

18 *W. und K.*, IV, p. 369.

19 *W. und K.*, III, p. 278.

20 *W. und K.*, II, p. 190.

21 'Die Berliner Gesellschaft in den Jahren 1789 bis 1815', in *Unbekannte Essays*, ed. H. Uhde-Bernays, Bern, 1955, p. 72.

22 *W. und K.*, IV, p. 543.

23 *Gesammelte Schriften*, XIV, p. 79.

24 Cf. e.g. *Freundin*, I, p. 175.

25 *Freundin*, I, p. 65.

26 *Briefwechsel zwischen Schiller und W. v. Humboldt*, 3rd ed., with notes by A. Leitzmann, Stuttgart, 1900, p. 176.

27 *W. und K.*, I, pp. 344f.

28 *Briefwechsel zwischen Schiller und W. v. Humboldt*, pp. 277f.

29 *The Limits of State Action*, ed. J. W. Burrow, pp. xxxvif.

30 Isaiah Berlin, *Two Concepts of Liberty*, Oxford, 1958, p. 14.

31 *Gesammelte Schriften*, I, p. 117.
32 *Ibid.* p. 158.
33 *Ibid.* p. 283.
34 *Ibid.* p. 151.
35 *W. und K.*, II, p. 260.
36 See Kurt Müller-Vollmer, *Poesie und Einbildungskraft, Zur Dichtungstheorie W. v. Humboldts*, Stuttgart, 1967.
37 *Goethes Briefwechsel mit W. und A. v. Humboldt*, ed. L. Geiger, Berlin, 1909, pp. 184–6.
38 *Briefwechsel zwischen Schiller und W. v. Humboldt*, p. 279.
39 *W. v. Humboldt und die Humanitätsidee*, p. 421.
40 *Ibid.* p. 419.
41 *W. und K.*, III, p. 158.
42 *W. und K.*, IV, p. 43.
43 *W. und K.*, V, p. 328.
44 *W. und K.*, III, p. 141.
45 *W. und K.*, II, p. 262.
46 *Gesammelte Schriften*, IX, p. 90.
47 *W. und K.*, II, p. 281.
48 *W. und K.*, III, p. 33.
49 *W. v. Humboldt*, p. 634.
50 E.g. *Freundin*, I, p. 334; II, p. 276.
51 E.g. *Freundin*, II, pp. 101, 354.
52 *Freundin*, II, p. 244.
53 *Freundin*, II, p. 208.
54 *Freundin*, II, p. 50.
55 Varnhagen von Ense, *Vermischte Schriften*, Vol. V, 2nd ed., Leipzig, 1843, pp. 118–42.
56 *Briefwechsel zwischen Schiller und W. v. Humboldt*, p. 318.

Chapter 2

1 For the emergence of the National Theatre see e.g. Bruford, *Theatre, Drama and Audience in Goethe's Germany* (General Index). London, 1950.
2 Book V, chapter 3.
3 Book III, chapter 9.
4 *Goethes Werke*, Hamburger Ausgabe, vol. VII, pp. 618ff.
5 See *Essays on Goethe*, ed. W. Rose, London, 1949, pp. 193ff.
6 *Goethe*, vol. II, Zürich and Freiburg i.B., 1956, pp. 167f.
7 Zweiter Teil, *Klassik*, Leipzig, 1930, p. 149.
8 Bruford, *Culture and Society in Classical Weimar*, Cambridge, 1962, p. 223.
9 See E. Trunz (editor), *Goethe und der Kreis von Münster*, Münster i.W., 1971, or my essay, *Fürstin Gallitzin und Goethe*, Köln and Opladen, 1957.
10 *Goethes Wilhelm Meister und die Entwicklung des modernen Lebensideals*, Berlin and Leipzig, 1913, p. 210f.
11 Roy Pascal, *The German Novel*, Manchester, 1956, pp. 27f.
12 Kurt May, '*Wilhelm Meisters Lehrjahre*, ein Bildungsroman?' in *Deutsche Vierteljahrsschrift für Literaturwissenschaft und Geistes-Geschichte*, XXXI (1957), p. 36.
13 *Ibid.* p. 34.

Chapter 3

Monologen. Good critical edition by F. M. Schiele, with introduction, bibliography and index (Philosophische Bibliothek 84). Leipzig, 1902. 2nd ed. by H. Mulert, 1914: *-Über die Religion. Reden an die Gebildeten unter ihren Verächtern.* ed. H. J. Rothert (Philosophische Bibliothek 255). Hamburg, 1958: *Gesamtausgabe der Werke* in drei Abteilungen, Berlin, 1835-1864: W. Dilthey, *Leben Schleiermachers* i, Berlin, 1870 (life to 1802). 2nd ed. by H. Mulert, 2 vols., Berlin and Leipzig, 1922: R. Haym, *Die romantische Schule.* Berlin, 1870. 4th ed by Walzel, Berlin, 1920 (3rd chapter, Schleiermacher, pp. 551-611): *Aus Schleiermachers Leben,* ed. L. Jonas and W. Dilthey, 4 vols, 1860-3 (letters and documents). Good introduction with recent bibliography: F. W. Kantzenbach. *Schleiermacher in Selbstzeugnissen und Bilddokumenten* (Rowohlts Monographien), Hamburg, 1967.

1 *Die protestantische Theologie im 19. Jahrhundert,* Zürich, 1947, p. 379.
2 *Ibid.* p. 386.
3 Letter to Eleonore Grunow, 19 August 1802.
4 *Ibid.*
5 Letter to Charlotte von Kathen, 5 May 1805.
6 Letter to sister, 4 August 1798.
7 *Op. cit.* p. 388.
8 Letter to Willich, undated (? May 1801).
9 Cf. *Culture and Society in Classical Weimar,* Cambridge, 1962, pp. 246ff.
10 H. B. Nisbet, *Goethe and the Scientific Tradition.* London, 1972, p. 57.
11 Paul Kluckhohn, *Das Ideengut der deutschen Romantik,* 3rd ed., Tübingen, 1953, pp. 53f.
12 *August Wilhelm und Friedrich Schlegel in Auswahl,* ed. O. F. Walzel (Deutsche Nationalbibliothek 143), Stuttgart, n.d., p. 266.
13 Lyzeumsfragment 55, quoted by Clemens Menze in his illuminating lecture: *Der Bildungsbegriff des jungen Friedrich Schlegel,* Ratingen, 1964.
14 H. S. Reiss, *The Political Thought of the German Romantics,* Oxford, 1955, p. 37.
15 *Die romantische Schule,* 4th ed., pp. 605f.
16 Kantzenbach, *op. cit.* p. 113.
17 Biedermann, *Goethes Gespräche,* 2nd ed., Leipzig, 1909, i, p. 291.
18 Dilthey, *Leben Schleiermachers,* 2nd ed., i, p. 499.
19 Letter to A. W. Schlegel, 28 November 1797.
20 Cf. e.g. Lilian R. Furst, *Romanticism in Perspective,* London, 1969, pp. 55-115.
21 Erich Franz, *Deutsche Klassik und Reformation. Die Weiterbildung protestantischer Motive in der Philosophie und Weltanschauungsdichtung des deutschen Idealismus.* Halle, 1937, p. 396.
22 F. Meinecke, *Weltbürgertum und Nationalstaat,* 6th ed., München and Berlin, 1922, p. 146.
23 Franz, *op. cit.* p. 400.
24 G. Kaiser, *Pietismus und Patriotismus im literarischen Deutschland. Ein Beitrag zum Problem der Säkularisation.* Wiesbaden, 1961, chap. 14.
25 Reiss, *op. cit.* p. 37.
26 Reiss, *op. cit.* p. 175.

Chapter 4

1 W. Mommsen (note 2) mentions: Karl Grün, *Über Goethe vom menschlichen Standpunkte.* Darmstadt, 1846. Ferdinand Gregorovius, *Goethes 'Wilhelm Meister' in seinen sozialistischen Elementen.* 1849; G. Radbruch, 'Wilhelm Meisters sozialpolitische Sendung', in *Logos,* vol. viii, 1919, expanded in *Gestalten und Gedanken,* Leipzig, 1944. There are long quotations from this essay in the notes to *Goethes Werke,* vol. viii, ed. E. Trunz, Hamburg, 1950.
2 *Die politischen Anschauungen Goethes,* Stuttgart, 1948, p. 247.
3 To Soret, 20 October 1830.

4 To Eckermann, 25 February 1824.
5 J. Falk, *Goethe aus näherem persönlichen Umgange dargestellt*. Leipzig, 1832, quoted by W. Bode, *Goethes Gedanken*, vol. I, Berlin, 1907, p. 371.
6 14 September 1826. From Hermann Fürst von Pückler, *Briefe eines Verstorbenen*, quoted by Bode, *op. cit.* p. 373.
7 *Mitteilungen über Goethe*, Berlin, 1841, quoted by Bode, *op. cit.* p. 372.
8 To Eckermann, 3 January 1827.
9 5 August 1815. S. Boisserée. *Seine Erinnerungen und Briefe*, Stuttgart, 1862, quoted by Bode, *op. cit.* p. 407.
10 To Kanzler von Müller, 3 February 1823. From *Goethes Unterhaltungen mit dem Kanzler F. von Müller*, ed. C. A. H. Burkhardt, Stuttgart, 1870, quoted by Bode, *op. cit.* p. 395.
11 *A Study of Goethe*, Oxford, 1947, p. 244.
12 Letter to F. Jacobi, 25 January 1795.
13 To Riemer, 24 November 1813.
14 From the *Noten und Abhandlungen zu besserem Verständnis des West-Östlichen Divans* (*Goethes Werke*, Hamburg edition, vol. II, p. 175), quoted by A. Harnack, *Goethe in der Epoche seiner Vollendung*, Leipzig, 1905, p. 259.
15 To Eckermann, 27 April 1825.
16 To Eckermann, 18 January 1827.
17 6 June 1825, quoted by Harnack, *op. cit.* p. 260.
18 Book I, chapter 6.
19 'Betrachtungen im Sinne der Wanderer', 165.
20 Kate Silber, *Pestalozzi*. Heidelberg, 1957, p. 173. Cf. also Humboldt's ideas about craftsmen becoming artists, p. 17 above.
21 Cf. p. 157 below.
22 *Goethes Werke*, Hamburg edition, vol. VIII, pp. 655f.
23 *Ibid.* pp. 657f.

Chapter 5

The text of Schopenhauer's works referred to is *Schopenhauers Sämmtliche Werke in fünf Bänden* in the Grossherzog Wilhelm Ernst Ausgabe, Inselverlag, Leipzig, n.d. The 'Aphorismen zur Lebensweisheit' are in vol. V, *Parerga und Paralipomena, Zweiter Teil*, ed. Hans Henning.

1 S.W. (*Sämmtliche Werke*) I, p. 907.
2 S.W. IV, p. 374.
3 *Ibid.* pp. 375f.
4 *Ibid.* p. 377.
5 *Ibid.* p. 394.
6 *Über die ästhetische Erziehung des Menschen*, 15th letter.
7 S.W. IV, pp. 399f.
8 *Allgemeine Literatur-Zeitung*, Jena, 4 Jan. 1796.
9 S.W. IV, p. 561.
10 *Ibid.* p. 578.
11 S.W. I, p. 270.
12 Stockholm ed., vol. XXXVIII, p. 62.
13 S.W. IV, p. 413.
14 *Ibid.* p. 395.
15 *Schopenhauers Leben*, 2nd ed., Leipzig, 1878, p. 622.
16 S.W. IV, p. 425.
17 *Ibid.* p. 424.
18 *Ibid.* p. 432.
19 *Op. cit.* p. 332.
20 S.W. IV, p. 501.

21 *Ibid.* p. 448.
22 *Ibid.* p. 500.
23 *Ibid.* p. 530.
24 *Ibid.* p. 528.
25 *Ibid.* p. 493.
26 *Ibid.* p. 423.
27 S.W. v, p. 603.
28 Gwinner, *op. cit.* p. 64.
29 S.W. iv, p. 501.
30 *Op. cit.* p. 60.
31 S.W. v, pp. 273f.
32 *Ibid.* p. 271.
33 *Ibid.* p. 267.
34 *Ibid.* p. 280.
35 *Ibid.* p. 279.
36 *Ibid.* p. 259.
37 *Ibid.* p. 277.
38 *Ibid.* p. 677.
39 *Ibid.* p. 282.
40 *Op. cit.* p. 64.

Chapter 6

1 Cf. Curt Hohoff, *Adalbert Stifter*. Düsseldorf, 1949, pp. 112ff.
2 Karl Privat, *A. Stifter. Sein Leben in Selbstzeugnissen, Briefen und Berichten*. Berlin, 1946, p. 49.
3 To Heckenast, 13 May 1854.
4 To Heckenast, 6 Dec. 1850.
5 Quoted by Karl Privat, op. cit. p. 272.
6 *Stifter als Dichter der Ehrfurcht*. Zürich, 1952, p. 17.
7 *Ibid.* p. 39.
8 E. Staiger, *Goethe*, vol. ii, Zürich and Freiburg i.Br., 1956. p. 260.
9 Letter to Albert Brenner, c. 1855, quoted by Rehm, *Der Nachsommer*, p. 114.
10 *Dichtung und Wahrheit*, Erster Teil, 4. Buch.
11 *Gesellschaft und Demokratie in Deutschland*, München, 1965, p. 447.
12 *Re-interpretations*, London, 1964, p. 361.
13 A. R. Hein, *Adalbert Stifter*, Prag, 1904. vol. i, p. 545.
14 Karl Viëtor, *Goethe*. Bern, 1949, p. 456.
15 Hohoff, *op. cit.* pp. 114f.
16 *Stifters sämtliche Werke*, ed. G. Wilhelm, vol. xxiii. Reichenberg, 1939, p. 200.
17 *Menschliches, Allzumenschliches*, ii, Aph. 109 of 'Der Wanderer und sein Schatten', pocket edition, vol. iv, p. 257.

Chapter 7

1 Anton Springer, 'Aus meinem Leben', 1892, in *Deutsche Literatur, Reihe Deutsche Selbstzeugnisse*, vol. xii, Leipzig, 1943, pp. 246f.
2 Erich Auerbach, *Mimesis*, Bern, 1946. pp. 397ff.
3 *Auch Einer*, ed. G. Manz, Deutsche Bibliothek, Berlin, n.d., p. 411.
4 *Ibid.* p. 412.
5 *Ibid.* p. 412.
6 *Ibid.* p. 478.
7 *Ibid.* p. 479.
8 *Ibid.* p. 480.

9 *Ibid.* p. 482.
10 *Ibid.* p. 482.
11 *Ibid.* p. 274.
12 *Ibid.* p. 411.
13 The theory is briefly summarized as follows by H. Wein in his article in *Nicolai Hartmann, Der Denker und sein Werk, Fünfzehn Abhandlungen*, herausgegeben von H. Heimsoeth und R. Heiss, Göttingen, 1952, p. 183; 'Organic life depends on inorganic processes and substrates. But in spite of that it has its own (organic) laws. Intellectual and historical life depends on the existence of living and conscious individuals and on the functioning of their organic and psychic life. Yet it too is autonomous life within its limits, in that dependence, but not in opposition to it.'
14 *Auch Einer*, p. 319.
15 *Ibid.* p. 343.
16 *Ibid.* p. 344.
17 *Ibid.* p. 344.
18 *Ibid.* p. 382.
19 *Ibid.* p. 44.
20 *Ibid.* p. 461.
21 *Ibid.* p. 451.
22 *Ibid.* p. 264.
23 *Ibid.* p. 187.
24 Fritz Schlawe, *Friedrich Theodor Vischer*, Stuttgart, 1959. Ruth Heller, '*Auch Einer*: the epitome of Friedrich Theodor Vischer's philosophy of life' in *German Life and Letters*, N.S. vol. VIII, 1954–5, pp. 9–18.

Chapter 8

Nietzsche's works are quoted from the Taschenausgabe in eleven volumes, Alfred Kröner Verlag, Leipzig, n.d. (vols. I-X, 1905–6, vol. XI, 1919). For quotations from the extensive manuscript material not published by Nietzsche himself, which takes up over 500 pages in volume III of the *Werke in drei Bänden*, edited by Karl Schlechta, München, 1956, and is printed there in roughly chronological order, a reference is given first to the Schlechta edition, and then to the place where the same passage can be found in the so-called *Wille zur Macht*, edited by Nietzsche's sister and her assistants. Abbreviations: Taschenausgabe, TA; Schlechta, Schl.

1 TA II, pp. 255f.
2 TA II, p. 259.
3 TA II, p. 263f.
4 Cf. Bruford, *Culture and Society in Classical Weimar*, p. 357.
5 TA II, p. 267.
6 TA II, p. 276.
7 TA II, pp. 198f.
8 TA III, p. 160. For the influence of religious feeling on patriotism, see: K. S. Pinson, *Pietism as a factor in the rise of German nationalism*, New York, 1934, and Gerhart Kaiser, *Pietismus und Patriotismus im literarischen Deutschland*, Wiesbaden, 1961.
9 TA III, p. 96.
10 TA III, p. 172.
11 *Ibid.*
12 TA V, p. 180.
13 'Characteristics of German Genius' in *Foreign Quarterly Review*, 1842. Reprinted in *Essays and Tales* by John Sterling, ed. J. C. Hare, 2 vols., London, 1848.
14 TA V, p. 181.
15 *Aristocracy and the Middle Classes in Germany, Social types in German Literature*, London, 1937, p. 109.

16 TA v, pp. xixf.
17 TA ix, pp. xff.
18 *Egotism in German Philosophy*. London and Toronto. n.d. (1919), p. 127.
19 Schl. iii, p. 751 (TA ix, pp. 366f).
20 Karl Jaspers, *Nietzsche*. *Einführung in das Verständnis seines Philosophierens*, Berlin and Leipzig, 1936. p. 346 (from Werke xii, p. 177).
21 TA x, p. 275.
22 TA x, p. 260.
23 TA x, pp. 262f.
24 Schl. iii, p. 730 (TA ix, p. 290).
25 Schl. iii, p. 862 (TA x, p. 213).
26 Schl. iii, p. 435 (TA ix, p. 100).
27 TA viii, pp. 323f.
28 Schl. iii, p. 742 (TA ix, p. 504).
29 Schl. iii, pp. 897f. (TA ix, p. 500).
30 Schl. iii, p. 846 (TA ix, pp. 169f.).
31 TA viii, p. 337 (*Zur Genealogie der Moral*); Schl. iii, p. 553, p. 809 etc.
32 Schl. iii, p. 660 (TA x, p. 21).
33 Schl. iii, p. 434 (TA ix, pp. 100f.).
34 Schl. iii, p. 432 (TA x, p. 168).
35 TA x, p. 365 (Schl. iii, p. 1169).
36 TA vii, pp. 13f.
37 TA vii, pp. 18ff.
38 TA vii, pp. 174f.
39 TA vii, p. 177.
40 TA vii, p. 230.
41 *Nietzsche, Zeitgemässes und Unzeitgemässes*, ed. and introduced by Karl Löwith (Fischer-Bücherei), Frankfurt and Hamburg, 1956, p. 9.
42 *Ibid.* p. 11.
43 'Nietzsche's philosophy in the light of recent thinking' in *Last Essays*, London, 1959. (First published in German, Berlin, 1948.)
44 Jaspers, *op. cit.* p. 374.
45 Hamburg, 1946, pp. 144–217.
46 *Plaudereien mit Lothar Engelbert*, Bamberg, 1948, pp. 116–27 ('Von der Erzählerkunst und der Humanität in Deutschland').

Chapter 9

1 Walter Müller-Seidel, 'Gesellschaft und Menschen im Roman Theodor Fontanes', in *Heidelberger Jahrbücher*, vol. iv, 1960, pp. 108–27.
2 *Briefe an Friedländer*, Heidelberg, 1954, pp. 147f. (May 1891).
3 *Ibid.* p. 114.
4 To his wife, 13 September 1898.
5 *Briefe an Friedländer*, p. 295 (22 March 1896).
6 *Ibid.* p. 243.
7 *Ibid.* p. 148.
8 To his wife, 10 August 1875.
9 *Briefe an Friedländer*, p. 257.
10 *Ibid.* p. 254 (1894).
11 25 August 1891.
12 *Zwischen Zwanzig und Dreissig*, chapter 1.

Chapter 10

1 *The ironic German*, London, 1958, p. 15.
2 *Der Zauberberg*, in 'Thomas Manns erzählende Schriften gesammelt in drei Bänden', Dritter Band, Berlin, 1924, p. 778.
3 *Ibid.* p. 505.
4 *Ibid.* p. 37.
5 *Ibid.* p. 199.
6 In his *Solzhenitzyn*, London, 1970.
7 *Zauberberg*, p. 71.
8 *Ibid.* p. 264.
9 *Ibid.* pp. 159-64 (section 'Hippe' in chap. 4).
10 *Ibid.* p. 136. John Sterling, in his article 'Characteristics of German Genius', 1842, said the main characteristic was 'a moral earnestness, conveying above all the idea of the worth of man'.
11 *Zauberberg*, p. 387.
12 *Ibid.* p. 405.
13 *Ibid.* p. 419.
14 *Ibid.* pp. 163ff.
15 *Ibid.* pp. 492-504.
16 *Ibid.* pp. 513-30.
17 *Lübeck als geistige Lebensform*, Lübeck, 1926.
18 *Lübeck*, pp. 47f.
19 *Zauberberg*, p. 641.
20 *Ibid.* pp. 646f.
21 *Ibid.* p. 669.
22 *Ibid.* pp. 677-85.
23 *Ibid.* p. 904.
24 *Ibid.* p. 667.
25 *Lübeck*, p. 45.

Chapter 11

1 Thomas Mann–Heinrich Mann, *Briefwechsel* 1900-49, ed. H. Wysling, S. Fischer-Verlag, 1968, intro. p. 1.
2 Thomas Mann, *Briefe*, I, 1889-1936, ed. Erika Mann. S. Fischer-Verlag, 1962, p. 354 (To Karl Kerenyi, 20 November 1934).
3 Thomas Mann, *Betrachtungen eines Unpolitischen*, Berlin, 1920, p. xxxii.
4 *Ibid.* p. 74.
5 *Ibid.* p. 79.
6 *Ibid.* p. 108.
7 *Ibid.* p. 118.
8 Thomas Mann–Heinrich Mann, *Briefwechsel*, pp. 25f.
9 *Ibid.* p. 104.
10 Thomas Mann, *Reden und Aufsätze* I, Stockholm, 1965, pp. 548f.
11 *Betrachtungen*, p. 244.
12 *Ibid.* p. 246.
13 *Ibid.* pp. 254f.
14 *Ibid.* p. 490.
15 *Reliquien*, quoted by F. Meinecke, *Weltbürgertum und Nationalstaat*, München and Berlin, 1922, p. 27n.
16 *Les deux sources de la morale et de la religion*, Paris, 1932, p. 33.
17 *Betrachtungen*, p. 517.

273

18 *Ibid.* p. 273.
19 *Ibid.* pp. 273ff.
20 *Ibid.* p. 267.
21 *Ibid.* p. 270.
22 See *Natural Law and the Theory of Society*, 1500–1800, by Otto Gierke, translated with an introduction by Ernest Barker, Cambridge, 1934. The 1922 lecture by Troeltsch is printed in translation at the end of vol. I and discussed in the introduction.
23 Ralf Dahrendorf, *Gesellschaft und Demokratie in Deutschland*, München, 1965, p. 442. See also 'Conflict and Liberty', *Brit. Journal of Sociology*, vol. XIV.
24 Now in *Reden und Aufsätze*, II, pp. 11–52.
25 *Dr Faustus*, Stockholm, 1948, pp. 522f.
26 *Mein Kampf*, München, 1933, I, p. 240.
27 *Reden und Aufsätze*, II, pp. 341–51.
28 *Briefe*, I, p. 202.
29 Published April 1928 in *Preussiche Jahrbücher*. Reprinted in *Reden und Aufsätze*, vol. II, pp. 387–97, Stockholm, 1965.
30 *Reden und Aufsätze*, II, p. 55.
31 *Reden und Aufsätze*, I, pp. 375ff.
32 *Ibid.* pp. 378ff.
33 *Reden und Aufsätze*, II, pp. 776ff.
34 *Briefe*, I, p. 278.
35 *Reden und Aufsätze*, I, pp. 431–519.
36 *Briefe*, I, p. 281.
37 *Reden und Aufsätze*, II, p. 394.
38 *Ibid.* pp. 426–32.
39 *Ibid.* p. 198.
40 *Ibid.* p. 516.
41 *Ibid.* pp. 432–514.
42 *Ibid.* p. 507.
43 *Ibid.* pp. 507ff.
44 *Ibid.* p. 534.
45 *Ibid.* p. 138.
46 Thomas Mann–Heinrich Mann, *Briefwechsel*, p. 339.
47 *Reden und Aufsätze*, II, pp. 313–35.
48 *Ibid.* p. 323.
49 *Ibid.* p. 333.

Conclusion

1 *The Perfectibility of Man*. London, 1970, p. 153.
2 *Georg Kerschensteiner–Eduard Spranger. Briefwechsel 1912–1931*. Edited and introduced by L. Englert. München, 1966, p. 49.
3 *Ibid.* pp. 62f.

BIBLIOGRAPHY

Works mentioned in the text and notes. A few other works are included which have been found particularly useful.

Arendt, Hannah. *Rahel Varnhagen*. London, 1958.

Auerbach, Erich. *Mimesis*. Bern, 1946.

Barth, Karl. *Die protestantische Theologie im neunzehnten Jahrhundert*. Zürich, 1947.

Bergson, Henri. *Les deux sources de la morale et de la religion*. Paris, 1932.

Berlin, Sir Isaiah. *Two Concepts of Liberty*. Oxford, 1958.

Bertram, Ernst. *Nietzsche, Versuch einer Mythologie*. Berlin, 1919.

Blackall, E. A. *Adalbert Stifter*. Cambridge, 1948.

Bode, W. *Goethes Gedanken*. 2 Bde., Berlin, 1907.

Braun, J. W. (ed.). *Goethe im Urteil seiner Zeitgenossen*. Berlin, 1884.

Dahrendorf, Ralf. *Gesellschaft und Demokratie in Deutschland*. München, 1965.

Dilthey, Wilhelm. *Leben Schleiermachers*. 2.A. ed. H. Mulert, 2 Bde., Berlin und Leipzig, 1922. (First edition in one volume. Berlin, 1870.)

Fairley, Barker. *A Study of Goethe*. Oxford, 1947.

Flitner, W. *Goethe im Spätwerk*. Hamburg, 1947.

Fontane, Theodor. *Gesamtausgabe der erzählenden Schriften*. Berlin, 1925.
Autobiographische Werke: Meine Kinderjahre: Von Zwanzig bis Dreissig. Ed. C. Coler. Berlin, 1961.
Briefe. Ed. K. Schreinert and C. Jolles, 4 Bde. Berlin, 1968–71.
Briefe an G. Friedländer. Ed. K. Schreinert Heidelberg, 1954.

Franz, Erich. *Deutsche Klassik und Reformation*. Halle, 1937.

Furst, Lilian R. *Romanticism in Perspective*. London, 1969.

Gardiner, Patrick. *Schopenhauer*. London, 1967.

Gierke, Otto. *Natural Law and the Theory of Society, 1500 to 1800*, translated with an introduction by Ernest Barker, 2 vols. Cambridge, 1934.

Goethe, Johann Wolfgang von. *Werke*. Hamburger Ausgabe in 14 Bänden. Hamburg, 1948–60. (*Wilhelm Meisters Lehrjahre* in vol. VII, *Wilhelm Meisters Wanderjahre* in vol. VIII, both ed. Erich Trunz.)
Gespräche. ed. Biedermann, 2.A., 5 Bde. Leipzig, 1909–11.

Gwinner, W. *Schopenhauers Leben*. 2.A. Leipzig, 1878.

Harnack, A. *Goethe in der Epoche seiner Vollendung*. 3.A. Leipzig, 1905.

Harnack, O. *Wilhelm von Humboldt*. Berlin, 1913 (Geisteshelden).

Hartmann, Nicolai. *Das Problem des geistigen Seins*. Berlin, 1933.

Haym, Rudolf. *Wilhelm von Humboldt.* Berlin, 1856.

Die Romantische Schule. 4.A. ed. Walzel. Berlin, 1920.

Heimsoeth, H. and Heiss, R. (eds.). *Nicolai Hartmann. Der Denker und sein Werk.* Göttingen, 1952.

Hein, A. R. *Adalbert Stifter, sein Leben und seine Werke.* Prag, 1904.

Heller, Erich. *The ironic German.* London, 1958.

Heller, Ruth. '*Auch Einer*, the epitome of F. T. Vischer's philosophy of life'. In *German Life and Letters*, N.S. vol. VIII, 1954–5, pp. 9–18.

Hillebrand, Karl, 'Die Berliner Gesellschaft in den Jahren 1789 bis 1815'. In *Unbekannte Essays.* Ed. H. Uhde-Bernays. Bern, 1955.

Hitler, Adolf. *Mein Kampf.* 2 Bde. München, 1933.

Hohoff, Curt. *Adalbert Stifter.* Düsseldorf, 1949.

Howald, Ernst. *Wilhelm von Humboldt.* Erlenbach-Zürich, 1944.

Humboldt, Wilhelm von. *Gesammelte Schriften.* Ed. A. Leitzmann and B. Gebhardt. 15 Bde. Berlin, 1903–18.

Schriften zur Anthropologie und Bildungslehre. Ed. A. Flitner. Düsseldorf und München, 1956.

The Limits of State Action. Ed. with introduction and notes by J. W. Burrow. Cambridge, 1969.

Briefe an eine Freundin. Ed. A. Leitzmann. 2 Bde. Berlin, 1909.

Wilhelm und Karoline von Humboldt in ihren Briefen. Ed. Anna von Sydow. 7 Bde. Berlin, 1906–16.

Wilhelm und Karoline von Humboldt in ihren Briefen. Ed. Anna von Sydow. Gekürzte Volksausgabe. 1 Bd., 2.A. Berlin, 1935.

Goethes Briefwechsel mit Wilhelm und Alexander von Humboldt. Ed. L. Geiger. Berlin, 1909.

Briefwechsel zwischen Schiller und Wilhelm von Humboldt. Ed. Leitzmann. 3.A. Stuttgart, 1900.

Jaspers, Karl. *Friedrich Nietzsche, Einführung in das Verständnis seines Philosophierens.* Berlin und Leipzig, 1936.

Kaiser, G. *Pietismus und Patriotismus im literarischen Deutschland.* Wiesbaden, 1961.

Kantzenbach, F. W. *Schleiermacher in Selbstzeugnissen und Bilddokumenten.* Hamburg, 1967.

Kerschensteiner, G.–Spranger, E. *Briefwechsel 1912–31.* Ed. L. Englert. München, 1966.

Kluckhohn, Paul. *Das Ideengut der deutschen Romantik.* 3.A. Tübingen, 1953.

Kohn-Bramstedt, E. *Aristocracy and the Middle Classes in Germany. Social Types in German Literature.* London, 1937.

Korff, H. A. *Geist der Goethezeit.* 4 Bde. Leipzig, 1923–50.

Leroux, R. *Guillaume de Humboldt; la formation de sa pensée jusqu'à 1794.* Paris, 1932.

L'anthropologie comparèe de Guillaume de Humboldt. Paris, 1948.

276

Löwith, Karl, ed. *Nietzsche, Zeitgemässes und Unzeitgemässes.* Frankfurt/M. und Hamburg, 1956.

Lukács, Georg. *Goethe und seine Zeit.* Bern, 1947.

Solzhenitsyn. Translated from the German by W. D. Graf. London, 1970.

Mann, Heinrich. *Im Schlaraffenland.* München, 1900.

Professor Unrat. München, 1905.

Die kleine Stadt. Leipzig, 1909.

Der Untertan. Leipzig, 1918.

Der Kopf. Leipzig, 1925.

Mann, Thomas. *Werke, Stockholmer Gesamtausgabe.* Stockholm, 1965.

Erzählende Schriften gesammelt in drei Bänden. Berlin, 1924. (*Der Zauberberg* is Band III.)

Briefe. Ed. Erika Mann, 3 Bde. Frankfurt/M, 1962–5.

Thomas Mann–Heinrich Mann, Briefwechsel 1900–49. Ed. H. Wysling. Fischer-Verlag, 1968.

Marrou, H.-I. *Histoire de l'éducation dans l'antiquité.* Paris, 1948.

May, Kurt. '*Wilhelm Meisters Lehrjahre*, ein Bildungsroman?'. In *Deutsche Vierteljahrsschrift für Literaturwissenschaft und Geistesgeschichte*, vol. XXXI (1957).

Meinecke, F. *Weltbürgertum und Nationalstaat.* 6.A. München und Berlin, 1922.

Menze, K. *Der Bildungsbegriff des jungen Friedrich Schlegel.* Ratingen, 1964.

Mommsen, W. *Die politischen Anschauungen Goethe.* Stuttgart, 1948.

Moritz, K. P. *Anton Reiser, ein psychologischer Roman.* 4 Teile, 1785–90.

Müller-Seidel, W. 'Gesellschaft und Menschen im Roman Theodor Fontanes'. In *Heidelberger Jahrbücher*, Bd. IV (1960), pp. 108–27.

Müller-Vollmer, Kurt. *Poesie und Einbildungskraft. Zur Dichtungstheorie Wilhelm von Humboldts.* Stuttgart, 1967.

Nietzsche, Friedrich. *Werke*, Taschenausgabe, 11 Bde, Leipzig, n.d. (I–X, 1905–6, XI, 1919).

Gesammelte Briefe. 5 Bde. Leipzig, 1902ff.

Nisbet, H. B. *Goethe and the scientific Tradition.* London, 1972.

Pascal, Roy. *The German Novel.* Manchester, 1956.

Passmore, J. *The Perfectibility of Man.* London, 1970.

Pinson, K. S. *Pietism as a factor in the rise of German nationalism.* New York, 1934.

Privat, Karl. *Adalbert Stifter. Sein Leben in Selbstzeugnissen, Briefen und Berichten.* Berlin, 1946.

Rehm, W. *Nachsommer, zur Deutung von Stifters Dichtung.* Bern, 1951.

Reiss, H. S. *The Political Thought of the German Romantics.* Oxford, 1955.

Rose, W., ed. *Essays on Goethe.* London, 1949.

Santayana, G. *Egotism in German Philosophy.* London and Toronto, n.d. (1919).

Sasse, H.-C. *Theodor Fontane*. Oxford, 1968.

Schaffstein, F. *Wilhelm von Humboldt*. Frankfurt/M, 1952.

Scheler, Max. *Die Formen des Wissens und die Bildung*. Bonn, 1925.

Schiller, F. von. *Sämtliche Werke*. Ed. Güntter and Witkowski. 20 Bde. Leipzig, n.d. (1910).

On the Aesthetic Education of Man. Translated and edited by Elizabeth M. Wilkinson and L. A. Willoughby. Oxford, 1967.

Schlawe, F. *Friedrich Theodor Vischer*. Stuttgart, 1959.

Schleiermacher, Friedrich. *Gesamtausgabe der Werke in drei Abteilungen*. Berlin, 1835–64.

Aus Schleiermachers Leben. Ed. L. Jonas and W. Dilthey. 4 Bde., 1860–3.

Über die Religion. Reden an die Gebildeten unter ihren Verächtern. Ed. H. J. Rothert. Hamburg, 1958.

Monologen. Ed. F. M. Schiele. Leipzig, 1902; 2.A. Ed. Mulert, 1914.

Schnabel, F. *Deutsche Geschichte im 19. Jahrhundert*. Bd. i, 4.A. Freiburg i.B., 1948.

Schneider, F. J. *Die Freimaurerei und ihr Einfluss auf die geistige Kultur in Deutschland am Ende des 18. Jahrhunderts*. Leipzig, 1909.

Schopenhauer, Arthur. *Sämtliche Werke in 5 Bänden*. (Grossherzog Wilhelm Ernst Ausgabe.) Leipzig, n.d.

Schücking, Levin L. *Plaudereien mit Lothar Engelbert*. Bamberg, 1948.

Schultz, Werner. 'Wilhelm von Humboldt und der faustische Mensch'. In *Jahrbuch der Goethegesellschaft*, Bd. xvi, 1930.

Die Religion Wilhelm von Humboldts. Jena, 1932.

Seuffert, B. *Goethes Theaterroman*. Graz, Wien. Leipzig, 1924.

Silber, Kate. *Pestalozzi*. Heidelberg, 1957.

Sombart, Werner. *Der Bourgeois*. München und Leipzig, 1913.

Spengler, O. *Der Untergang des Abendlands*. 2 Bde. München, 1918–20.

Spranger, E. *Wilhelm von Humboldt und die Humanitätsidee*. Berlin, 1909.

Wilhelm von Humboldt und die Reform des Bildungswesens. Berlin, 1910.

Springer, Anton. 'Aus meinem Leben', 1892. In *Deutsche Literatur in Entwicklungsreihen, Reihe Selbstzeugnisse*. Bd. xii. Leipzig, 1943.

Stahl, E. L. *Die religiöse und die humanitätsphilosophische Bildungsidee und die Entstehung des Bildungsromans im 18. Jahrhundert*. Bern, 1934.

Staiger, Emil. *Goethe*. 3 Bde. Zürich, 1952–9.

Stifter als Dichter der Ehrfurcht. Zürich, 1952.

Sterling, John. *Essays and Tales*. Collected and edited with a memoir by J. C. Hare. 2 vols. London, 1848.

Stern, J. P. *Re-interpretations*. London, 1964.

Idylls and Realities. London, 1971.

Thomas Mann. (Columbia Essays on modern writers, 24.) New York and London, 1967.

Stifter, Adalbert. *Sämtliche Werke und Briefe*. Prag, 1901–7, Reichenberg, 1927–39.

Stöcklein, P. *Wege zum späten Goethe*. Hamburg, 1949.

Sudhof, S. *Von der Aufklärung zur Romantik*. *Die Geschichte des 'Kreises von Münster'*. Berlin, 1973.

Troeltsch, Ernst. 'Die deutsche Idee von der Freiheit'. In *Deutsche Zukunft*. Berlin, 1916.

Deutsche Bildung. Berlin, 1919.

Naturrecht und Humanität in der Weltpolitik. Berlin, 1923.

Trunz, Erich (ed.). *Goethe und der Kreis von Münster*. Münster i.W., 1971.

Varnhagen von Ense, K. A. *Aus dem Nachlass*. Ed. Ludmilla Assing. Bd. I, Berlin, 1867.

Vermischte Schriften. Bd. v, 2.A. Leipzig, 1843.

Viëtor, Karl. *Goethe*. Bern, 1949.

Vischer, Friedrich Theodor. *Ästhetik*. 3 Teile. Reutlingen, 1846–53.

Dichterische Werke. 5 Bde. Leipzig, 1919.

Auch Einer. Ed. G. Mann (Deutsche Bibliothek). Berlin, n.d.

Kritische Gänge. 2.A., 2 Bde. Berlin, 1920.

Walzel, O. (ed.). *A.W und F. Schlegel in Auswahl*. (Deutsche Nationalbibliothek, Bd. 143.) Stuttgart, n.d.

Weber, Alfred. *Abschied von der bisherigen Geschichte*. Hamburg, 1946.

Weil, Hans. *Die Entstehung des Bildungsprinzips*. Bonn, 1930.

Wundt, Max. *Goethes Wilhelm Meister und die Entwicklung des modernen Lebensideals*. Berlin und Leipzig, 1913.

INDEX

Abbé, the (*Wilhelm Meister*), 50f., 55, 75, 98, 102, 104–6
actors, as social type, 33, 35ff.
Allgemeine Literatur-Zeitung, 61
Aprent, J., 131
Arnold, Mathew, viii, 147, 156
Aschenbach, Gustav (*Der Tod in Venedig*), 36, 229
Athenäum, 29, 76f.
Auerbach, B., 172
Auerbach, E., 153f., 270
Aurelie (*Wilhelm Meisters Lehrjahre*), 41, 44, 46, 51
'Ausbildung' (full self-development), 16, 37, 56f., 82
Austin, Sarah, 42
Austria: contrasted with North Germany, 161, 248; Benedictine schools in, 128f.

Baden, Prince Max of, 240
Bagehot, W., 42
Balzac, Honoré de, 132
Barby, 59f., 73
Barker, Sir E., 274
Baron, the (*Wilhelm Meisters Lehrjahre*), 38f.
Barrès, Maurice, 249
Barth, Karl, 58, 69, 72
Baudelaire, Charles, 188
Beccaria, C. Marchese di (1738–94), 97
Beerbohm, Sir Max, 42
Benthamism (Goethe on), 89f.
Bergson, Henri, 232
Berlin, Sir I., 16, 266
Berlin: its society in the 1880s, 192–200; the University of, 164
Berliner Nachtausgabe, 249
Bertram, Ernst, 186, 228, 243
Biedermann, F. von, 268
'Bildung' (self-cultivation, culture), vii (Mann); 14–18, 22–7 (Humboldt); 40–57 (*Lehrjahre*); 68, 70, 76–8, 80–4 (Schleiermacher); 104 (*Wanderjahre*); 115–18

(Schopenhauer); 129–37, 140–6 (Stifter); 159–63 (Vischer); 167–9, 180ff. (Nietzsche); 191–4, 198ff., 204f. (Fontane); 207, 209ff., 215–22 (Mann); 228–33 (Mann), 236f. (Troeltsch), 245, 250, 256 (Mann); 264
'Bildungsroman' (novel of personal cultivation and development), vii, 29f., 32–57, 98, 190, 206–25, 246
Bismarck, Otto, Fürst von, 152, 178, 188, 229, 233f., 242, 262
Blume, G., 241
Blumenbach, J. F., 75
Bode, W., 269
Boisserée, S., 91, 269
Boy-Edd, Ida, 239, 244
Boyen, H. von, 11, 235
Brenner, A., 270
Brentano, Clemens, 36
Brockes, B. H., 83
'Bund, der' (the league – *Wilhelm Meisters Wanderjahre*), 52, 95
Burkhardt, J., 184
Burrow, J. W., 266
Byezukhov, Pierre (*War and Peace*), 54, 110
Byron, Lord, 127

Campe, J. H., 3, 9
Carlyle, Thomas, viii, 29, 104, 147, 156, 170, 211
Castorp, Hans, 207–25, 229, 247
Catholicism, 77, 218
Charité (Berlin hospital), 64
Charron, P., 264
Chauchat, Clawdia, 210f., 213–15
Chekhov, A. P., 139
Chesterfield, Lord, 37
Civilization ('Kultur'), 70, 157, 159f., 165–8, 181f., 184, 250
Clough, A. H., 156
Coleridge, S., viii
Comte, Auguste, 168, 177
Countess, the (*Wilhelm Meisters Lehrjahre*), 39, 44f., 51

281

INDEX

Romanticism, German, 29f., 58, 65f., 74–8, 81f., 84, 89, 104, 262
Rome, 21f.
Rose, W., 267
Rossetti, D. G., 29, 42
Rothert, H. J., 268
Rousseau, J. J., 36, 51, 55, 91, 104, 165, 184, 235
Russell, B., 219
Ryle, G., 175

Sack, F. S. G., 64, 66
Salem (school), 108
Santayana, G., 172f.
Scharnhorst, G. von, 235
Schelling, F. W. J. von, 147, 164, 170
Schickele, R., 240
Schiele, F. M., 268
Schiller, F. von, 4, 11, 13, 15f, 18f., 21, 23, 28 (Humboldt); 31, 39, 48, 55ff. (*Lehrjahre*); 78 (Schleiermacher); 91, 110 (*Wanderjahre*); 132 (Stifter); 147, 151 (Vischer); 170 (Nietzsche). WORKS: *Maria Stuart*, 204; *Wilhelm Tell*, 85; *Ästhetische Erziehung*, 55f., 73; Poems: 'Die Götter Griechenlands', 21, 'Das Ideal und das Leben', 72, 117, 119, 159, 236, *Die Worte des Glaubens*, 68
Schlawe, F., 151, 162, 271
Schlegel, A. W., 118, 268
Schlegel, F., 29, 36, 65f., 75–8, 82f.; *Lucinde*, 36, 65f.
Schleiermacher, F. D. E., 3f., 26, 104, 118, 150, 154, 164, 170, 173, 176. *Monologen*, 58–87. The work of a reformer second only to Luther, 58; early years and Herrnhut education, 59f.; inner conflicts at Barby, 60f.; their resolution through study at Halle, 61; rewarding tutorship with the Dohnas, 62f.; after experience as a country pastor, six exciting years in Berlin, 64f.; the *Vertraute Briefe* on *Lucinde*, 66; *Über die Religion. Reden an die Gebildeten unter ihren Verächtern*, the immediate awareness of divinity in ourselves and in the world, 66–9; immortality, not outside time but in this life, seems like 'Bildung' in a new guise, 68; elaboration of some ideas in the *Monologen*, 69–83; the corporeal world 'has no influence on me, the influence is exerted by me on it' (cf. Humboldt), 70; self-contemplation and its lessons, 71–3; the ideas of humanity and individuality, 73–5, influence on *Athenäum* group. 'Bildung' their shibboleth, 75f.; Frie-

drich Schlegel's rapidly changing views, 76ff.; Schleiermacher's criticism of contemporary society in the third Soliloquy, 78–80; personal hopes and fears in fourth and fifth, 80f.; the key ideas of 'development' and 'humanity', moral, not aesthetic standpoint, 81–3; the idea of the individuality of groups and nations, 84–6; the heirs of Pietism as 'preachers of patriotism', 86f.
Schliemann, H., 196, 200
Schlobitten, 62, 69
Schnabel, F., 266
'schöne Seele', the (*Wilhelm Meisters Lehrjahre*), 48–50
Schopenhauer, Arthur, 150, 160 (Vischer); 164–8, 170, 173–5, 184 (Nietzsche); 230, 232, 250 (Mann). *Aphorismen zur Lebensweisheit*, 113–27. Early life and studies, 114; in this work, empirical advice on the sources of happiness, strictly speaking inconsistent with *Die Welt als Wille und Vorstellung*, his main work, written at the age of 30, 114–18; the inward life contrasted with philistinism, 114; health, an even temper and a commonsense regimen important for happiness, 115; play as an index to human types, the physical, the irritable and the intellectual, 116; joys of the intellectual life, 116f.; comparison with Schiller, Humboldt, Schleiermacher, 118; paradox of the happy pessimist, 119; the bourgeois and the quietist in Schopenhauer, 120f., 125; views on women, love and marriage, 121f., 124; attitudes shared with other Germans of his time, authoritarianism, 125; dislike of progressives, 126; insistence on the rights of the male, and especially of the genius, 126f.
Schröder, F. L., 40
Schücking, L. L., 187–9
Schultz, W., 13
Schumann, Clara, 129
Schwerte, Hans, 150
self-cultivation, *see* 'Bildung'
Serlo (*Wilhelm Meisters Lehrjahre*), 41
Settembrini, *see* Thomas Mann (*Der Zauberberg*)
Shaftesbury, Anthony Ashley, third Earl of, 74, 264
Shakespeare, W., 31, 39ff., 151
Sidgwick, H., 42
Silber, Kate, 269
Smith, Adam, 73, 84
social democracy, 251f., 254

288

INDEX

socialism, German (Marxism), 251
Socrates, 105 (Goethe's form of 'Know thyself!')
Soret, F., 268
Sombart, W. (*Der Bourgeois*), 94, 135, 229
Spectator, The, 34, 135
Spengler, O., 186, 238, 242
Spielhagen, F., 172
Spranger, E., 22f., 83, 265f.
Springer, A., 147f., 270
Stael, Germaine de, 20, 93
Stahl, E. L., 266
Staiger, E., 47, 132f., 270
Steffens, H., 86
Stein, Charlotte von, 6
Stein, Freiherr vom, 52, 235
Sterling, J., 170, 211, 271
Stern, J. P., 138
Stifter, Adalbert, 125, 154, 187; *Bunte Steine*, 131; *Der Hochwald*, 131; *Das Haidedorf*, 131; *Der Nachsommer*, 128–45: influence of Benedictine schooling and of the German classics on an Austrian provincial, 128ff.; a missionary of 'Bildung', the 'gentle law' 130f.; but *Der Nachsommer* is more utopian than a normal Bildungsroman, 132; an abstract ideal of beauty in carefully selected figures and stylized conversation, 133f.; a merchant's patriarchal domestic life, his collections, his careful guidance of his children, 134f.; similar atmosphere at a retired official's country home, with its 'temple' of books, 136; Heinrich's education. Ideas of Rousseau and Goethe, 'a man here for his own sake' and only indirectly for society, the life of women a dependent one. Paternalism and unquestioning acceptance of traditional way of living, 136f.; persistence of such ideas perhaps partly explains the Stifter revival of the 1920s, 138; consistent idealization, with hints from a vanished Austria, 139f.; Heinrich samples many studies before choosing his line, natural history, but we hear of no history proper. The arts come very late, through Risach. The final grand tour seems an anachronism, but this is utopia, 140–3; 'a suggestion of heathen feeling' in the novel for Catholics, but its timeless 'Geist' attracted Nietzsche in spite of himself, 144–6
Strauss, D. F., 147, 149f., 157, 167
Stresemann, G., 248, 251
'Sturm und Drang', 18, 74

Superman, the, 179–82
Swinburne, A. C., 189
Switzerland, 248
Sydow, Anna von, 266
Symonds, J. A., 156

Teutsche Merkur, Der, 61
Thaer, A., 97
Therese (*Wilhelm Meisters Lehrjahre*), 53f.
Three, the (*Wilhelm Meisters Wanderjahre*), 106, 108f.
Toller, E., 241
Tolstoy, Count Lev, 131; *War and Peace*, 54, 110, 143
Tower, the (*Wilhelm Meister*), 43, 50, 53–5, 75, 95, 98
trial by jury (Schopenhauer), 126
Troeltsch, Ernst, 194; *Die deutsche Idee von der Freiheit* (1916), 234–7: the British idea of freedom, 235; contrast with the German idea, freedom as service to the whole, 235f., link with the idea of 'Bildung' and its religious roots, 236; historical background, 236f.; *Naturrecht und Humanität in der Weltpolitik* (1922). Romantic Germany's rejection of the Natural Law theory, 237f.; author's doubts about this after the First World War, 238
Trunz, E., 40, 109f., 267f.
tube post, 204
Tübinger Stift, 147f.
Türck, J., 130
Tugendbund, der, 5–9
Turgeniev, I., 229, 232

Uhde-Bernays, H., 266

Varnhagen von Ense, K. A., 27f., 266f.
Veit, Dorothea, 3, 5, 65
Vercors (*Le silence de la mer*), 228
Vischer, Friedrich Theodor, 107, 119, 205; *Auch Einer* (147–63): Swabian clerical background and education, 147f.; early poems, inner conflicts, 148; the professor at his 'Stammtisch', 148f.; break with theology, cultural influences, 149; Hegelian attitude to religion, switch to aesthetics, 150f.; unorthodox from Inaugural Lecture on, role in 1848, a patriotic enthusiast for 'Bildung', 152; form of *Auch Einer*, diverges from typical Bildungsroman in not avoiding public issues, 153f.; autobiographical fea-